Torah Through a Zionist Vision

Avraham Feder

Torah Through a Zionist Vision

Avraham Feder

Volume I
BEREISHIT
SHEMOT

gefen
publishing house בית הוצאה לאור גפן
JERUSALEM ♦ NEW YORK

Layout: Marzel A.S. — Jerusalem
Cover Design: S. Kim Glassman

ISBN: 978-965-229-395-4
Edition   1 3 5 7 9 8 6 4 2

Gefen Publishing House Ltd.	Gefen Books
6 Hatzvi St.	600 Broadway
Jerusalem 94386, Israel	Lynbrook, NY 11563, USA
972-2-538-0247	1-516-593-1234
orders@gefenpublishing.com	orders@gefenpublishing.com

www.israelbooks.com

Printed in Israel   *Send for our free catalogue*

Contents

Volume I

Volume II

VA-YIKRA

BA-MIDBAR

DEVARIM

Dedicated to
Leona Posner Feder z"l
and
Tzipora Ne'eman Feder

and to
Bracha, Nehama and Tzvika, David and Maayan
and
Lielle, Batya, Etai, Hila, Lianna

ACKNOWLEDGEMENTS

In putting my signature to a book of this kind, I offer its contents as a summary of my learning and thinking over many years with many teachers and students of Torah. It has been said that a student has truly made a bit of learning his own when he has forgotten from whom he learned it. Where I could attribute insights to specific teachers of Torah, I have done so by name. Where I have spoken in my own name, it is with full appreciation for the opportunities I have had to absorb Torah and general studies from many others whom I do not name but whom I thank for their wisdom and imaginative insight.

In my years in the rabbinate as teacher, preacher, and fellow student I have been privileged to serve two congregations — Beth Tikvah in Toronto, Canada, and Moreshet Yisrael in Jerusalem, Israel. Over the years the members of these two communities have given me a forum for the vital interchange and cultivation of ideas so indispensable for producing serious discussions of Torah.

The MAOR Foundation has provided the material sustenance that has allowed me to write this book. Many individuals have supported this effort. I single out for particular thanks Philip and Nancy Turk, Shelly and Sharon Wiggins, Ben and Malka Hayeems, Morris Justein, and Joe Dubrofsky. Isaac Silverstein and Norman Stern have offered their friendship and eager support in seeing through this project as well as others over the years.

I owe a debt of gratitude to my long-term friend, colleague, and fellow student Dr. Lewis Rosen for his ongoing advice, critical suggestions, and shared visions for Torah and the Zionist future. Arlene Kaplinsky was of invaluable help in typing the manuscript and guiding me through the new world of word processing.

I appreciate the efforts of Mr. Ilan Greenfield and the staff of Gefen Publishing House in producing the book, with special thanks to Fern Seckbach for her excellent editing of the manuscript.

PRELUDE

In the Book of Deuteronomy the future Israelite king is commanded to have a copy of the Torah written for him (Deut. 17:18-20). Why? Granted, it is to remind him of his obligations to fear the Almighty and to abide by the Almighty's Torah laws! But why is the king obligated to have a copy of the Torah written especially for himself if not to impose on the king's individual "self" the task of penetrating the text personally, to make the text his very own? Indeed, ever since Sinai, what can it mean for a student of Torah to listen to Torah if not to have his individual "self" be engaged totally by that Torah. One's "self" can only mean that it is not someone else's. It cannot even mean someone else's *peirush* (interpretation), unless that *peirush* has been made his very own.

Every witness to the Torah is a king — a creaturely king, to be sure, compared to the King of Kings — but a king nevertheless. He listens to the hermeneutical advisors of the past: the imaginative authors of the *midrashim*, and the medieval, modern, and contemporary *parshanim* (interpreters). But then he must attend himself to the sonorities of the text, to the renewed resonances of its songs and stories, promises and commands, blessings and threats, imprecations and consolations. Based on the text, he must listen anew, constantly, eagerly — and then orchestrate or perhaps even originate his own insights. If Moses endured for forty days and nights the fiery demonic sparks that choreographed the composition of the Torah as Moses understood it and attempted to transmit it to the Children of Israel, then I — as sovereign of my "self" — must endure a lifetime of seeking to understand what the "burning bush" of Torah is saying to me and the children of Israel of my generation.

❧   ❧   ❧

What is the Torah saying to me if I am a product of a post-Emancipation way of looking at things, of thinking of things? There is a talmudic lament *"Oy li mi-yotzri; oy li mi-yitzri"* ("Woe is me if I am afflicted by my Creator and woe is me if I am afflicted by my instinctual desire"). Anticipating Freud's insight, the Talmud recognizes that I am compelled to surrender in all aspects of my life either to my superego or to my id. But it is also clear that in all aspects of life, wedged in to a space between the superego and the id — narrow as it may be — is an ego, "I." In the struggle to iron out my *peirush* of Torah, this "I" battles the interpretive *yeitzer* (id), i.e., my gut impulses to interpret a text spontaneously, almost without thinking. At the same time, this "I" confronts and wrestles with the interpretive *yotzer* (superego), i.e., the allegedly acceptable traditional interpretation of a text. And in the crucible of my struggle with both interpretive influences, I arrive at my own *peirush* of Torah, *my* understanding of Torah.

What is this struggle? Would it not be arrogant, if not obtuse, to say that I am totally free to interpret the Torah as a fresh, newly introduced revelatory text? My instincts — not to mention my genes — have already determined certain things about me and my capacities for absorption of Torah! My parents, teachers, and a legion of other commanding forces have already injected me with and subjected me to an abundance of information and set attitudes, opinions, and predilections about Torah! Indeed, the war between my *yeitzer* and *yotzer* to determine what Torah should mean to me is unremitting. Yet it is "I" who will direct myself to participate actively in this "war-of-interpretation," and it is "I" who will hope to emerge with my own fully committed response to the call of Torah.

"I" plunge, therefore, into this two-front struggle. I fight to extricate myself from the blandishments of the *yeitzer*, from its vertiginous pull on me to give in to an accustomed spontaneous mode of thinking, feeling, and living. At the same time I challenge the *yotzer's* texts and traditional interpretations of the texts to illuminate my life anew. Not because I *ought* to let the Torah do so as an uncritical surrender on my part to the tradition, but because my post-emancipated self, my critical ego, insists that it must be so! In other words, my claim for autonomy — even if complete autonomy is an illusion — is not to make myself opaque to the influence of traditional Midrash or homiletics. On the contrary, I insist on asserting my critical autonomy so as to renew my belief in the vitality of traditional Midrash and its supple susceptibility to contemporary experiential renewal.

My insistence on autonomy also means that my individual identity as a Jewish human being must be a blatantly proud self-assertion. I assert that my hearing of Torah must help me to face my people, to be with my people, and to be inspired to communicate with my people. And through the communication of Torah between me and my people I intuit the possibility as well as expectation that we shall all rediscover what new revelatory insights to the Torah we have to share with humanity-at-large.

🦗 🦗 🦗

What is the Torah saying to me at the beginning of a new century and a new millennium? As a Jew, this past century — in truth, the entire millennium or both millennia since the destruction of the Second Temple — has witnessed two apocalyptic events that have branded themselves into my consciousness and conscience: the Shoah and the rebuilding of a Jewish sovereign state in Eretz Yisrael. I cannot reflect upon the Shoah without contemplating the malodorous near-reality of national extinction. All now know that there was a plan to bring to an end the flesh-and-blood existence of the House of Israel. It was an eminently rational plan, efficient, effective, and nearly successful. The Shoah has become the paradigm for humankind's capacity for spiritual and moral degradation — with my people, the Jewish people, as the hounded and tortured victim. It has pointed quintessentially to the flaw inherent in humanity's pretense at spiritual and moral mastery of itself. One cannot but be struck dumb by the capacity of the Torah to envision cataclysms of the dimensions of the Shoah and to have anticipated it so early in human history.

But at the same time, the Torah's dimensions in this same apocalyptic century have expanded to embrace the resurrection of Israel from the near-extinction of the Shoah. And this national resurrection has released energies long dormant in a people fettered to the "straits" of *galut* (exile) thinking and feeling. The experience of listening to the Torah in the light of such a resurrection has to have about it the aura of revelation. If revelation bespeaks an experience of spiritual transport somehow translated into a vocabulary which inserts itself into my understanding as I see myself, my people, and the world, in the here and now, today, then whatever Israel's limitations, disappointments, frustrations, there is about its resurrection meaning much beyond the immediate. Torah becomes a searing flame, as vividly present as one's sympathetic imagination will allow.

❦   ❦   ❦

A Jew living today in Diaspora and listening to Torah must be hearing, therefore, a Zionist call. The Zionist call is sifted through a prism of Diaspora existential living — culturally, socially, spiritually. The Diaspora Jew cannot deny where he is living any more than Jacob could deny living with Laban for twenty years in Mesopotamia, earning a living there while raising a family. Will such a Diaspora Jew go on *aliyah*? The same question was asked of Jacob several times: when in Mesopotamia his idealistic dreams of the ladder joining heaven and earth had turned into materialistic dreams of speckled and mottled flocks; when he sent his sons down to Egypt to buy provisions in order for the family to survive the famine in Canaan; and when he himself went down to Egypt to be with his beloved Joseph and to begin building and nurturing a people — in exile.

A Jew living today in Israel and listening to Torah is also hearing a Zionist call — a call for a renewed Zionist vision informed with a post-Emancipation, post-Shoah, post return-to-sovereignty covenanted Judaism. And such a Judaism needs more to be freshly explored than to be artificially "protected" by dogma. For through the prism of having returned as a tiny sovereign nation to the arena of political, cultural, and "religious" history, one hears revealed Torah. But it cannot be a Torah from and for another age. It cannot merely repeat. It cannot merely imitate. This renewed Torah must be a beam of spiritual, moral, political, and cultural light that inspires the Israeli Jew to invest his total self in the realization of Jacob's ladder joining heaven and earth in *his* land, in *his* society today and tomorrow. Nothing less!

The Diaspora Jew's Torah enmeshes him in the agonizing question of horizontal movement to and from Israel which in Hebrew is also vertical movement of *aliyah* and *yeridah*. The Israeli Jew's predicament — notwithstanding obvious existential differences in kind — is not terribly different in degree. Now that Israel provides the ground on which to place the ladder joining heaven and earth, can the Jew climb it, ascend it and keep ascending it — or is the descent inevitable as long as one is human? And again it must be noted that the ascent and descent are not just vertical. Jewish history has been a history of horizontal "ascent" and "descent" — redemption and exile, exile and redemption.

❦   ❦   ❦

The Torah thus keeps asking Jacob-Israel — wherever he lives — that question. And Jacob-Israel is "I," an earthly "king" ruling my "self," searching for mature self-understanding as a Jew. Jacob-Israel is every one of us, if every one of us is truly and authentically listening...

BEREISHIT

בְּרֵאשִׁית

God in Search
of a Family-Nation

What does one consider a beginning when one is thinking about one's origins? One's birth? The genealogy of one's parents? How far back does one go, can one go? To a beginning, *the* beginning! And the beginning for a Jew is the biblical beginning. It has always been so. The biblical beginning is not a geological-astronomical beginning. It is a primitive perception of the beginning; but as Gaston Bachelard once said, "for primitive man thought is a centralized reverie." By reverie a believing Jew means *yirat shamayim*, and *yirat shamayim* encompasses large visions superintended by an omnipotent omniscient overwhelming Presence. Such is the biblical beginning.

The poet who wrote Psalm 19 was experiencing creation and revelation through his own centralized reverie. Had he not been a poet but an ordinary witness to the natural light of day, he might have said something as scientifically ludicrous as "the sun is trying to come out." But his poetic sensibility painted images of a sun emerging from its tent "like a groom coming forth from the chamber, like a hero, eager to run his course." And this natural light, the psalmist says, is paralleled by the light of God's Torah. Just as the first part of the psalm is not a meteorological forecast, neither is the second part a calculatedly prosaic listing of the Torah's qualities. That the "Torah of the Lord is perfect, renewing one's life…making the simple wise…rejoicing the heart…" is a statement aimed right at one's center of enrapturement. The reverie — the *yirah* — bespeaks a readiness, an eagerness, to respond to the Presence.

The beginning is perceived as a point in the pristine past — distant, but not so distant as billions or millions of years ago. One's personal imaginative horizon would find it difficult to reach out beyond a few thousand years at the most. The reverie, the *yirat shamayim*, is that of a single human being — not yet Jewish or Israelite or even Hebrew. The Torah understands that there is a level of creaturely consciousness which is pre-Jewish-pre-Abrahamic. For with Abraham we begin to establish a family and with the family is born the beginning of a tradition and with the tradition comes the cultivation of memory. With Adam-Eve there is no memory; there is only a Presence.

And so we begin with Adam-Eve, an image of first man, first woman. What else but an image of ourselves, naked in the universe! We are overwhelmed by all the sights, sounds, smells, tastes, and feel of things. We cannot stop feeding on the sights and sounds and smells and tastes and feel of things even though we *know* that they are really not ours, that we were created just as all "things" were. Our *knowledge* of our senses already separates us from all other things and other creatures; yet like all other creatures we feed on everything. And then we dare to hide from ourselves that dimension of our knowledge which should remind us of our own creatureliness, our own dependence.

The more we hide from our total selves the more we sink into the undifferentiated foliage of reality. If not for the overwhelming voice addressing us with "*Ayeka!*" ("Where are you!"), we would never emerge from the straits of our natural creaturely habitat. And we must emerge, we must begin to establish the ground from which a later Abraham will *journey* so that his Isaac will *settle* in order for his Jacob-Israel to continue the paradigmatic *struggle* to build a ladder integrating human creatureliness and creativity.

The Book of Bereishit studies the emergence, the journey, the settling, and the struggle until a single family — a large family — of Hebrews who will become the Children of Israel will go down to Egypt in order to survive, to become a nation, and to set the scene for the later dialectic of servitude and emancipation, of *yeridah* and *aliyah*, of descent and ascent.

Bereishit   בראשית

There is God. There is Adam. There is Eve. And there is the Serpent. And then there are Cain and Abel. For Adam and Eve there is a question. For Cain — once he has killed Abel there is also a question. Each question has an answer which the Serpent's agenda seeks to subvert. The question addressed to Adam and Eve — *"Ayeka!"* ("Where are you!") — probes their human readiness to respond to their Creator-Revealer-Redeemer with worshipful love, as the future Children of Israel will be charged: "You shall love your God with all your heart, with all your soul, with all your everything." Why aren't Adam and Eve ready to love God Who has given them life? Instead they disobey Him and then surmise that they can hide from Him!

The question addressed to Cain *after* the slaying of his brother might have better suited, in retrospect, God's desired response had it been posed *before* the slaying. For to God's question *"Ey Hevel ahikha"* ("Where is your brother in your life"), the longed-for response is certainly not "Am I my brother's keeper" but an acceptance of the injunction "you shall love your brother — the significant other in your life — as yourself." But the Serpent has insinuated itself into these critical moments of human awakening, whether it be Adam and Eve's crisis or Cain's. And this Serpent, this adversarial force — created by God for the purpose of tempting Man into disobedience — has gone further. The Serpent has declared itself to be an independent "secret sharer" in the grand plan of Creation-Revelation-Redemption.

The Ultimate Sin

The Serpent is not merely our "id" or "instinct." If tradition has associated it with the *yeitzer ha-ra* (the evil drive), this dare not limit our appreciation of its power. This power of the Serpent is much beyond customary meanings given to clinical terms like id or instinct. There is more to the representational function of the Serpent in the Garden than mere animal drive. There is a near-irresistible deliberative and volitional strength in the Serpent's machinations. God has created the Serpent to function as the ultimate *meisit* (the inciter to idolatry). The Serpent's machinations are part of God's plan or need to test Man's ultimate loyalty. For the idolatry of primary concern to God is not focused on forces alternative to God and Man — but on Man's temptation to announce himself as an alternative god to God.

The talmudic tractate *Sanhedrin* (29a) has caught the essence of the Serpent's malevolent role in its discussion of the judicial necessity to defend criminals in capital cases even if they refuse to defend themselves. One of the cardinal principles of an enlightened jurisprudence is that every human being under God should receive a defense even in the face of his own wickedness. All, that is, except the *meisit*. And the model for such a case is the biblical Serpent.

The biblical Serpent, argues the Talmud, could have defended himself. He could have pleaded: *"Divrei ha-Rav divrei ha-talmid, divrei mi shome'in? Divrei ha-Rav shome'in!"* ("If the master gives one opinion and the student gives another, whom does one obey if not the Master!"). The Serpent could have defended himself by arguing that the sin was totally Eve's and Adam's. They had heard the opinion or instruction of the Master, i.e., God, and then had listened to the contrary word of the student, i.e., the Serpent. They chose to obey the student. It was *their* disobedience, *their* violation of cosmic protocol. Moreover, the Serpent could have claimed that he was doing God the Master a service by testing this new creation, the human being, to see if he was ready to acknowledge an authority above him.

But this defense is precisely the one which the Serpent rejects. For adopting it would require an acknowledgment and admission on his part of God's absolute authority over all of creation — including the Serpent himself. And this acknowledgment, this admission, the Serpent will not entertain — let alone adopt. This is the essential idolatry. The student insists on being master! The Serpent agrees to no alternative sovereignty beyond himself. But worse: He incites Adam and Eve to a similar self-idolatry in that they disobey God in choosing to capitulate to the counsel of the Serpent. The Serpent — and now Adam and Eve — have become guilty of the ultimate heresy. Such heresy brooks no defense. For the essence of the heresy is not just the rejection of God as true and exclusive sovereign. It rejects God as critical

Ultimate-Superego Who must serve as unremitting therapeutic corrective to the Serpent's own self-deification and now — more crucially — to Adam and Eve's.

From *Ayeka* to *Eikha*

The Serpent's challenge to God is pure insolence. Adam and Eve at this stage lack the Serpent's audacity. And so they hide, trying to eclipse themselves in the face of God's critical scrutiny. But their sin — the first sin of humanity — is not just disobedience. In hiding from God they are attempting to deny His Presence. Later humanity will aggravate this denial with an audacity and an insolence beyond the Serpent's. But all that Adam and Eve are able to do at this juncture in the evolution of self-idolatry is to fall into a pit of confusion and self-deceit.

God as omnipotent can put Himself into a situation of eclipse vis-à-vis His creation and still retain His supernal light. When Adam and Eve put themselves into eclipse, they descend into an abyss of sightless bewilderment and terror. As *Midrash Shir ha-Shirim Rabbah* puts it, before Adam and Eve's sin, they are able to hear the voice of God while standing erectly and without fear. But after their sin of incipient self-idolatry they cannot attend to the Commanding Voice without losing their own anchor, albeit an anchor grounded in self-deception. They have rejected the Commanding Voice by blocking it out of their consciousness. They are determined to walk in the footsteps of the Serpent. But they learn quickly that by shutting out God's illumination they have sentenced themselves to an existence mired in fear and shame. Adam and Eve are now left in hiding — huddling close to one another while not trusting one another — groundless, helpless.

The pathos of Adam and Eve has been their refusal to accept the blessedness of their state in Eden as "little less than the angels." Given the power to name the particles of reality surrounding them, they have been incited to believe that with this primordial power, this "language capacity," it follows that they should possess the comprehensive answer to all questions. Their self-deception hides the truth that whatever power/capacity they have has not originated with them; it has been totally derived from God.

In their utter aloneness, their response to God's call *"Ayeka"* ("Where are you?") is not tragic. It lacks tragic nobility. Adam gives an embarrassed response: "I heard the sound of You in the garden, and I was afraid because I was *eirom* ('naked'), so I hid." *Eirom* (naked) evokes its twin attribute *arum* (cunning) associated with the Serpent. This verbal echo cannot help but arouse God's wrath beyond His initial tragic disappointment in His creatures. What answer should Adam have given to the question *"Ayeka?"* He could have said "I have heard your voice, O Lord, and thank you that I am not alone to bear the illusion that I am perfect; for I now know that I am imperfect, that whatever illumination I can bring to the reality about me is derived from You, my Creator and Revealer."

God's *Ayeka* is the ultimate tragic interjection — vowelized elsewhere in the Bible as *Eikha!* ("Woe!") It will encapsulate Moses' agony over the burden of shepherding Israel through its wilderness of disbelief. It will burst out of Isaiah as he views Jerusalem playing the harlot and out of Jeremiah lamenting the solitary Jerusalem, now abandoned, now forsaken. But God's sense of woe, God's *ayeka-eikha* — here — at the very beginning of His creative enterprise will expel Adam and Eve from His and — it had been hoped — their Garden of Eternal Life.

Adam's self-idolatry will turn the Garden into a "wilderness." At the very appearance of the Garden and Adam's placement in the Garden he had been charged with the task of cultivating it — *"le-ovdah u-le-shamrah"* ("working it and guarding it"). This labor was not intended to be "by the sweat of the brow." It was to be an exhilarating, uplifting, rapturously creative effort. But as with any work of art, the artist required self-control. Whatever was in the Garden — from the foliage to the food — was to be tended by Adam. It was why he had been put there. It was his opportunity to share in a pristine attempt at existential cosmic harmony. In Adam's inability to control his appetite, however, in his loss of control — done so casually, so irresponsibly — he has surrendered his right to the Garden.

His only place henceforth will be the "wilderness." And he will not deserve the sympathy which Moses will deserve when he cries *"eikha"*; for Moses will have been given the "wilderness" to begin with — never the Garden. The later Israel will be warned — like Adam and Eve — not to let their eyes wander indiscriminately after anything and everything. It will be the later Jerusalem's having become a "wilderness" of untended, unsupervised idolatrous growth, a repository of lust and rapacity, which will evoke Isaiah's *"eikha."*

That Adam and Eve have failed to control their appetite and have turned their nude innocence into lustful embarrassment brings them not only into adversarial conflict with their Creator. They have now become adversaries of each other with accompanying mutual condemnation leading to separate solitudes. Thus Adam and Eve as separate lonely creatures have now become the antithesis of God's original intention. Eve had been created, had been put there, in the Garden, for the explicit purpose that Adam should not be alone; that they should represent together an incipient community. But their togetherness is illusory. Confronted by their first "crisis of trust," Adam blames Eve for the sin. Yet in his acceptance of the forbidden fruit he has been no less guilty than she. In truth he is more guilty in that he has now separated himself from her in the moment of joint peril.

If Isaiah will see the later Jerusalem as a harlot — an image sufficiently defamatory — Jeremiah will capture the tenebrous solitude of Jerusalem sunken deep in her harlotry. And that solitude in its abjectness is the true despair. Whatever sin Adam and Eve have been capable of committing before God, standing at least together before the common judge could somehow, even slightly, mitigate the verdict. But the "divorce" — and the blaming is the cutting edge of divorce — isolates each of them instead of shielding both of them, even ephemerally. For in moving apart, leaving themselves to face God, each alone, they imitate the paradigmatic Godless rebel — the Serpent.

God cannot permit this ultimate challenge to His sovereignty. He cannot permit it to the Serpent who — arrogant to a level of super-pretentiousness — must be made to crawl literally, or worse, to slither into eternity. God cannot permit it to Man and Woman who may have been chosen to rule the world, but only as God's deputies. And so God will issue His edict of expulsion, an edict etched in truth, searing in its just affirmation of a Godly decision which has no alternative but to determine exile for those who would reject so abjectly the perfect harmony of Eden.

At the same time, Adam and Eve — notwithstanding their sin and the severity of the decree of exile — will not be rejected totally by God. God will lament their fate just as His *eikha* will lament the fate of the later Israel when they are similarly forced into exile as punishment for their rebellion against God. And Moses, Isaiah, and Jeremiah will all lament Israel's fatal flaw of collective self-idolatry. But Israel, though an unbearable burden to Moses, a harlot to Isaiah, the solitary scorned of Jeremiah's lamentations, will never be rejected totally by God. Like Adam and Eve, exile, yes! Total rejection, never!

Justice and Mercy: Adam, Eve, and Cain

Adam and Eve are driven out of Eden. But they are still the exclusive progenitors of humanity. They will become wedded again — but now in the "wilderness." What will be the essential difference between the Garden and the "wilderness"?

A rabbinic *midrash* has a debate going on within God's inner circle of angels. Truth argues against the creation of Man; for Truth anticipates the coming creature called Man as a creature of lies. But God throws Truth to the ground and creates Man anyway. Abraham Joshua Heschel has expressed the thought in Yiddish: *"Di kise-ham'lukha funem mentsch shteit oifn kever fun emes. Der mentsch is a kaysar, veil der emes ligt bagruben. Az okh un vei tzu aza memshalah."* ("The throne of Man stands on the grave of truth. Man is a king as long as the truth is buried. Woe to such a kingship.") And in the *midrash* the angels protest against God having thrown his own seal (truth) to the ground. In the words of Psalm 85:12: "Truth shall (must?) spring up from the earth, even as justice looks down from heaven."

Man will thus have to struggle to discover the truth not in a heavenly Eden but in a terrestrial "wilderness" which will lend itself only to a painful sweat-filled labor. A "wilderness" of dissonances daring Man to seek harmony! Is Man up to this destiny? Will Israel be up to it? Can justice look down from heaven as an unmoved Mover expecting Man to succeed in such a "wilderness"?

Another rabbinic *midrash* has God originally seeking to create the world according to His *middat ha-din* (attribute of justice) exclusively. Seeing that the world can never be sustained according to such a standard, God alters His plan of creation by introducing His *middat ha-rahamim* (attribute of mercy) as an adjunct to the process. It will be God's *middat ha-rahamim* that will enable Adam and Eve to survive the expulsion. The blessing of the *middat ha-rahamim* will enable them to resurrect their own sense of partnership and move on to their "wilderness" — but a "wilderness" of continuing possibility.

They will need constant reminding that they have survived because of

God's attribute of mercy. And they dare never forget that mercy is not only a deviation from strict justice; but that showing mercy, and asking for mercy means looking for compromises with the truth. For truth demands justice, rightness — not mercy for wrongness. There will be later teachers who will remember, as souls scorched by truth, that there is a difference between receiving justice and receiving mercy. Justice is done when human beings receive reward for something good because they have earned it, as opposed to — out of mercy — receiving something good even though they have not earned it. What are Adam and Eve to learn from their expulsion from Eden and subsequent amnesty? What will they be trying to teach their offspring Cain and Abel — to seek and demand justice, equity, and fairness because they deserve it or to beg and plead for mercy because they do not!

And yet how can the descendants of Adam and Eve — the exiled from Eden — not learn that as human beings their destiny will be conditioned by an oscillation between standards calling forth justice and errors banking on mercy. The oscillation will be socially, politically, and morally indispensable for survival. It will also unfortunately hide much self-deception as human beings seek to dispense justice and mercy to themselves and others or at times withhold justice and mercy from others and even themselves. The future Cains and Abels will be destined to go about justifying actions at all costs, or showing mercy to themselves at all costs.

And if it will be Cain, left alive in mortal struggle with his brother, where will he be in response to the question "*Ayeka?*" Or will that question now be superseded by the more relevant socially imposed question: "Where is your brother?" What should Cain have said when confronted with the question: "Where is Abel your brother?" Rashi sees God's intention in asking the question as a merciful attempt to give Cain an opportunity to confess before being accused. Instead of taking advantage of the opportunity, however, Cain gives the worst possible answer. He surely knows that God knows what has happened. His answer, therefore, is not just brazenly ingenuous: "I do not know; am I my brother's keeper!" In essence, his homicidal act and seeming lack of regret underscore his resentment that God had created someone else besides him, like him (one tradition has it that they were twins), someone else to share with him, to compete with him. Cain has demanded exclusivity.

Cain cannot address himself to the "where is your brother" question appropriately when he has not known how to answer the more pristine question addressed originally to his parents — *"Ayeka!"* Cain may lack the insolence of the Serpent in entirely denying God as Master, as Sovereign. But Cain is sufficiently cunning in his alleged acceptance of God as Creator, Master, and Sovereign to nevertheless challenge God's creative effort. The *Midrash Tanhuma* puts into Cain's mouth the following argument: "You are the keeper, the guardian of all creatures and you ask me where my brother is? To what is this like if not a thief who steals vessels during the night and is not caught. By morning, however, he *is* caught. And to the guard's challenge: 'Why did you steal these vessels?' the thief retorts, 'I am a thief — by profession, so to speak — and therefore was doing my job. But you, O guard! Your job is to guard and you failed to do so! Why hold me responsible for the consequences of your failure!'"

Cain is not the offspring of the wholly self-idolatrous Serpent who will not countenance the idea or reality of a being superior to him. Cain accepts God; but he has not reached a level of understanding that will enable him to respond honestly to the living Presence of a superior being. The realization that acknowledging a Presence is not merely a cognitive or affective process, but is an activating sociomoral commitment has not begun to pierce Cain's consciousness. He has as yet no conscience. Conscience would give him the moral grounding to respond to *"Ayeka"* and *"Ey Hevel ahikha."* Thinking in terms of justice and mercy in the new "sharing" environment which he inhabits with others has been beyond Cain. Not that he isn't intelligent! But his intelligence bestows upon him, morally speaking, nothing more than the capacity to rationalize his wrongdoing!

Cain argues that it must be something in God's creative plan which has led to the homicide. After all, says Cain, You O Lord are the Ultimate Conscience! If I've done something wrong, if "stealing" (from the *Tanhuma* analogy above) or killing — as I have done in this case out of my natural instinct — is now judged by You to be wrong, then You are responsible for creating me as I am. And now it is clear that You have manipulated me — Your creature — a manipulation which is utterly arbitrary!

But there is a flaw in Cain's argument. It lies in overlooking the reconciliation of Adam and Eve orchestrated by God's *middat ha-rahamim.* Adam and Eve have indeed been driven out of the Garden; but they have come together again in intimacy — "conceptually," as the pun would have it, in two senses: (1) Adam has acknowledged Eve by *naming* her, *conceiving* her in the abstract as the mother of all living human beings; but (2) he also "knows" her in the fullest personal psycho-physical sense which makes possible the *conception* and birth not just of humankind in general but specifically Cain and Abel. This means that Adam and Eve have learned to respond to one another. They will know henceforth how to respond to God's *"Ayeka."* They certainly know what God's response has been to them, a response calibrating justice and mercy sufficient to give them another chance — albeit outside of Eden. But Adam and Eve have now also learned what "response-ability" entails for them: a similar allegiance to the twin attributes of justice and mercy.

Cain's sin, therefore, is a retrogression to the solipsism of pre-exiled Adam and Eve. He has rejected the injunction which he should have implicitly known: "Love your human brother as yourself." He has eliminated his brother and he knows the implications of his deed. He knows that he is guilty! He cannot deny knowledge of his guilt! But now the question becomes: Is he thereby to be condemned totally, completely, absolutely? Has God's attribute of justice condemned him — utterly, finally, absolutely? Or in Cain's readiness to plead for mercy, is he patently admitting that he has committed a wrongdoing and is thereby deserving of some mitigation of sentence?

Rashi adds a footnote to the *midrash* from *Tanhuma* in which Cain is seen to be presenting a wholly amoral argument accusing God of bearing the responsibility. But Rashi has Cain adding: "You Who shoulder the weight of all supernal and terrestrial beings — why can You not bear my sin as well, since it is too much for me to bear!" Cain, according to Rashi, is hereby acknowledging that he has sinned! Will such a claim now bring Cain respite? The Ramban adds a further dimension of remorse to Cain's defense, bestowing upon the protagonist more and more of a human face: "You have driven me out of any terrestrial space as I must wander from place to place. Moreover I must hide from Your Presence for I am irretrievably ashamed. Indeed my sin according to You Who are perfectly just is utterly unforgivable."

Cain's remorse is a self-condemnation subjectively superimposed upon the guilt which is an objective consequence of the deed. Cain has now become a judge of himself and is immeasurably more severe than even God. And it is with this human superimposition of a starker justice than God seeks — for perhaps Cain didn't realize the blow or blows with which he struck Abel would lead to death — that the attribute of mercy must manifest itself, even for Cain.

Ibn Ezra senses the poignancy in Cain's predicament by identifying the word *avon* (sin) with the punishment. Indeed, it is the sin-as-punishment which is too heavy to bear. It is God's attribute of justice that if unmodified or unmollified by the attribute of mercy will sentence Cain to a fate so stark as to leave a residual sense that something is missing in the judgment — that this is not quite what is intended for this first criminal within the biblical cosmos. Ibn Ezra thereupon humanizes Cain further by having Cain not only admit the crime but acknowledging that some punishment must and will follow. Once his confession is made, however, Ibn Ezra has Cain looking for some show of sympathy, some promise of possible atonement. There must be some way for this first criminal who is still a human being created in the image of God to maintain his connection with God.

God's attribute of mercy will thereby grant a degree of sympathy to a Cain whose horror at being hidden from God's Presence is indeed too much to bear. God's attribute of mercy will together with His attribute of justice mark Cain as untouchable to other blood-lusts. In short, God's Presence will protect him as long as he lives. But that is all! Justice must demand its punishment. Therefore, Cain's "destiny" will be to wander through the "wilderness" without *destination*. Such a "destiny" will lack redemptive hope. The angst of hopelessness is necessitated morally, after all, by the finality of the crime for the victim.

Cain, in other words, in his wandering — without hope of destination — will still have life to possess, to relish, as long as it is granted to him with God as his protector. A long-term future, however, cannot lie ahead for Cain. His genealogical line can have no future; for the echo of the Psalm will be affirmed: "...the way of the wicked is doomed to extinction." He has destroyed any possibility of loving his brother — his relevant other — as himself. He has frozen his humane potential into an idol of self-worship. He has closed himself off from sharing the earth's largesse through the care of another human being — his brother. This largesse exists even outside of Eden in a pre-cultivated "wilderness." He has thus condemned himself to permanent exile; and an exile which is permanent must lead to extinction.

Condemned to the "Wilderness"

God's *ayeka* has indeed been His *eikha*. As soon as He uttered His *ayeka* to

Adam and Eve, it was tantamount to lamenting His own failure. It didn't matter what they said, whom they blamed. They have shattered God's dream of a Garden of faultlessness. God's subsequent questioning of Cain as to the whereabouts of his brother — knowing that Abel's blood cries out from the earth — is the distraught moan of a Creator whose artistic masterpiece has been shown to be critically flawed. Among the many anthropomorphic passages in the Bible, is there a more sad-hearted one than the depiction of God viewing His creation and realizing "how great is Man's wickedness on earth, and how every plan devised by his mind is nothing but evil all the time." Under such circumstances how can God's "heart not be saddened;" how can God not "regret that He has made Man on earth."

So reclaiming God's own sovereignty is the motivating force for exiling the rebellious Adam and Eve from the Garden and condemning Cain to a pointless wandering through a "wilderness" with no exit. Abel has been forgotten, relegated to "Hevel-ness" — sheer nullity. And Cain, having lusted after everything and having lost everything, will wander and wander until there is no path left for him.

As for Adam and Eve, what of their future? Their line through Abel has been severed. Their line through Cain — in justice — has similarly been cut off. But Adam and Eve in being exiled from the Garden into the "wilderness" are granted the hope that had been taken from Abel and has been forfeited by Cain. Their surrogate son — granted to them, "posited" for them (as his name "Seth" suggests) will carry the line into a future where there will be a stopping-place within the wandering, an end-place, a destiny focused on a destination beyond the "wilderness."

Adam and Eve as Adam-Humanity have been expelled from God's ideal Garden. As Adam-Humanity, they cannot get back into the Garden. God's cherubic-guardians reinforced by the flaming revolving sword will prevent any such return. But a return to Eden is not Man's mandate. Man will now be destined to journey through a "wilderness" of *testing, temptation, and tribulation*. The *testing* will be abstracted in a much later injunction by an Israelite prophet Micah, although the injunction will be aimed not exclusively at Israelites but at universal Man: "He has told you, O Man, what is good, and what the Lord requires of you: to do justice, and to love mercy, and to walk humbly with your God." The *temptation* will continue to be provided by deviant impulses seeking to distort the sound of the Presence calling out to Man

"Ayeka." The *tribulation* will characterize the struggle to discover the response to the *ayeka* concretized in the equally weighty struggle to live out the dialectical justice-mercy response to "Where is your brother in your life?"

The ongoing test will trace the journey of biblical Adam through a particular history in its search for a place beyond the "wilderness." It will be the particular history of Israel whose envisioned destiny through the length of the journey will model the dream of a universal Man who feels redeemed when called by God to respond in love to Him as he lives out covenanted loving relationships within the Brotherhood of Man. Eden is now closed. The "wilderness" now beckons. It is a threatening "wilderness," where the omens of discontinuity are already hovering over the descendants of Seth. In this pre-redeemed earth-wilderness, is there a place for Seth, for Noah, for Man...?

Noah נח

God's *eikha* is an *ayeka* hurled at Himself. *Where is God at* now in His planning? To begin with, self-criticism is in order: In His characterization of the creation in general as "good," as "very good," what did He expect, once He had created Man and placed him in charge of this earth which was "very good"? God expected harmony as orchestrated by Himself the composer and conductor. As composer He had laid out the entire original composition. A masterpiece! But was God envisioning Himself as conductor — visible, active, up front, in performing the "composition"? Or was God to remain behind the scenes, leaving the "performance" in the hands of Man? The answer was clear! In His original charge to Man to have dominion over all the living things on earth, was God not placing in Man's grasp the free will and responsibility for assuming sovereignty in the "performance" of the composition with all its attendant risks?

And so after God's disappointment with Adam and Eve and Cain a fresh new beginning is made. Seth is born. He is to serve as a new focus for creative assertion, the progenitor of Enosh, the new Man, the weaker but more mature replica of the original model of humanity. God has attempted a refashioning of harmony — in the more mature environs outside of Eden! The plan of creation has been modified. Humankind is to be given a "wilderness" — but a "wilderness" ready to be cultivated. God will recede somewhat from this modified undertaking, abandoning utopian dreams to an undetermined future. In His mercy, He has given the descendants of Seth another chance.

But no! God's *eikha* will presently roar again — this time rending His creation entirely. For this time a huge amorphous collective of human beings has replaced the original tiny family as the destroyer of Godly harmony, as the mocker of God's creative spirit. God's reaction is an eruption of devastating power. Everything must be turned upside down, not only Eden, but the "wilderness" itself. All must be swept away, crushed, atomized.

Yet, at the same time, sensitive to His own self-critical *ayeka*, God does not surrender completely to His righteous anger, to the explosive expression of His *middat ha-din* (attribute of justice). He has not given up totally on Man — although the apocalyptic dimensions of the Deluge might testify otherwise. God chooses one post-Eden family, the family of Noah, to survive. This saving of one family is God's *middat ha-rahamim* (attribute of mercy) manifesting itself again not only to humanity, but this time to Himself.

Noah is described as "a righteous man, blameless in his age." The phrase "blameless in his age" will serve to stimulate a later rabbinic debate as to his genuine moral credentials. Was he blameless only in contrast to the extreme wickedness of his age or was he truly a righteous man for all ages?

The debate has Noah's defenders arguing that had he lived in an age of exemplary righteous people, he would have achieved even greater moral heights. The basis of the claim is that God selected him to justify the saving of future humankind. He must have somehow been worthy. Didn't he exhort the people for 120 years to mend their ways as he built his redemptive ark in public, enduring their taunts and threats? Noah's accusers among the interpreters, on the other hand, see Noah as a fairly dim model of moral rectitude. Had he lived in a generation blessed by Abraham's spiritual and moral effulgence, Noah would have fallen into the shadows, indistinguishable from the conventionally less than righteous masses. Doesn't Rashi underscore Noah's lack of faith in that he did not enter the Ark until the torrential waters forced him to? Moreover, what kind of moral exemplitude does Noah represent in not pleading with God to save humanity? He is ready to sail away to private salvation without uttering a word!

What shines forth through the later rabbinic debate, however, is not that the defense and the prosecution disagree on whether Noah measures up to standards of absolute righteousness, blameless "for all seasons," as it were. It is that both sides agree on what Noah must measure up to as an affirmation of God's creative purposes. The defense says he was worthy in God's eyes to be selected; the prosecution says that even he lacked total faith in God's announced decree. But what both sides agree upon is the reality of God's Providence as a force for determining the world's destiny and the fullness thereof. The defense argues that Noah exhorted mankind to repent; the prosecution maintains that he was content to escape alone. But what both sides are claiming implicitly is that compassion for the rest of humanity must be an integral part of one's own sense of self if one is to be a wholly righteous person, worthy to participate in God's creative enterprise.

In their commentary the Rabbis have thrust into God's calculus for viewing the future of His creation the role of His *middat ha-rahamim* even as He has prepared to destroy this creation. Noah's family is selected to serve as the foundation for a new attempt at building a world not only committed to God's purposes, but a world hospitable to human beings. As such, a primary condition for God to set for Himself is to "never again doom the earth because of Man"…nor to "ever again destroy every living being." God will now "accept" the reality of Man as a creature "whose devisings are evil from his youth." The removal of Man from the harmony of Eden is thus not merely to a cosmic-mythologically grounded "wilderness"; it is to a *sociomoral* "wilderness" waiting to be cultivated, requiring specially endowed individuals and groups who will lead in the sociomoral cultivation. Eventually it will be Abram the model individual leaving for the model Land chosen for sociomoral cultivation; and it will be Israel the model family-tribe-nation chosen to people that Land and live out in paradigmatic fashion the challenges of the sociomoral cultivation.

The New Beginning and the Necessary Secular

God Himself will be careful never again to permit His own concern for creation and the constant mending necessary to modify creation to bring Him to the threshold of anger — an anger which in its omnipotence is necessarily apocalyptic. In a carefully modulated fashion He will "alienate" Himself from the world as part of His reconciliation with that world. He will perform what the later Jewish mystics will call *tzimtzum* — a necessary self-limitation, leaving the created arena, the post-Eden, post-Deluge "wilderness" free for human action. This human action will only be free to exercise itself in a world which is thereby secular, that is, mundane — released, if only moderately, from God's embrace, but sufficiently free to be responsibly human.

The pressure towards secularization is intrinsic to the post-Eden human-God encounter. It was this drive towards secularization which had served as the background for Man's first disobedience in the Garden itself. The Hebrew words *hol* or *hilon* or *hillul* are all associated with the root for secular, mundane and profane. But the root (*hll*) also means "beginning," as in the Hebrew word *hehel*. The common root suggests that secularization characterizes every beginning, a phenomenon which is functionally necessary in order to allow Man the freedom to work the earth, to cultivate it in order to produce blessings. God understood this in placing Adam and Eve to work the Garden and to guard it. God's *ayeka-eikha*, however, has lamented Adam and Eve's following the Serpent's counsel and thereby turning the necessary secularization into a gratuitous profanation of God's will.

The same would be true for antediluvian Man. The later Rabbi Shimon will teach that there are three places in this early biblical material where the word *hehel* signifies not just neutral, colorless "beginning," but profane rebellion. And the rebellion in each case is against pre-conceived Godly visions of harmony. The first citation comes from the period of Enosh: *"Az huhal likro be-shem Adonai"* ("Then they *began* to call on the name of God"). Rabbi Simon sees this *beginning* of worship, however, as a profanation in that it is in truth the beginnings of idolatry. The second citation refers to the increase in population: *"Va-yehi ki* hehel *ha-adam la-rov al penei ha-adamah u-vanot yuldu lahem"* ("When human beings *began* to multiply on the earth and daughters were born to them"). This is the introduction to the mysterious mythological passage in which the so-called "divine beings" consort with these daughters to produce the "giants." These acts are profane, perversely so. The third citation alludes to Nimrod: *"Hu* hehel *lihyot gibor ba-aretz"* ("He *began* to be mighty in the land"). His thrust towards mightiness leads him along the profane path of political authoritarianism.

All these rebellious "beginnings" culminate in God's characterization of the attempt to build the Tower: *"Ve-ze* hahilam *la-asot"* ("And this these rebels *begin* to do"), i.e., to rebel out of their profane arrogance. But the arrogance has been there tragically from the beginning. God has insisted on human autonomy, for how can the human being manifest love for God if not as a free agent exercising his autonomous will. But at the same time, God now knows that any assertion of human autonomy is in danger of tipping over sooner or later into rebellion, as Rabbi Shimon's three examples underscore: (1) Humankind begins to call on the name of the Lord? Calling on the name of the Lord will lead to repeated attempts of one religious group — through the necessarily limited teachings of its theology, cosmology, ideology — to dominate others, to persecute others, to exterminate others; (2) Humankind begins to multiply on earth and "daughters are born to them"? The world will witness the agonizing struggle to establish institutions to regulate sexual relationships, to harmonize differing needs, yearnings, desires, passions among persons, families, tribes, and peoples; (3) Humankind will begin to be "mighty in the land"? History will record the successive growth of empires at the expense of smaller nations. Power undedicated to transcendent purpose but strapped to its own unsatisfied lust to envelop all will inevitably overextend and feed the seeds of its own disintegration, only to invite a new power to swallow it up. And then that new power will in turn push itself to new levels of imperial aspiration — with ultimate disintegration to follow.

In short, the human tragedy with God as tragic witness will not be a result of Creation requiring a secular dimension. But that the secular dimension invites profanation will become the overarching bane of human existence and the recurring goad to God's *eikha*.

Man's Categorical Right to Life

The builders of the Tower of Babel presume to challenge Heaven itself. The presumption is a natural extension of the rebellious proclivities of Man at every turn. The rebelliousness is illegitimate not just because it denies any possibility of fulfilling the first love which God the Creator has been seeking: "You shall love the Lord your God..." And this spiritual rebelliousness itself could be enough to draw forth another cosmic *eikha* from a God who has again been abused — now in this new post-Eden situation. But in addition, the sociomoral vice which accompanies the rebelliousness negates any possibilities of fulfilling the second "love" commandment — to love one's fellow human being as a brother. For in each of the three cases cited above by Rabbi Shimon, whether religious, social, or political, one human being is seeking to dominate another.

Man as rebel against God is seeking to substitute himself for God — a serious enough heresy. But such a substitution exposes humankind to a danger more horrific than that brought on by the "mere" challenge to the Presence, the Presence Who, though all-powerful, may in any case restrict His concern to the celestial realm. God may just decide to abandon the earth to the devisings of the rebels. The horrific outcome of such abandonment, however, would be an earth left to those human beings who fancy themselves as gods "whose devisings are evil from youth." These man-gods would show a capacity for fiendishness which would so thirst to victimize all humankind that God's dream for the terrestrial realm — harmony-on-earth — would be scarred irretrievably.

A new grounding, therefore, must be posited for the human being's spiritual and sociomoral development. It must precede and undergird any hope for cultivating the capacity to love God and human beings. This new grounding has in fact existed since Creation. It is the biblical "fact" that humankind, i.e., all human beings, have been created in the image of God! It isn't that God will surrender the first injunction "to love Him" which evoked His original *ayeka*. God looked for that love from Adam and Eve, failed to get it — with fateful consequences. And God will continue to seek that worshipful love from other individuals, families, the Children of Israel, and eventually all humankind. It is the second injunction "to love your fellow as yourself" that, after Adam and Eve's initial "failure of trust," and Cain's murder of Abel, and the wholesale wickedness of the antediluvians, has been shown to be dangerously utopian.

Granted, God surely knows that "you shall love your fellow as yourself" is an inspiringly uplifting injunction. As an overriding moral principle, however, it has already proven itself less than adequate. At first look it could be considered a sound utilitarian foundation for a rational approach to morality and the basis for a valid sociomoral educational agenda. But it fails to confront the potent reality of a human being "whose devisings are evil"; as such, its purview is limited. The human being may not be imprisoned from birth in the shackles of the implacable *yeitzer ha-ra*. But the serpentine blandishments of this *yeitzer ha-ra* are there and increase the more the human being grows.

God will not conclude that Man, His creature, *must* be evil. Such a proposition cannot be correct; but to say that Man *can* be evil — a sufficiently ominous characterization — has been shown already in this early period of the growth of humankind to be painfully true. Man can not only be evil; he can be irrational, he can be a sadist and masochist, a self-hating, self-destructive creature who in his own desperate lust for achievement or happiness (as he imagines it) or salvation (as he dreams of it) is quite prepared to abuse others, to subjugate them, to liquidate them.

Again, this does not mean that Man *will* be evil; it *does mean* that he battles his *yeitzer ha-ra*, the allurements of the Serpent, without respite. Aiming to love one's fellow is a worthy effort. It is a necessary effort, but God now knows that it is not sufficient as a moral grounding for building a humane society. The *Midrash Rabbah* records the search of Ben Azzai and Rabbi Akiva for an overriding moral principle found in the Torah. Akiva chooses "thou shall love thy neighbor as thyself." Ben Azzai prefers "*ze sefer toldot ha-adam*" ("this is the record of the line of Adam") as more fundamental to God's spiritual and sociomoral agenda.

At first look, Ben Azzai's maxim does not seem to be a sociomoral injunction at all. Yet, its sociomoral grounding is categorical; for it postulates that all human beings are equal and inviolable; not because human beings choose to love other human beings, but because they are all creatures of God. A human being's life, therefore, is an independently sacred entity, not contingent upon whether he is worthy of love. One does not oppress a fellow human being. One does not take another human being's life — except to ward off a lethal attack by that other human being who in his attack has thereby forfeited his own right to live.

In other words, the right to live as a necessary gift of every human being — not a contingent one — is the most essential of gifts in that it is derived from Man's having been created in God's image. All creatures in the universe are to fear Man — including human creatures vis-à-vis each other — because any attempt to injure Man is a blow aimed at the "image of God."

God has thus chosen to reiterate this message, first given at Creation, to the post-Flood generation. For He knows that Man must struggle to have that Godly "image" of his neutralize the relentless temptations to sin, to commit to evil, which the *yeitzer ha-ra*, the Serpent, places in his path. The talmudic tractate *Hagigah* quotes a phrase from the prophet Micah (7:5): "*Al taminu be-re'a*" ("Do not trust a certain type of friend"). It adds: "If the *yeitzer ha-ra* should urge you to sin assuring you that the Holy One Blessed Be He will forgive, don't believe him, as it says, 'don't trust this friend,' since this 'friend' — *re'a* — is the *yeitzer ra*." The search for a mode of social living which can then somehow make it possible to approach the messianic fulfillment of loving a friend as oneself instead of unleashing either in oneself or in the friend impulses to do evil must become then the burden of the post-Noah generations.

But again, the grounding for such a mode of social living cannot be dependant on as illusive a moral injunction as "love your fellow as yourself." It must be a regulative system that recognizes the *ra* — the evil which persists in disguising itself as Man's friend. And so what becomes known eventually as the Seven Commandments of the Descendants of Noah is revealed as part of a covenant with Man. It is revealed, but it has been part of the intrinsic nature of Man as understood by God from before this covenanted revelation — from God's very creation of Man in His image. For if the Seven Commandments — prohibition of bloodshed, for example — had not been assumed to be known to Cain, then why was he punished?

Building a society then is expected to be doable by natural law. Establishing courts to mete out justice, prohibiting bloodshed, robbery, blasphemy, idolatry, incest, and the eating of flesh cut from a living animal are understood to be basic pillars for a society of human beings seeking to live together. This natural law should be sufficient as a ground for building and socialization, even if it had not been revealed explicitly. But since the *yeitzer ha-ra* — the diabolical "friend" — battles to turn every human initiative, every human beginning, into a profanity, a self-indulgent arrogation of power for corruption, the indispensability of the Seven Noahide Commandments must be proclaimed as God's revealed word. And even then, the autonomous human being will decide whether or not he is to live according to God's revealed word or to defy that word and continue building "towers" of self-deification.

The Drive to Totalitarianism

Has Noah then been chosen to carry forward a Godly mandate for humankind? God has entertained the notion. For had He not stated before the Flood: "You alone have I found righteous before Me in this generation." But Noah, after the Flood, forfeits his sociomoral potential as he is also described by the word *va-yahel*, i.e., he began, but began profanely, in planting a vineyard which would lead him to drunkenness with licentious consequences. Instead the descendants of Noah are charged with committing themselves to cultivating the post-Eden "wilderness" and to dedicating their efforts and achievements to the Source of Creation. But as a collective they also fall short in committing two elemental sins — or more particularly — one elemental sin, the sin of hubris, in two different directions: (1) they try to storm the Heavens; and in so doing (2) they disobey God's order to fill the earth.

Adam and Eve have been driven out of the Garden of Eden because in having succumbed to grasping at the forbidden tree they had seen themselves as gods and thereby sought to live forever. God had to make certain that they could not eat of the Eden Tree-of-Life. God would not countenance a life-into-eternity for a rebellious humanity. Nevertheless, this post-Eden Babel collectivity, untrammeled by doubt, decides to invade the upper realm in order to overturn the verdict. Furthermore, it is determined to reverse God's commandment to fill the earth by centralizing its "civilization" in one area. As Eliezer Schweid has described it, the people of Babel defy God's expulsion from Eden by seeking in hubris to build their own Eden.

They elect arch-rebel Nimrod — a name derived from the root *mrd*, *"mered"* (revolt) — who has risen to election by being the hunter par excellence. As the most single-minded, the most aggressive, the most ruthless figure in his society, he is perceived as the natural leader to interpret natural law according to the self-serving standards of the post-Eden "wilderness-Eden" of Babel.

The medieval commentator Sforno sees the building of the Tower as the program of the society's oligarchs. It is they who urge the building of the Tower in order to acquire a name — *the name*, the essence of human civilization. For it is their imperialistic drive which overrides, according to Sforno, the desire of the simple people to use bricks in order to build adequate homes and fences for their flock. Schweid then sees the rebellion against God as a refusal to truly share with God in creation. For God's plan is to spread out and make the whole world fruitful and all of humanity blessed. The contrary plan of the oligarchs is to find the valley between the two rivers and then turn it into an urban "Garden of Eden" for themselves and their class, thus defying God by building a city upwards instead of spreading outwards; i.e., focusing on their own narrow self-aggrandizement instead of the well-being of all. As Schweid puts it: "Man has been intended from his creation to be in God's image (purpose) to work the entire earth and guard it; instead he now seeks to limit his interest to one place on earth jutting upwards for *his own* purposes."

God expresses His "anxiety" in the words: "If as one people with one language for all, this is how they have begun to act, then nothing that they may propose to do will be out of their reach." God realizes that Man or the institutions of Man must never have complete power; for Man will misuse the power, principally to enslave others. What is most deceptive about the search for power is that at first it *appears* and in fact *is* for human good. Power is an indispensable component in creating and building and cultivating. Power gives security. Power lends confidence. Power contributes to overall well-being. Yet, at the same time, power can destroy. It can enslave, debilitate, decimate.

Why? Why should what starts out as an otherwise rational exercise of natural intelligence, strength, and will degenerate into an irrational compulsion for brutal centralized authority and mechanistic control for its own sake? According to the oft-repeated maxim *"ma'aseh avot siman la-banim"* ("that which happens to the parents is repeated with the children"), the biblical Joseph will save Egypt and the entire Middle East from famine by centralizing authority and control. This ingenious and courageous plan becomes, however, the structural foundation of a future totalitarian state which, precisely because of its monopoly ownership of all goods and services and centralized bureaucracy with easy and total access to all means of control, can enslave peoples eventually under one human but diabolical sovereign. And the later Pharaoh — he who "will have forgotten Joseph" — will serve as the model for later Caligulas and Ghengis Khans; Stalins and Hitlers; Mao Tze-Tungs and Saddam Husseins.

Babel is the precursor of Egypt, which in the crucible of the history of Israel and the Jewish people is the demonic model for all later imperialistic bondages. Assyria, Babylonia, Rome will follow and be followed by all the later economic-military cultural colossi which will seek and partially achieve suzerainty over the known world or large parts of it and will enslave among others Israelites and Jews.

Babel also serves as the paradigm — in its attempt to storm the Heavens, to challenge God — for the attempts of organized religious "brotherhoods," e.g., radical Islam, to repudiate diversity in ideas, to squelch novel spiritual explorations in the name of predetermined human projections of unity. The great imperialistic religions will sweep across the world spreading civilization — and destruction; enlightenment — and ignorance. All effected with the same strokes of the double-edged sword of human aspiration and pretentiousness!

Cassuto looks upon the genealogical listings following the flood not as a lesson in ethnology, but to emphasize that the progenitor of mankind after Noah is meant to represent a principle similar to that hoped for after Adam and Eve — a unity, i.e., one couple reproducing mankind. Yet, the Babel story smashes any thoughts of human unity as a desideratum. The Mishnah *Sanhedrin* stresses the dialectical lesson to be learned from the single-source-of-mankind theory. "If a man strikes many coins from one mold, they all resemble one another; but the supreme King of Kings fashioned every man in the stamp of the first man, and yet not one of them resembles his fellow. Therefore every single person is obliged to say: the world was created for my sake."

This teaching is a variation of the more familiar condemnation of Cain in the Mishnah for not just having destroyed Abel — but the future world descended from Abel, "to teach us that whosoever destroys a single soul of humankind is as though he has destroyed a complete world, and whosoever preserves a single soul of humankind, is as though he has preserved a complete world." The variation speaks in the name of Abel — lamenting the world's loss of any Abel with his own uniqueness for whom the world was created. But the variation also speaks in the name of Cain who, left alone in the world after slaying Abel, the other half, has proclaimed in existential fashion his act of murder (or any act of his) as the norm, as the way to behave, e.g., "the world was created for my sake" — to commit murder! Or is the world not totally dependent upon my every act because every act does establish a norm for this world and for all who dwell therein? Therefore, how can I dare to establish a norm which sanctions murder? How can I arrogate to myself the right to "correct" God's world by killing my brother?

How else can one describe the destiny/fate of Nimrod! Nimrod's plan is not to imitate Cain totally. It is not to slay everyone besides himself. Instead, it is to model everyone to fit his pre-conceived need for them in his scheme for ruling the world. Those who don't fit or won't fit he is indeed prepared to slay. He is, after all, the hunter par excellence. But those willing to fit in, those eager to deny their own uniqueness in order to attune themselves to Nimrod's uniqueness, are welcome to become the mortar for Nimrod's Tower!

Nimrod builds a huge civilization as will all the later hunters from Pharaoh to Hitler who build empires only to see them speedily or gradually but inevitably disintegrate. The disintegration is a splintering — literally — of the humanly imposed unity which has sought to blot out individual difference, individual creativity, individual claims on the world. Isaiah Berlin will offer the analogy of every future Nimrod's dream of cooking the ideal "messianic" omelet for which millions of eggs will have to be broken — and yet the ideal future omelet never gets cooked. Pity the millions of broken eggs!

The Emergence of Abram

Following the Flood, God has "matured." He fully understands and accepts that humanity's jurisdiction over the "wilderness" demands a secular conditioning of Man's potential — albeit dedicated to the Author of Creation. God has hoped that the Seven Noahide Commandments, i.e., the proto-covenantal legislation for universal humankind, will suffice to make of the "wilderness" an adequate home for all human beings created as they are in the image of God. But again, God's *eikha* will cry out in the face of Babel's totalitarian revolt.

Therefore, out of the forging of Nimrod's empire, which in defiance of God sought to hammer into a single perfectly tuned mechanism for human self-aggrandizement all the creaturely components necessary, must emerge an Abram. God must see to it. Abram will have rejected being forged or sculpted or molded by human invention. He will have seen, heard, felt, lived in the crucible of Nimrod's "high" civilization. Yet midrashic tradition has it that Abram is saved by his faith from being incinerated in the flames of this "high" civilization. Abram will thereupon remove himself not just from the larger, dictatorially secure civilization into which he has been born and by which he has been nurtured — but from the very bosom of his own family.

Indeed, Abram leaves! The father of the future Israel will prefer the unknown "wilderness" to the known, to the already welded, to the already finished and completed human "civilization" which is Babel-Mesopotamia. He must leave, he must go, for the command to fill the earth is a command to be obeyed even and particularly when the destination is as yet unknown. God knows. For Abram, that is enough! Abram's intuition will lead him to seek to fill the earth with the knowledge of God. To do that, he will be mandated to go to a specific place, a place which a later people, his descendants, will claim, conquer, and settle, not as an Eden-on-earth, but as a "wilderness" made humanly livable. That will also be enough!

Lekh Lekha   לֶךְ לְךָ

Abram is the first *oleh* ("one who goes up to the Promised Land") — and the first *yored* ("one who leaves the Promised Land"). The dialectical movement of *aliyah* and *yeridah*, going up and going down, *kenisah* and *yetzi'ah*, going in and going out, *hityashvut* and *galut*, settlement and exile, is the paradigmatic national myth of Israel. The command to go is absolute, although the reasons are embedded in the text reinforced by rabbinic interpretations. Abram must break out of the imperial prison that Nimrod has built. The initial thrust is to leave, to go, to get out. There *is* an exit! The mausoleum that is Babel is not hermetically sealed, even if on the surface the society that has spawned Nimrod and the Tower glitters with single-minded material and cultural purpose.

The purpose ostensibly has been to provide "everything" — at least for the oligarchs. For Abram, there does not need to be an *ayeka*. He is ready to be seen by God and ready to be commanded by God. He is commanded to leave, to escape from Babel and to go to a place where whatever he does will be considered a long-term blessing for himself, for the family he will raise, and for all the families of the earth.

At the same time Abram is not a superman. Material lack will compromise his staying power — at least for the short run. If the land which God has shown him cannot sustain him economically, he will "go down" temporarily — even if it is to the spiritual and moral straits of Egypt. Abram will be criticized by some later rabbinic critics for having succumbed to normal materialistic concerns. *Yeridah* in the face of famine may be understandable where ordinary people are concerned, but not for an extraordinary leader like Abram. But Abram retains his idealistic radiance because his *yeridah* is never justified beyond the material fact of famine in Canaan. It is never transformed into an ideology for exile. That will come later among some of his distant descendants.

Abram-Abraham the Extraordinary

Abram *is* extraordinary. He has responded to God's command to leave his land, his cultural birthplace, his familial home. And he has done it alone, not as part of a mass of people, but as head of a small family unit with no children of his own. This act by itself marks him as extraordinary no matter how many other tests and trials he will face and survive.

The Ramban sees the order within the command to Abram as particularly wrenching. The normal order of psychological concerns in a physical move for any individual is to realize first that he is leaving the family home. He then begins to understand that he is abandoning his cultural birthplace. Finally he is struck with the knowledge that he is going beyond the very borders of his country — to the treacherous unknown. But with Abram, there is a particularly painful psychologically grounded agitation involved in the order that God has chosen for His command. Abram is told in the following reverse order: to cross over his national borders — an opportunity which Abram will not resist in any case, considering the nature of totalitarian Babel. Then, however, he is to realize that in so escaping he will be shutting the door forever on his previous cultural identity — never a casual prospect. Finally he is to become fully sensitive to the cruelest truth of all: that he has said a final farewell to his parents, to his personal patrimony.

It can be argued — and must be argued — that notwithstanding the Ramban's psychological insight, the point of the command is precisely to override normal psychological hesitations, let alone the normal reaction of recoil before something unnatural. For the command of God, the overwhelming immediate Presence addressing Abram, is at least as incontrovertible as the *ayeka* has been to Adam and Eve or the *"ey Hevel ahikha"* has been to Cain. Except that with Adam and Eve and Cain the "questions" were condemnations for what they had already done! With Abram the command constitutes an all-encompassing commission and empowerment to act! If Abram the addressee of this command has accepted that it is a command from God, if an Abram has the *yirat shamayim*, i.e., the centralized reverie sufficient to experience the call of the outer Voice commanding him, then he has already neutralized his normal psychological misgivings and is ready to carry out an extraordinary mandate.

Abram is extraordinary not just because in the face of the overwhelming

Presence he does not hide from God like Adam; nor seek to outwit God like Cain; nor blatantly rebel against God like Nimrod. Abram is extraordinary because he is the first among the gallery of biblical personalities to grow into being a full autonomous human being, while accepting nevertheless that he continues to walk before God not as an equal but as a dependent creature. He has accepted his creatureliness in two ways. On the one hand, he is the appreciative recipient of God's largesse in having been created. But, on the other hand, he is a fully responsible human sharer in that creation, sufficiently confident in his own reverence for God and His purposes to commune with God humbly and discreetly, but openly and frankly.

Pirkei Avot (Ethics of the Fathers) speaks of Abram undergoing ten tests of his faith. And in all of them he is found to be "whole." He is wholehearted in that *"she-lo hirher ahar midotav me-rov ahavato"* ("He did not question the attributes of God because of his abundant love for God"). Such an interpretation cannot be insensitive, however, to at least two seminal episodes reported in the Torah which record explicitly Abram's "questioning." Abram will question God's justice in the face of the coming destruction of Sodom. And even more basically, Abram will challenge God's very logic, as it were, when He has promised that Abram's seed shall be as countless as the stars in heaven. Surely it is obvious that he and Sarai are well beyond the normal years of fertility.

Abram's faith, however, is not a simple ordinary faith, a childishly blind sense of security in the face of threats, unpredictabilities, and evidences of injustice in the world. The summary verse containing the first mention of faith in the Torah in general and of Abram as a man of faith in particular is Gen. 15:6: *"Ve-he'emin ba-Shem va-yahsheveha lo tzedakkah."* ("And because he had faith or put his trust in the Lord, He — the Lord — reckoned it to his merit.") But a number of commentators have noted the alternative possibility that the subject of *va-yahsheveha* is not the Lord but it is Abram. The verse may be understood as follows: He had faith or put his trust in the Lord because he — Abram — reckoned justice to be a fundamental attribute of God.

At the same time, because he had faith in God's attribute of justice he would allow himself to question God rigorously. If the destruction of Sodom would include the wanton destruction of righteous individuals — no matter how few — how could such an act be consistent with a just God? It should be noted that Abram himself did not argue below the number ten as a minimum quorum for a viable community. At first he couldn't believe that there weren't fifty righteous citizens in Sodom. And so he challenged God's alleged attribute of justice — politely but stubbornly — until his surrender at ten.

More immediately and more personally and crucially, if at the very beginning of Abram's career as an *oleh* it was promised that he would become a great nation even though at an advanced stage of life he and his wife were still barren, what criteria were being applied in seeing God as just or rational or even minimally comprehensible?

Yet the mature *emunah* (faith) of Abram rests on a sense of intuitive certainty and consequent security tested by experience in the caldron of life-on-earth. Unlike Cain, for example, who has been sentenced to wander from place to place never to know his place, Abram is commanded to leave his place in order to go to another specific place which God will show him. He and his descendants will face in turn obstacles denying their claim to the place; but they will know for certain where the place is and that it is a place which has been promised to them. For Abram's *emunah* has reconstructed for him — and later on for his descendants — the world in an image of confirmed confidence that there is a Creator, that Providence rules, that whatever negative images appear in order to deny the truth of Creation and Providence, they will be dispelled. God's promises will be fulfilled!

The tests thrust at Abram will be prodigious, beginning with the burden of loneliness. Carving out a new path and settling in to it, when there are no precedents and no confirmatory supporters, demands single-minded and iron-willed determination. But the clarity of his vision illuminates his lonely journey. He is thereby able to act decisively in a number of domestic, sociopolitical, and military crises.

Abram has a keen understanding of his environment. His self-awareness as a *yerei Elohim* (God-fearing) person is able to mold his understanding into an integrated whole projecting a will that will drive itself into a new totally unfamiliar situation ready to make a claim for a share in the consequences of his actions in that situation. Along the way, he will endure cruel domestic trials. He will be asked to choose between sons in the interest of assuring the safe transfer of the covenantal birthright and blessing. Eventually, he will have to reject and drive out the son who will be perceived to be a threat to the continuity of the covenant. He will then be given an unthinkable test bordering on absurdity, bringing him to the threshold of madness as he perceives

the necessity for obeying a transcendent command to offer up his remaining
son, his future, as a sacrificial offering. But Abram-Abraham the extraordinary will endure these trials. They will push him and pull him to greater and
greater commitments of self to God's vision, which had sent him out of the
crucible of Babel in the first place.

Along with these personal domestic crises Abram will move onto the
larger political stage as he has arrived at the place that someday, it has been
promised, will be his. There is recorded his battle against the kings. The biblical description of Abram's entrance into the war against the four strong kings
on behalf of the weak confederacy underscores the decisiveness that will have
to be his as he faces a formidable military coalition. His apparent motivation
to save his nephew Lot — who is less than deserving of his largesse — leads
him to attack and vanquish a far superior force. As such, he is recognized as a
formidable new "player" on the scene in this new place.

And then there is recorded perhaps the toughest test of all — tougher
even than the *akeidah* (binding) of his son! The promise to Abram has an
extremely lengthy projection, way beyond Abram's personal length of days.
This is why the *Brit bein ha-Betarim* (the Covenant of the Pieces) has a particularly awesome significance for the promise. How blessed can a promise be if
it is accompanied by a "great dark dread descending upon him!" Moreover,
the content of the promise will be: "Know well that your offspring shall be
strangers in a land not theirs, and they shall be enslaved and oppressed four
hundred years." What possible relief can there be found within such a horren-
dous forecast? What future blessed foreground can possibly compensate for
such a grim background?

The compensation and ultimate comfort will come from the *place*. As
cited earlier, the promise has focused on a future place — Abram's place,
Abram's land. Later Jewish tradition will see this particular land as God's special place, His chosen Land. This land is part of the created unfinished "wilderness" waiting for human cultivation. But it has been set aside by God for
special exemplary attention. The Amorites and Canaanites and Hittites possess the land now. Abram cannot be accused, therefore, of a lack of faith in
questioning God's promise in the face of the current settlement of these
indigenous tribe-nations on the land. But according to God's providential
prescience these tribe-nations are headed to perdition. Meanwhile, Abram's
descendants will be ground down in their own incubator of suffering,

waiting, weeping, wallowing in formless, aimless bondage. But they will be raised up someday, and they will be brought up from bondage to a Wilderness and then into their chosen part of the beyond-the-Wilderness "wilderness" — into the Land — and be given their opportunity to "work and guard it."

The great dark dread that has enveloped Abram-Abraham is explained by the long-term prediction of enslavement for his descendants. Yet Abram-Abraham's extraordinary faith does not waver. In a much later era, a non-Jewish theologian, Paul Tillich, will refer to one's faith or religion as one's "ultimate concern." Reflecting on the human condition, it will be suggested that every human being — if pressed by circumstances — will be brought to an existential threshold of admitting to an ultimate concern. Moreover, the human being — in his behavior — will show that he is hanging on to this ultimate concern. It may at any time be food, money, fame, sex, play, power, an ideology, a religion. Among the existentialists in Tillich's day there will be those who will attempt to contradict the unifying religious concept of an "ultimate concern" by substituting splintered momentary experiences as the be-all and end-all of the human condition.

But Abram-Abraham has laid the foundation of a view of reality which is postulated on an intense degree of *yirat shamayim* (centralized reverie) having the capacity to unify, to harmonize all the dissonances — not to mention consonances — of human experience under one supervening Presence. Living and walking before this Presence is to be Abram-Abraham's ultimate concern. And the long, arduous, and enduring history of Abram-Abraham's descendants will prove an undeniable testimony to that special *emunah*.

From God's initial command to leave Babel — the *galut* (exile) of Babel — Abram-Abraham's allegiance to the *lekh lekha* ("go forth") mandate is to be marshaled into the working-guarding-cultivation of the place called Canaan but soon to be renamed Israel. The Land is to become Abram-Abraham's way of fulfilling God's will in sending him on his *lekh lekha*. The Land is to become his and his descendants' preoccupation. For God has made the land-as-laboratory a corollary necessity for Abram-Abraham and his children — the Children of Israel — in which to practice the exercise of their total humanity.

A much later exiled teacher of the Children of Israel will summarize the place of Israel as *the* place for full religious expression: "While I am breathing and alive, I must go to Israel. Absolute spirit and wisdom are found only in Israel. There a man can attain his highest estate, to be like Him, Praised Be His Name." It is said that the disciples of this teacher, the Bratzlaver, will ask him if he is thinking and speaking of a spiritual Israel. He will answer: "No, I mean the real Israel, with its houses and streets, as we see it with the human eye. Whatever life we possess is due only to once having been in the Land of Israel."

Abram-Abraham's Fears

Abram-Abraham is thus the living, acting link between God and God's experiment in creation. He has now been assigned a specific place on earth for himself and for his descendants. He will have to fight for this place, for this land — as will his descendants. He will have to settle it and resettle it — as will his descendants. His view will have to have a projective thrust far into the future. It will also have to have the grounded faith in a long-term program which has the stamp of enduring approval of the Creator-Revealer-Redeemer. God has been perceived from the beginning as the originator of the program. His delegation of authority to Abram-Abraham has been the choice of a given individual whose faith has thus far proven itself capable of enduring not only external challenges and threats but internal doubts — and fears. What are these fears?

At a critical juncture following Abram's victory over the four kings, God consoles him with the words *"Al tira Avram, Anokhi magein lakh, skharkha harbei me'od"* ("Do not be afraid, Abram, I will protect you, your reward will be very great") (Gen. 15:1). The question arises: Militarily Abram has been totally successful. Morally speaking, he has gone out of his way, placing himself in harm's way, in order to save Lot despite the latter's having separated himself from his uncle. Psychologically as well as morally Abram must be feeling "good" about his rejection of the King of Sodom's offer of goods as payment for his decisive contribution to the victory. Why then should God have to soothe Abram's fears? What is Abram afraid of?

In general, Abram will have much to be afraid of once God effects the *Brit bein ha-Betarim* with him in which the "great dark dread" will descend upon him, seeing his descendants enslaved for four hundred years. But even before the awesome ceremony of the *brit*, Abram shows extreme anxiety. The

Midrash, studying this hero who despite his successes is fearful, gropes for an understanding of the darkness in Abram's soul.

It discovers misgivings, questionings of self which are moral, psychological, and theological. It first records Abram's awareness of the moral ambiguities of war. "What if on the opposing side, there was even one righteous person who was slain in battle!" Abram knows that he and his troops fought at the side of Sodom. How then could his side be thought of as unblemished, as morally worthy of prevailing in battle? To these sorts of doubts God answers: "Those whom you have slain were already 'thorns to be cut down!'" In other words, collectively they were already doomed to military disaster on their own evil account.

Yes, there are ambiguities in war, in human conflict. But in this case, in this specific case, the four kings have been imposing tribute upon the weak kings. But more crucially, the fact that a segment of Abram's family has been imprisoned by the four kings has made these four kings automatically Abram's enemy. Future history will dictate to a participant in that history the difficult lesson that political theory and its attempt to understand reality have to cope with moral ambiguities. Decisions will still need to be made. And the decisions will need to take into account the teachings of Machiavelli as well as Isaiah.

Another source for Abram's fear is his awareness that those whom he has defeated have descendants of their own who will hope for revenge, who will seek to renew the battle. In other words, hostilities have in effect not ended. They may never end! Whereas his first fear derives from his appreciation of the moral ambiguities associated with life's conflicts, this second fear is the emotionally charged anticipation of the certainty of an ongoing conflict-filled future — for him and his descendants. In the face of this second fear, God has to urge Abram again "not to be afraid." God will be with him as He will be with the future Israel so that the fear will not paralyze him or them but will rather energize a covenanted people to maintain constant alertness, toughness, and long-term courage.

The Midrash records a third type of fear which Abram betrays when he considers his relative good fortune within the conflicts he has already experienced. He is thankful for having been saved from the fiery furnace of Nimrod. He is thankful for having survived unscathed the war against the kings. That he is indeed alive, he never takes for granted. He knows that life with its complexities, hurdles, traps, does not offer anyone an unbroken series of joys and blessings. There lurks before every human being a balancing diet of bitterness, pain, and gall. Abram feels that perhaps he has already exhausted the blessings due him. How long can he rely on the fickleness of dangerous situations turning a favorable eye to him? Life often reflects an "unbearable lightness of being" when one thinks about accidents in peacetime, let alone casualties in war. Abram is afraid that the good fortune which has already been his must inevitably give way before its antithesis. God again has to show him that no matter what the "short-range" future may hold for him and his descendants — four hundred years of enslavement — the long-range future promises redemption.

The charge, which in the future will be given to Joshua as he stands ready to bring Abram's descendants into the Promised Land of Israel, will address itself similarly to the reality of fear: "I charge you, be strong and resolute; do not be terrified or dismayed, for the Lord your God is with you wherever you go." But the fear which Joshua will have every right to manifest cannot really compare — in kind — to Abram's; for Joshua will be following a road already paved by Moses — and initiated by Abram. But Abram — the initiator — has had no Moses as precursor, as teacher, as mentor. Abram has had to discover and uncover for himself and by himself the resources necessary to confront his fears and override them. A much later Israel will resurrect itself out of the near-extinction of Auschwitz in order to return to its Land and fight for it again and again and again. It will need to draw comfort and inspiration from its living memory of Abraham — and the God of Israel who will have been cited in prayer through the ages as the shield of that Abraham, that unique extraordinary pioneer of faith.

Abram-Abraham's Autonomy

It may be argued that Abram has had an extraordinary precursor — Noah. The biblical texts which connect — and contrast — the attributes of Noah and Abram focus on the two words *tamim* (wholehearted) and *hithaleikh* (walk). Noah is described as righteous and wholehearted (in his generation) and as walking *with* God. Abram is described as being told by God to walk *before* Him and to be wholehearted. The Midrash offers two pedagogic analogies which contrast Noah and Abram, following the interpretations of Rabbi Yehudah and Rabbi Nehemiah.

Rabbi Yehudah talks of a king who has two sons. One is more mature; one is less mature. To the less mature son, the father-king says, "Walk *with* me." To the more mature son, the father-king says, "Walk *before* me." Similarly with Noah and Abram: Noah needs the consistent support of being *with* God in a fully heteronomous relationship. Abram who is more mature spiritually, psychologically, morally — plainly speaking, is a greater person — can walk *before* God. For Abram walks through life with a considerable degree of autonomy, independence, never leaving God's Presence, experiencing God as Superego and often as Alter-ego — but never losing his own formidable sense of "I."

Rabbi Nehemiah — in considering the ego-strength of Noah — talks of a king's favorite who is sunken in thick clay or mud. The king sees him in his plight. He invites him to walk safely with him so as to avoid becoming trapped in the mud. Similarly Noah cannot be left to himself; he must walk *with* God, on the *derekh ha-melekh*, the royal path. Only with the close, immediate protection of God can Noah remain on the royal path — protected from the "mud" of human existence. Abram, on the other hand, is to be compared by Rabbi Nehemiah to the king's favorite who, peering through the window of his home, sees the king walking in dark alleyways. The favorite, seeking to assist the king, to insure that the king won't lose his way, shines light through the window which the king cannot help noticing and appreciating. The king thereupon invites his favorite to come out of his home into His very Presence in order to continue to light the way *before* Him. So it is with Abram.

The contrast between Noah and Abram is much more radical in Rabbi Nehemiah's interpretation. For whereas God's largesse is predominant in Rabbi Yehudah's analogy — whether God is relating to Noah or Abram — Rabbi Nehemiah dares to suggest that God needs Abram to help Him find the "light." Abram's "I," in other words, is not merely an expression of Abram's own egoistic self-appreciation. God Himself requires this independent creaturely source of light to illuminate the darkness that God Himself experiences, i.e., God's "despondency" following Eden, the antediluvians, and Babel, and from which He must emerge.

But Rabbi Nehemiah adds a further note. The Holy One Blessed Be He says to Abram: "Instead of showing a light for Me from Mesopotamia and its environs, come and show one before Me in Eretz Yisrael." Again, Rabbi Nehemiah's more comprehensive analogy has Abram's autonomy being further and further defined. We've seen that in Rabbi Nehemiah's analogy Noah is utterly passive in his state of sunkenness. God is the exclusively active force. Abram on the other hand sees God in a less than admirable situation — "sunken" Himself, as it were, in the darkness. And, as we've noted, Abram's autonomous light provides the active illumination to guide God through the darkness. But God, according to Rabbi Nehemiah, still has the last word vis-à-vis Abram's autonomous light. It is a mediated light, complains God, because its source is the Mesopotamian "exile." A pure light can only come from the Land of Israel, Abram's destined place.

In summary, Abram's relationship with God, entirely different from Noah's, translates thereby the attribute *tamim* (wholehearted) differently. There is a symbolic change of Abram's name to Abraham in which the numerical equivalent of the letters in Abram add up to 243 and the additional *he* (numerical equivalent: five) brings the total to the 248 organs of the body, making Abraham now *whole*. His wholeness must include the dimension of individual autonomy, the kind of autonomy which will not only relate to God out of a sense of *yirah* (fear), but with *ahavah* (love) born out of a sense of faithful empathy with God's purposes. It will be an autonomy which will stand, when deemed necessary, before God not just to give illumination but to demand illumination — as in the case of Abraham's negotiations with God over the fate of Sodom. It will also serve as an autonomous demanding model for later defenders of Israel ranging from Moses through the Prophets through latter-day Levi Yitzhaks and other plaintiffs seeking justice for the Jewish people.

Abraham's Particularist Universalism

There is yet a further dimension to Abram's wholeness which is now to be signified by his name Abraham. He will represent God who has had from the beginning a universalist purpose in His creation. Therefore Abraham is to be known as "Father of a Multitude of Nations." He will be covenanted as "*u-netatikha la-goyim*," given over to the nations; by definition he will be involved with the nations. Abraham's descendants will be charged similarly with the burden and opportunity of participating fully among the nations as part of a Godly mission. Hadn't God's opening *"lekh lekha"* included the promise that all the families of the earth would be blessed through Abraham!

At the same time, Abraham and his descendants will never abandon their own particularistic destiny, which will be as fundamental a component of the terms of the covenant as its universalistic dimension. The *Ha'amek Davar* commentary will agree that Israel's mission to the nations is to educate them in wisdom as the injunction says: *"u-netatikha la-goyim."* But lest any descendants of Abraham should see this mission as the exclusive purpose of the covenant, they are to be reminded by the immediately following verses which mandate the future Israel to build its own sovereign nation in its own land by itself and for itself. The *"Brit-Milah"* will represent for Abraham, for his house, for his clan, and for all future descendants a covenanted-circumcision which is to be tied irrevocably to Zion and to the Land of Israel.

In order to maneuver one's sense of double purpose — the universalist and the particularist — Abraham has to be strong enough to resist surrendering to the temptations of losing himself to either purpose while disavowing the other. It will require a sacrificial dedication, a hard-nosed demand on self to prepare the way for building a nation solidly secure in its own sense of place and purpose of place. At the same time it will understand in a variety of ways that the world in its entirety is God's creation and God's concern. Israel therefore must consider all of God's creation, i.e., all of humanity, as its concern.

That the covenant has as its sign circumcision of the reproductive organ argues for the concerned attention to Abraham's future. The future of his family will signify the state of the world at any given juncture. Whether the direction in which this family will be moving vis-à-vis the Land is up or down, in or out, the sacrificial dedication to be demanded will be total. In this sense, the future of Israel is irrevocably connected to a sacrificial binding commitment — not in death, God forbid. It is to be a commitment to life, but a life always lived in the breach representing before God an unqualified uplifting hope for humanity even when humanity descends into darkness. Always in the breach... always on the brink....

Va-Yera וירא

The "men" — messengers, angels, deputies of God — come to visit Abraham as he is recovering from his physical discomfiture following the covenantal circumcision. What they are doing in and of itself is a *mitzvah* (a sanctified good deed), i.e., visiting the sick. But they have a twofold purpose beyond the immediate *mitzvah*. They are heralding events which will bring Abraham great joy, on the one hand, but great sadness, on the other.

The joy — and *laughter* — comes from the announcement that he and his wife Sarah will have a son. And it will be this son who will carry the covenant into the next generation. Moreover, it will be this son Isaac who — unlike his father Abraham or his own future son Jacob — will never leave the Land and will set thereby the precedent for permanent residency in the Land. The sadness which the "men" are bringing along with the joy is not related to Abraham directly. But the additional mission of these "men" will motivate Abraham to protest. For once Abraham realizes that these "men" are on their way from a birth announcement to a decree of mass destruction of the city of Sodom, he must react, he must do something. He must confront God directly, uninhibitedly.

Justice and Sodom

The Psalmist (30:6) will capture the swiftness of God's change of mood and material consequence in the verse: *"Ki rega be-apo hayyim bi-rtzono"* ("For He is angry but a moment; but when He is pleased there is life"). Except that here, the mission of the "men" is sequentially reversed. God is pleased to bring life to the barren and skeptical Sarah and to the faithful but curious Abraham. Abraham's overall faith has been strong, to this point unshakable. He is confident that there is a future, even though he knows that at his and Sarah's age they will need an abundant measure of God's supportive will to

47

bring new life into their lives. God has promised and the promise shall be fulfilled!

But now the "men" are on their way to wreak God's anger on Sodom. The anger needs but a moment's activation; for the agitation spewing forth from Sodom's wickedness has long been very great. God does not need to justify to Himself any act. In utter free will, He is *"meimit u-mehayeh"* ("He deals out death just as He gives life"). God does need to justify Himself, however, to Abraham. If Abraham is to be a blessing to all the nations…if, moreover, it is to be assured that his own future descendants who will become a nation, the nation of Israel, will *know* what is entailed in building a life-giving society, then Abraham must learn to *know* why Sodom is being destroyed.

It will be Ezekiel the later prophet who will attempt to summarize (16:49, 50) Sodom's crimes: "Arrogance! She and her daughters had plenty of bread and untroubled tranquility, yet she did not support the poor and the needy. In their haughtiness they committed abomination before Me…" A more subtle and demanding appraisal of Sodom will be made in *Pirkei Avot* (Ethics of the Fathers): "He who says, 'What is mine is mine and what is yours is yours,' this is average; some say that it is the *attitude of Sodom*…." What can possibly be meant by an epigram in which on the one hand the "laissez-faire" attitude is considered average, yet on the other hand is no better than the immoral attitude of Sodom?

What God wants Abraham to know is that there is a tension which exists and must exist between conventional civic and moral behavior and the need to push beyond the letter of the law to post-conventional models of moral autonomy and creativity. That Sodom may be guilty of normalizing gross perversions would certainly warrant destruction — in the pattern of the Flood generation. Such indeed is the description given in the Written Torah regarding the attempt of the townspeople to "know" Lot's visitors, i.e., intending gang rape and sodomy! But what Abraham must learn in order to educate the peoples in general and his future Israel in particular is that conventional standards of morality and humaneness are sometimes "enough," but not always "enough." The prophet Isaiah will compare and then identify his generation of Israelites as "chieftains of Sodom." Will he thereby be berating his society for being wickedly perverse or for encouraging its citizenry to maintain no more than conventional "laissez-faire" standards? Might Isaiah be anticipating the later rabbinic condemnation of Jerusalem to destruction for not going *beyond* the letter of the law?

What of Sodom and the cause of its destruction? Is the episode of intended gang rape and sodomy at Lot's door meant to indicate that the entire city is hopelessly corrupt and therefore deserving of destruction? Or is the emphasis to be — as Ezekiel will later see it — on Sodom's opposition to strangers sharing their prosperity, a somewhat lesser "crime" in the eyes of God and Man — yet still serious enough to condemn Sodom to destruction! Whichever the cause, is Sodom worse than Isaiah's later Jerusalem or Jonah's later Nineveh?

Abraham stands before God pleading for the *tzaddikim* (the righteous) of Sodom. By "righteous" let us assume that Abraham is referring to those among the citizens who have been pressing for some normative standards of civic morality. Abraham pleads for justice. He negotiates on a plane in which he challenges God Himself to act justly. As mentioned earlier, the minimum kernel which Abraham suggests at first is fifty. If there are fifty righteous, God agrees to "bear the sins," i.e., to forgive the sins of the entire community. Abraham will argue God down to a *minyan* (quorum) of ten righteous persons making up what Abraham himself intuits is a requisite minimum number for constituting a viable community. Generations later in the Wilderness it will be a fatal *minyan* of *meraglim* (spies) who will sabotage the mission of the slave generation of Israelites to reach the Promised Land. In the case of Sodom Abraham realizes soon enough that this iniquitous city lacks even ten righteous persons (by whatever minimum definition one might give to the word "righteous"). And so a disconsolate Abraham "returns to his place."

But now, why doesn't Abraham address God's attribute of mercy in this dialogue of life-and-death for a community? Is the model of Sodom meant to teach Abraham as simple a theological lesson in reward and punishment as Noah was meant to learn from the cataclysm which destroyed his generation? Namely, that the calculus which God uses can be seen at times to be as clear, as hard, and as final as a sentence of death! Granted, God has an attribute of mercy which, according to the Midrash, has worked diligently to create humankind to begin with. In the very motivation to create, God has had to show mercy or an anticipatory empathy for what He now knows will be an imperfect humanity. But when everything which the Flood generation and the people of Sodom do mocks God's purposeful empathy, all that is left for God is to activate His attribute of justice and bring on the cataclysm.

On the other hand, if Abraham is meant to be taught to *know* the terms for life and death survival in the post-Eden "wilderness," i.e., humaneness for mankind in general and for his later descendants the Children of Israel in particular, then it cannot be that the lesson for Abraham is meant to be as simple as Noah's. Abraham's Sodom, as Isaiah's Jerusalem and as Jonah's Nineveh, may be — according to God — ordinary cities which are corrupt, at times depraved, lacking in palpable evidences of righteousness. Nevertheless these cities embody conventional "acceptable" laissez-faire standards for organizing collectivities of people. In other words, they may not be irretrievably wicked. And yet they are failing or are perceived to be failing when prophets like Abraham, Isaiah, and Jonah are sent to them.

Isaiah's imprecations before the people of Jerusalem to change their ways, to repent, and Jonah's eventual surrender to God's command to teach Nineveh to repent, seem not to be available to Abraham's arsenal of arguments as he stands before God. God has not yet taught the possibilities of repentance to Abraham. Abraham's best effort on behalf of Sodom is to plead for justice in an increasingly minor tone emphasizing his own "dust and ashes" unworthiness. Perhaps in this tone we hear Abraham's plea for mercy as he implies that all human beings are "dust and ashes" and therefore incapable of standing up before God's attribute of justice.

But then Abraham lets go. There is an intuitive realization within him that if the aspiration to build the world in God's image is truly serious, then there are times when the attribute of justice must clearly and emphatically prevail. There are critical points in human history and in the history of Israel when compromise in the name of exercising mercy on those who wish to abandon the strictures of the covenant is unacceptable, is lethal, perhaps suicidal. In the not too distant future of Israel Moses and Aaron will represent, in the eyes of some rabbinic sages, the two attributes of justice and mercy in their dealings with their people. Aaron will be known as the lover and pursuer of peace, always prepared to compromise with standards in order to "make peace" or "keep the peace." Moses' attribute will be summarized as *"yikov ha-din et ha-har"* ("may the standard, the law, God's uncompromised command, cut through the mountain"). Aaron becomes for later Israel the paradigm for arbitration in dealing with problems. Moses, however, becomes *the* teacher of all Israel — Moshe Rabbenu!

God's command to Abraham to break out of the incarceration of Babel in order to bring forth a new light to the world has been an uncompromising command. God *does* have an attribute of mercy, which He has already shown that He will exercise when He chooses to exercise it. Moses himself will appeal to it when he has no recourse. But for the fulfillment of God's vision for Israel and the world, God needs an Abraham and later a Moses who are prepared to live a life of severe, painful, sacrificial choices. And the choices will often hold the risk of death so as to make possible life. The choices will often be between: (1) following God's command — being absolutely loyal to God's attribute of *justice* in the name of long-term life; or (2) compromising God's command while appealing to His attribute of mercy, rationalizing the need for compromise, but thereby risking the nullification of the command — unto sociomoral death.

Living with the *"Akeidah"*

There is a tradition that asks why wasn't the Bet ha-Mikdash ("the Holy Temple") built on Mount Sinai. The answer given is that the *akeidah* ("the binding of Isaac") took place on Mount Moriah, not on Mount Sinai. But the Torah was given on Mount Sinai! True, but Torah or *hora'ah* (teaching) has come forth from Mount Moriah as well, an indispensable part of Torah and its lesson urging sacrificial commitment to Torah. (Torah, *hora'ah*, and Moriah may be seen as having common verbal roots.) For what Abraham — and Isaac — are prepared to offer on Mount Moriah to the point of risking death is an uncompromised total giving.

The test of Abraham is spiritually light-years beyond Adam's shameful hiding from God's Presence in Eden. Adam avoids accepting God's vivid immediate demanding Presence; and so in ridiculous fashion hides. Abraham knows exactly where God is and — equally important — he knows where he himself is. He is postured fully and uncompromisingly within God's field of vision. He knows it and accepts it. His *"hineini,"* his "being here," before God, is an oath of allegiance. It is qualitatively different from responding in Hebrew *po* or *kan* which announces one's objective locus, i.e., I am here just as every other object in the field of vision is here. *Hineini* means much more than *po* or *kan*. It means that I am here prepared to activate my total personhood into becoming more than I could have ever imagined. I am here to act on your command, O Lord. You do not have to ask me, *"Ayeka!"*

But must the test of the *akeidah* (binding) be so ultimate? From even God's point of view doesn't it forfeit the importance of God's other concern embodied in the question, "Where is your brother, your son, your beloved other?" Or if it must be a test which truly does measure serious commitment to purpose, why can it not be a hypothetical test?

It cannot be hypothetical, for then it wouldn't be a true test. The Ramban explains the difference: "The test gives Man the opportunity out of his utter free will to choose to do or not to do and the ensuing reward results from the actual *doing*, not from the mere *intention* to do." In moving from a hypothetical test to a categorical test, one progresses from potentiality to actuality. At Sinai, Israel would promise what they were prepared to do — potentially. At Moriah, Abraham — and Isaac — are on the brink of actually doing, acting clearly and decisively.

A special prayer will be composed long after the era of Abraham and Isaac in which the circumciser or *mohel* of a Jewish child will say: "Creator of the Universe, may it be your gracious will to regard and accept this performance of circumcision as if I had *brought* this infant before your glorious throne...." The Hebrew word for "brought" in this prayer is "*hikravtihu*," as if I have sacrificed him to you. The prayer will be a vestige of a memory which has some traditional support, namely that Isaac was actually offered up on the sacrificial altar. Whether or not Abraham carries through with the sacrifice is academic, since the command itself is appalling, and the consequence of the command will be enough to kill Sarah the mother of Isaac and leave Isaac permanently scarred, spiritually and psychologically.

Sarah will have suffered a maelstrom of ups and downs in her life ranging from her need to cope with barrenness to her sudden shock at hearing what at first is a laughable promise of fertility. She has endured the haughtiness of Hagar. She has had to confront her husband insisting that he exile his older son Ishmael from his homestead and patrimony. She has given birth to her precious son, her only son Isaac, only to hear that he is being placed on the altar of what has to be for her as a mother tantamount to extinction.

Isaac of course will not be sacrificed. He will become the land-bound link between two titans of the spirit, Abraham and Jacob. But the categorical nature of the test will leave Isaac traumatized. Abraham and Isaac's descendants will continue to bear the trauma of the *akeidah*. They will experience the realization of Isaac's sacrifice in their own blood-drenched history. They will be called upon to offer up their lives and the lives of their children *al kid-dush Hashem* (for the sanctification of God's Name). They will be called upon to do it not as a hypothetical test, but as a categorical one. They will see their own lives — and deaths — as actualizations of God's command. They will learn that there are times when one's faith does require a supreme sacrifice; but that after Isaac's "death" — having been brought to God's throne — there is the salvational hope of resurrection for the righteous.

The *hineini* readiness to die and to bring others to die for one's faith, religion, ideology, is the essential paradigmatic message of the first part of the *akeidah* story. But there is a second and third *hineini* in the story. Abraham's second *hineini* is in response to his son's call to him: "Avi!" ("My Father")! Isaac sees the trappings for the offering; but where is the offering? The son is crying out to his father who is the rock of his security. The younger human being created in the image of God is addressing the older human being who represents life and hope, a future for humankind. How can Isaac's cry not pierce the heart-mind of Abraham! It must! True, a readiness under certain circumstances to die for one's religion may be a manifestation of true faith and commitment to faith. But is the price to be paid for such faith the slaying of a son who is after all, objectively speaking, a creature of God! And subjectively speaking, even more to the emotional point, to slay one's hope, one's future — before all and after all — one's son, one's beloved son!

The third *hineini* comes as a cosmic resolution of what has appeared to Abraham as a dilemma, but in God's view was always understood as a test *not* to be carried out to its bloody denouement. Rashi, basing himself on the Midrash, will argue that a priori God never intended a sacrificial slaughter. For in His instruction God doesn't use the word "slaughter." The word used is "offer him up" with the apparent intention that as soon as Isaac would be offered up he would be taken down. Long before Rashi, Jeremiah (19:5) will censure the residents of Jerusalem who "...have built the high places of Baal, to burn their sons in the fire for burnt-offerings unto Baal which I *commanded not, nor spoke it, neither came it into My mind.*"

The Talmud in the tractate *Ta'anit* interpreting the end of the verse in Jeremiah will say, "I *commanded not* Mesha the king of Moab, nor *spoke it* to Jephthah regarding his daughter, *neither came it unto my mind* regarding Isaac the son of Abraham." This rabbinic interpretation, in other words, lumps together the slaying of Isaac, if it were to have taken place, with two other repulsive examples of similar "sacrifices" — Mesha's son and Jephthah's daughter.

In the tractate *Sanhedrin* in a discussion regarding the punishment of a person who does not obey the words of a prophet, the *Gemara* will ask how would we know that the individual assumed to be a prophet is indeed one. The answer is that if he is *known* to be a prophet, then he must be obeyed and the example given is that Isaac would have only considered the command because it came from a *known* prophet, Abraham. From anyone else it would have to be rejected as horrifically criminal. In other words, the Rabbis will have become sensitive to the possibility of madness for the sake of Heaven. They will declare prophecy to have ceased. Henceforth no one will be able to justify an a priori sacrificial suicide or murder by claiming that he has received a command by God or by a prophet of God. There are no longer any *known* prophets. An overreadiness to offer up oneself or one's loved ones in the name of faith — when prophecy no longer exists, when God's voice is hidden — may indeed be madness! And clearly from a legal and moral point of view — murder!

The third *hineini* thus resolves the dilemma; in essence it dissolves it, because Abraham will not slay his son. He will not "suspend the ethical," a suspension which Kierkegaard will understand as the demand of the authentically "religious" in the name of "faith." Milton Steinberg will explain the Jewish viewpoint that "the ethical is never suspended, not under any circumstances, and not for anyone, not even for God. Especially not for God. Are not supreme Reality and supreme Goodness one and co-essential to Divine nature? If so, every act wherein the Good is put aside is more than a breach of His will; it is in effect a denial of His existence." It may be that the history of Israel will require dying *al kiddush Hashem*, but only when there is no choice. As a norm, a moral norm, a religious norm, the mandate is to *live al kiddush Hashem* and to let others live *al kiddush Hashem*, a prescription not to be violated — certainly not a priori.

The Re-testing of Abraham

In the final analysis has the test been necessary? There is evidence to show that indeed this test of Abraham's faith is required. Abraham's faith in the total enterprise which has begun with "*lekh lekha*" has perhaps not been absolutely firm — at least not to Rashi's grandson, the Rashbam. The medieval commentator will point to the passage immediately preceding the *akeidah* which records Abraham signing a treaty with Abimelech of Gerar and Philistia. God has promised the Land to Abraham. And the Philistines — before and after the treaty — will persist in stealing as well as stopping up wells. Notwithstanding Abimelech's apology, they will remain an enemy of Israel. After Abraham's death, they will stop up the wells again and they will compel Isaac to renegotiate a workable arrangement for water. They will be a threat to Israel at the Exodus, an oppressive presence during the period of the Judges, and the constant menacing force to be fought and defeated eventually by Samuel and David.

And yet Abraham settles in Gerar-Philistia and "remains a long time." Indeed, the verse immediately preceding God's test of Abraham is precisely the verse citing Abraham's sojourning in "the land of the Philistines many days." The test is signalized in God's repetition of the portentous *"lekh-lekha"* (go forth). Only this time Abraham is charged to go forth to Mount Moriah in order to offer up everything which is most precious to him — his son. It is a re-testing of Abraham's faith in the face of what appears to be a vacillation, a hesitation in relating to adversaries. How strong is Abraham prepared to be in a world of Nimrods; for there are other Nimrods outside of Babel, and a host of them will be from Philistia — through the ages. And they must be addressed with the confidence born of primordial faith. Abraham will need that faith if he is to be charged with shouldering a prophetic destiny which sees enslavement for his descendants for four hundred years followed by the struggle for redemption. Why then does Abraham let himself be seduced into a treaty with the faithless untrustworthy Philistines — of any age?

The dialectical perception of enslavement and redemption within the *"Brit bein ha-Betarim"* (the Covenant of the Pieces) bespeaks an unrelieved struggle to tame the Philistine "wilderness," to predispose it to human civilization. But humankind cannot tame its own bestial drives, its craving to dominate. Human civilization, therefore, does not yet exist in the sense of its humanity reflecting humaneness. Abraham will have to live and work in this "wilderness" and will often have to fight for survival within the patterns of behavior normative to the "wilderness." God has to know how determined Abraham really is to bear the burden of permanent "follow-up" on his first *"lekh-lekha."*

Is Abraham possessed with the importance of destiny? Is he single-minded in his dedication to the covenant of new birth even if the dialectic terms of the "wilderness" determine that when necessary he must destroy as well? Sarah has had no hesitation in determining that Ishmael is a threat to Isaac and thereby a threat to the covenant. Therefore he must go! Abraham has been promised the land by Divine Will. He is confronted by an Abimelech who has learnt that Abraham has the seal of a prophet; yet Abimelech's shepherds, without compunction, steal Abraham's wells. Can Abimelech's apology be trusted to have any long-term credibility? Signing a treaty with a Philistine may mark Abraham as either a shrewd pragmatist or an uncertain knight of faith. How is God to know? How is Abraham to know?

The test lays Abraham himself on an altar of severe introspection. Abraham must realize that to be human is to continue God's creative labor; but to be human is to combat the schemes of the Serpent and of those human beings who have signed themselves over to those schemes. To go into combat is to risk destroying or being destroyed. Sodom must be mended or destroyed. Abimelech and the Philistines must prove their sincerity before treaties are signed with them. To decide how to relate to Sodomites and Philistines is the ultimate complexity. The human being may avoid the sacrificial decision in human terms by offering up the nearest available scapegoat, the ram, in the *svakh* (the thicket). But all that the human being will achieve is to leap into the thicket of complex human decision-making himself.

Isaac's Trauma

The yoke of living with complexity is not exclusively Abraham's. It is to be shared and ultimately transferred entirely to the next generational link — Isaac. The offering, the potential sacrifice, is not to involve one person merely. It must involve two, two who will walk together and talk together. The bridge among the individual *hineini*s must be the companionship-leading-to-community-of-spirit of the two: Parent and Child.

André Neher notes in his *L'Exile de la Parole* that Adam doesn't talk to Cain and Abel; that Noah blesses and curses his sons but shares no dialogue with them. But Abraham and Isaac do address each other: "My father.... Here am I, my son." Fully present to one another they are able to walk together, to face any test, any predicament, any adversity.

Not that Isaac will ever be immune to the trauma of what is swirling about him! There is the *midrash* which records the mood among the angels in Heaven as Isaac is being placed on the altar for sacrifice. They weep and their tears float down into the expectant eyes of Isaac blinding him permanently. It is a partial blindness, but it is enough to play a critical role in the later drama surrounding the transfer of Isaac's blessing to the generation which will succeed him. The blindness will be responsible for Isaac's love for Esau, notwithstanding the latter's inappropriateness for the role of Abraham's covenanted grandson.

It may be that there is an indirect consequence of the dialectic of birth and destruction which has sent the "men," i.e., the angels, to promise at the same time Isaac's birth and Sodom's destruction. It will contribute to the eventual blinding of Isaac to the impossibility of his hunter-son Esau, a latter-day Nimrod, being the carrier of the covenantal yoke. That Isaac will even consider the possibility of preferring Esau underscores the trauma of his own "sacrifice" at the hands of his father Abraham.

The yoke of living in the thicket of things as a partner to God in cultivating the "wilderness" is indeed a traumatic yoke. Isaac in his own way will be as heroic as Abraham and Jacob. He will — after all — dig the wells which will dispense the life-giving waters to the parched Promised Land. But for Isaac, the tears of the angels, the knowledge that his father has been willing to offer him up, to risk his son's life, to give his son's life, if necessary, cannot be forgotten. It can be condoned or repressed *consciously* by an Isaac who is eventually brought in to the covenant himself by means of his own separate revelatory moments with God — without Abraham at his side. But *unconsciously* Isaac can never recover fully from the trauma.

If Jacob will limp as a result of his wrestling with his own angel at a key crossroad in his life, Isaac will be forever circumspect about every step he takes even if he walks steadily and erectly. Whereas Abraham and Jacob are secure enough in their dedication to their destined attachment to the Land so as to allow themselves to leave the Land when perceived necessary, Isaac will never leave the Land. He does not trust his unconscious storehouse of memories, dreams, and nightmares.

Hayei Sarah   חיי שרה

Abraham responds to two prodigious *lekh-lekha*s in his life: the command to leave his land, his birthplace, and home, and then the command to offer up the life of his beloved son. Between the two *lekh-lekha*s comes another variation on the theme of "walking" or "going." At the *Brit bein ha-Betarim* (the Covenant of the Pieces) in which Abraham is informed of a portentous future for his descendants — a future of enslavement followed by redemption — God enjoins him: *"Hithalekh lefanai ve-hyei tamim"* ("Walk [go] before Me and be whole"). Abraham's walking-in-wholeness will empower him to face an "up-and-down" (*"aliyah-yeridah"*) existence for himself and his descendants.

In contrast to Abraham, Isaac is never described as "walking" or "going" — except during the episode of the *akeidah*. There it is written twice: *"Va-yelkhu shneihem yahdav"* ("And they walked together"). Father and son, Abraham and Isaac, walked together sharing the ordeal of the *akeidah*. Isaac will continue to need someone to walk with him before God in order to be whole.

Walking together with his father has formed a bracket around the critical dialogue between father and son. Whatever limitless power God's command has had over the faithful Abraham, neither God nor Abraham can shut out the elegiac call of Isaac: *"Avi!"* ("My father!") A deep dark foreboding has enveloped Isaac as he begins to suspect that he himself is meant to be the offering. Nevertheless, he is comforted by Abraham's *"Hineini bni."* ("Here am I, my son.") He is more than comforted. He is sustained. One is comforted in the face of loss, pain, regret, angst. Isaac is sustained as he walks to face his destiny — whatever it may be — together with his father. His father has been promised continuity. It will be a continuity that includes tragic adversity along with majestic triumph. But whatever God intends, however it will play itself out, whoever walks with Abraham must be and will be an indispensable link in that continuity. For Isaac this is the comfort and the sustenance that he needs and seeks with his call: *"Avi!"*

As noted earlier, the linkage has not been enough to carry Sarah through the ordeal. Tradition has it that she dies as a result of the traumatic event — even if Isaac does come out alive. At the same time, however, Sarah has made possible through her giving birth to Isaac the clear removal of Ishmael the *pere-adam* ("the wild man") from consideration as Abraham's spiritual heir. And thereby she has also participated — albeit passively — in the mysterious working-out of this necessary period of transference of the covenant from Abraham to Isaac.

The Resident-Alien

Sarah's death is instrumental in making a legal land claim on the Promised Land well in advance of the conquest by Joshua. Abraham will purchase a burial site for his wife which will serve as the signpost for the future settlement of the Land of Israel. Abraham's right to the Land has come from his "subjective" revelatory experience at the *Brit bein ha-Betarim*. The sin of the Amorites (or Hittites in this case) may "not yet be full," so that they still have rights to the land; but ultimately — in God's good time — Abraham's descendants, the Children of Israel, will be given the right and the opportunity to possess the Land.

There is a more fundamental "objective" reason and justification for Abraham's claim to a piece of territory in this Land. For the initial right given to Adam to claim the whole world as his to "work and to guard," whether it be Eden or the "wilderness" — is henceforth shared by all of Adam's or Noah's descendants, including Abraham. Rashi will summarize the geo-political view of Torah in his very first comment on the very first verse of Torah: "The whole earth is the Lord's; He created it and gives it to anyone who is just in His sight to have it given to him…" God's utter free will "giveth and taketh away."

Abraham's description of himself as a *"ger-toshav"* ("a resident-alien") is a useful nomenclature for legal purposes within the framework of his particular civic situation. In theological-moral terms, it is a value-laden term bespeaking the eternal predicament of Man wandering from place to place in the "wilderness" seeking a home, finding it, settling it, but never certain that it is his because he is never certain that he is worthy in God's eyes of possessing it wholly. After all, the "earth is," before all, after all, and *during* all, "the Lord's!" All human beings wherever they find themselves on God's earth are hyphenated as residents and aliens at the same time.

There will be an additional appellation which for civic and internal national or tribal convenience will be useful: citizenship. The Hittites are citizens in the area in which Abraham seeks to settle and a piece of which Abraham seeks to claim. And the future teaching of the Torah: that *"Torah ahat yihye la-ezrah ve-la-ger"* ("one Torah shall be for the citizen and the alien") will serve as a critical guideline for jurisprudence. With Abraham, however, at this juncture in his residency in Canaan — not as a citizen, but as a resident-alien — the hyphenated identity captures most accurately his existential situation.

Abraham is an alien — but not a visitor. He is a resident — but not a citizen. In short, he is not a Hittite. He admits immediately that he is a hyphenated person — as if to say that he is not expecting absolute civic equality. He will pay for whatever largesse he may be given. He will pay for his minimal land-claim. He will reside with the local citizenry. But he will not assimilate to their ways. His is a self-imposed alienation — whether or not they might consider inviting him to be one with them. In any case, he cannot link himself to any group when he has been charged to "walk before God" sufficiently alone so as to guarantee single-minded wholeness in his working out the fulfillment of the covenant.

Moreover, the living Isaac — and his future as the bearer of the covenant — cannot be compromised through assimilation into the ways of the Hittites. Isaac cannot, must not, marry a Hittite. But does it make sense for Abraham to send his servant Eliezer to seek out a wife for Isaac beyond the river — even if those living there are his relatives? Is that a better solution considering that they are as idolatrous as the Hittites? Abrabanel will sharpen the question: "At least when Isaac and Rebecca send Jacob away from Canaan, it is based on their experience with Esau's Hittite wives Judith and Basemath who are described as a source of bitterness to them. But Abraham has had no such experience as yet. The experience which Abraham has had with his local non-Hebrew allies Aner, Eshkol, and Mamre has been positive. Why then forbid marriage with their daughters in favor of daughters of idolaters 'across the river'?"

The *Midrash Hagadol* answers the question in the name of Abraham:

"Since in any case I am converting people to my new faith, I may as well begin with my own family, fulfilling the words of Isaiah (58:7) *'U-mi-bsarkha al titaleim'* ('Do not ignore your own kin')." The Rabbis will articulate the principle of being concerned first with that which has been placed in one's immediate charge — himself, then one's closest relatives, and only then beyond, i.e., humanity-at-large.

Looking beyond his local environment is part-and-parcel of the peculiar self-definition of Abraham as a resident-alien. How does Abraham understand himself and his current situation among the Hittites in Canaan? He has been informed by God that someday in the distant future his descendants will be landlords, owners, majority citizens in this Land. He must in his own mind retain, therefore, his separate alien identity and make sure that his son and grandchildren and their children retain it so that their covenantal vision is still alive when the moment will have arrived for their claim to be fulfilled.

At the same time, he will not prejudge the Hittites as enemies. Their sin, as stated, "is not as yet full." God will judge them as He has judged the Flood generation, as He judges Babel, Sodom, Nineveh, and someday Jerusalem. He will judge Nineveh, first for survival, as he will give its inhabitants the opportunity to repent even as the city will someday serve as God's rod of anger against another sinning society — Israel. But when someday Nineveh's sin will become intolerably "full," it will then be judged for condemnation like any other society, tribe, nation, or empire.

In the meantime, this community of Hittites inhabits a section of the Promised Land. And at this stage it is God's will that their settlement be respected. And so, Abraham's civic status, as an alien who is at the same time a resident, requires him to be fully participant in the socioeconomic and general cultural activity of this community. He will live out this hyphenated existence in anticipation of what myriads of the Children of Israel after him will live out in Gentile environments throughout the civilized world — from Pharaoh's Egypt to Hellenistic Egypt, from medieval Spain to post-Emancipation France and Germany. Abraham's challenge and the challenge facing his descendants, wherever in exile they will find themselves, will be as clear as it will be intrinsically problematic: How to transmit the blessing of a covenanted identity to offspring while residing in a society where the non-covenanted constitute the majority? How to maintain a spiritual and sociomoral equilibrium between civic loyalty to that majority and a commitment to a covenant which demands a clear dimension of culturally responsible alienation from that majority?

Concern for the Covenant

On the surface, Abraham's life will come to a close *"be-seivah tovah"* ("dying at a good ripe age"). He will be described as having been blessed by God with "everything." He has actualized the original command of *"lekh lekha"* by settling in the Land which God has "shown him." Even his sons, Isaac and Ishmael, erstwhile enemies, will have made sufficient peace between themselves to allow them to come together for their father's burial. Indeed the name of the burial place of Abraham *"me'arat ha-makhpeilah"* serves the Midrash as a play on the word *kaful* (double) indicating that whoever is buried there is certain to have double rewards.

Yet on the basis of the verse (Gen. 25:11): "After the death of Abraham, God blessed his son Isaac..." Rashi raises a comment which focuses on an anxiety which has plagued Abraham in his later years as he has contemplated transmitting the blessing to Isaac. Rashi has a hidden question which may be stated as follows: Why does Abraham not bless Isaac himself? Why does he leave it to God? Rashi says two things in his comment on the verse: God's blessing of Isaac is first manifested in His visiting the mourner in order to comfort him. But secondly, and more revealing, even though the Holy One Blessed Be He has given over the blessings of the covenant to be delivered to whom Abraham will deem fit, the first patriarch *is afraid to bless Isaac* because he foresees Esau coming forth from this Isaac. Abraham concludes, therefore, that he will leave the blessing with God Himself to bless whomever God will deem fit to bless.

On the basis of Isaac's later life we will see that Abraham has good cause for anxiety. In the future, Isaac will appear ready — in his blindness, physically and spiritually — to hand over primary blessings to Esau. The text notes Isaac as loving Esau — despite Esau's undisciplined, even violent character.

The late nineteenth century commentator the Malbim will sense the difficulty in Abraham's anxiety over Isaac. If Isaac is expected to be the second of the great pillars of Jewish biblical tradition, how is it possible for this great second patriarch to be on the threshold of such error! The Malbim will argue that the entire later episode relating to Isaac's giving over blessings to his sons is unconnected to Abraham's special *covenantal blessing*. Isaac will mean no more than to give both Esau and Jacob personal-parental blessings of well-being, e.g., dew from heaven, abundant corn and wine. The *covenantal blessing* — having to do with possessing the Land and having God's full attention to the ongoing destiny of Israel — Isaac will only transmit later to Jacob. According to the text it will be recorded precisely in 28:3, 4 as the later blessing of Abraham given to Jacob to possess the Land as promised.

Granted, the Malbim's explanation in defense of Isaac is inventive and convincing. (More of this in the comments on the portion of Toldot!) But Abraham's anxiety is psychologically and spiritually well founded. Abraham is concerned about the "Esau-ness" which is latent in all humankind and which can explode at any time and can destroy any chance of moving through history with a vision of covenantal peace, security, and tranquility. He is concerned enough even and especially as he contemplates leaving Isaac alone to face his destiny, particularly since they have been living as resident-aliens in an enveloping culture not theirs. Abraham concludes, therefore, that he himself lacks the confidence to give over the covenantal blessing directly to Isaac. He will leave it to God. God will know better than Abraham how prepared Isaac is to carry on. Only God will truly know what lasting effects living with the Hittites, not to mention the experience of the *akeidah*, will have had on Isaac.

Are we to conclude, therefore, that Abraham's "ripe old age" and his having been blessed with "everything" is irretrievably blemished by these anxieties? Does Rashi's interpretation reflect an element of despondency as Abraham contemplates the future? Not necessarily! Let this "anxiety" rather be seen as symptomatic of an eleventh test imposed by God on Abraham following the climactic tenth test of the *akeidah*. This eleventh test is the test of *"hit'apkut"* ("restraint" or "forbearance"). Abraham has to accept the unalterable fact that whether he dies *"be-seivah tovah,"* in a mood of serenity, or afflicted with anxiety, he *will* die. He *will* leave the scene — the arena of human striving. All the promises made to him will be left to linger on in the imaginations, considerations, and aspirations of those who will be alive after him. But *he* will be gone! Isaac — or somebody else whom God may choose (and God will choose Isaac) — will be center-stage in this covenantal drama, not Abraham.

The test then is whether Abraham can trust Isaac to discover his own mode of relating to the preservation and concretization of the covenant. We have seen the workings of the test on Abraham earlier as he could not repress his concern that Isaac might not be fully ready to assume responsibility for the covenant, that Isaac might not be secure enough to fill his father's role. It was for this reason that Abraham had sent Eliezer his servant to seek a help-mate for an Isaac who was perceived as not being able to stand or walk alone. Since the *akeidah*, it was Abraham's intuition that Isaac had to have a partner if he was to continue Abraham's task of walking before God in covenantal wholeness. Thus the role to be played by Rebecca would be critical.

A Rebecca for Isaac

Much is made in the sources regarding Rebecca's concern for the camels of Eliezer. That she waters the camels on her own initiative is for Eliezer a sign that she is the chosen one for Isaac. This extra indulgence on her part — with-out waiting to be asked — is brought as evidence to illustrate her tender concern for animals; how much more will her tender concern for human beings be manifested in the future. Yet tender concern is hardly the character trait which the text projects as it reviews the major decisions Rebecca makes in her life as matriarch in Israel. She decides to go on her own *"lekh-lekha"* with this stranger — the servant Eliezer. She opens herself to a destiny which has not yet been revealed to her.

In the fulfillment of that destiny, she will be asked to choose between twin sons as to who is to be blessed with the redemptive task of carrying forward the covenant. In the process of choosing and seeing through the granting of the blessing she will rely on a deception of her husband who is blind to the consequences of his own preferences. Finally she will send her beloved son Jacob away while alienating her other son Esau — the rejected one. From all textual evidence, she will not live to see Jacob again when he delays returning home in favor of building his family and his wealth in "exile."

Rebecca's *lekh-lekha* is a *lekh-lekha* of the dimensions of Abraham's. There is a midrashic suggestion that her family led by the likes of Laban are less than enthusiastic about her venturing forth. Their question to her "Will you go with this man" provides her with the opportunity to give an autono-mous response: *"Elekh!"* ("I will go!") This serves as her decree of auto-eman-cipation. In certain ways her *"lekh-lekha"* may be considered a greater manifestation of courage than Abraham's. Abraham's *"lekh-lekha"* is a revealed command, a bare absolute heteronomous instruction giving him no choice. One cannot but hear the stentorian voice of God calling out *"Lekh-lekha!"* Can Abraham hesitate? Would he dare to refuse? Rebecca's *"elekh,"* on the other hand, is an autonomous expression following reflection upon what has been presented to her by a servant. Perhaps he has shared with her and her family the terms of the covenant — perhaps not!

How can the servant adequately present to Rebecca an image of Abraham as the lonely pioneer of faith? How can the servant even know the full spiritual parameters of what has taken place between father, son, and their God on Mount Moriah? How can the servant begin to discuss the *Brit bein ha-Betarim* — assuming he has even been apprised of it by Abraham — with its long-term promises and forebodings. At the same time, it is reasonable to assume that Rebecca's family, descendants of Nahor, Abraham's brother, would have recalled old and revered stories of Abram's mysterious departure many decades before. There may very well have been a certain aura of mystery and portent underlying Eliezer's offer of marriage to Rebecca — an offer of marriage to Isaac the scion of this obscure distant relative Abraham. There certainly would be good cause for Rebecca to pause at length for consideration and reconsideration! But no, undaunted, unhesitant, Rebecca goes!

She goes to join herself to Isaac and to be brought into his mother's tent. The sublime choreography of the meeting of Rebecca and Isaac inspires the great epic of Jewish mysticism, the Zohar, to compare the couple to Adam and Eve. The Zohar associates Rebecca's coming into the tent with the *Shekhinah* ("God's Indwelling Presence"); and then it views Rebecca as paralleling Eve coming towards Adam. Since the expulsion from Eden, there has been no description of Man and Woman coming together. When Abram and Sarai are introduced to us they are already together. But here, Isaac is alone and Rebecca is alone. They meet in the twilight of Isaac's meditative solitude. Rebecca's own solitude has been a consequence of her autonomous self-directed *"lekh-lekha"* or *"elekh."* Isaac doesn't initiate a new path. It has been done for him. It is for him to settle within the already carved parameters of the new path. Whatever initiative or modification of Abram's prior *"lekh-lekha"* will be necessary will depend on Rebecca — a new embodiment of Eve as truly *ezer ke-negdo* — both a helpmate for him and a helpmate confronting him.

The expulsion from Eden has left the entire originally perceived relationship between Man and Woman under a cloud of embarrassment and shame. In casting blame for the sin in the Garden on each other — or, more accurately, he on her and she on the Serpent — they have aborted any possibility of bonding for mutual growth. If each of them is unable to face up to his and her individual guilt, his and her individual responsibility, then how can either of them consider being a helpmate to the other? Accepting responsibility is a corollary of independence. And only as independent personalities are they capable of love. If they are not independent, then the relationship which they build can only be parasitic, each one dependent on the other, ultimately enslaved to one another.

Isaac being described as loving Rebecca is then a restoration of Eden which hadn't really been given a chance to flower in its first incarnation. And since the failure of Eve as woman, no woman has approached Rebecca in moral and psychological stature. Noah's women — wife and daughters — have no name in the text and no separate function. Lot's daughters are moralistic instruments whose roles within the Bible's ironic mode are totally passive on the one hand and almost perversely active on the other, i.e., first they are offered up by their father to the bestial lusts of the townspeople of Sodom; later they initiate the incest which will conceive Moab and Ammon. Sarah is, of course, a complex figure, but with only moments of decisiveness piercing her otherwise overall self-subordination to her husband's will.

In contrast, Rebecca stands "tall" and walks "tall," and, in a sense, "atones" for Eve's sin. If Eve has blamed the Serpent — her *yeitzer ra*, her lower self — for her misdeed, Rebecca will be called upon in all the critical decisions in her life and the life of her family to go against her *yeitzer* or maternal and connubial instincts. She will assume full responsibility for rejecting one son in favor of another. She will send her beloved son away from her (never to see him again). She will deceive her husband and override her husband's wishes in the process. Rebecca's "atonement" for Eve's sin makes possible Isaac's "atonement" for Adam's sin. Adam has blamed Eve rather than face up to his own weakness, his own failure. Isaac in the final analysis — whether he knows or doesn't know what Rebecca is doing — will permit Rebecca to assert herself and not feel threatened or betrayed when she in effect goes against his wishes. Thus Rebecca and Isaac, in their coming together — in love — bring to fruition after Eden and outside of Eden the possibilities of Man and Woman fulfilling each other, compensating for each other's weaknesses, redeeming each other.

In the biblical account, Isaac — unlike Abraham and Jacob — has no additional wives or concubines. If Adam and Eve in the Garden represent the primordial man-woman relationship as one of monogamy, Isaac and Rebecca continue the monogamous ideal in the post-Eden "wilderness" which the Abrahamic covenant is to realize on earth. The successful linkage between the patriarchal giants Abraham and Jacob is only made possible by the symbiosis of Isaac and Rebecca. Their coming together restores to relevancy the moral injunction of "loving the significant other as oneself" so egregiously violated by Cain. Isaac will have found his Rebecca, and thereby enabled both of them to walk together before God in synergistic wholeness.

Adam-Eve for the "Wilderness"

The marriage of Isaac and Rebecca as living post-Eden surrogates for what might have been realized in Eden itself by Adam and Eve also provides a living counterpoint to the purchase which Abraham has made of the gravesite *me'arat ha-makhpeilah*. The Zohar considers the cave to be the entrance to the Garden of Eden. Whether one approaches the word "entrance" from an "aggadic" (didactic-theological) or a "halakhic" (legal) point of view, one is not talking about a clear demarcation dividing territories. In *Pirkei Avot* Rabbi Jacob will teach "aggadically": "This world is only a corridor." It is only a prelude. The real life is in the world beyond. Yet in the very next verse, he teaches: "One hour spent in reflection and in helpfulness in this world is more precious than all eternity in the world to come." Are the two teachings irreconcilable? The coming together of Isaac and Rebecca as *"ish ve-isha"* ("man and woman") argues in favor of reconcilability. The two worlds — the ideal and real — are bridgeable through the connectedness of Isaac and Rebecca.

There is a "halakhic" definition of "entrance" which strengthens the "aggadic" teaching of Rabbi Jacob. Speaking of "entrance" or threshold which divides private domain and public domain, the *Gemara* says: "When the door is open, the 'entrance' or threshold is considered part of the house inside; when the door is closed, the 'entrance' or threshold is considered part of the public thoroughfare." The "entrance," therefore, is a link joining two areas.

Again the marriage of *"ish ve-isha"* is a link between the real "wilderness" world of striving between irreconcilables and the ideal Eden garden of loving unity.

As tradition has it, Isaac and Rebecca will be buried together in *me'arat ha-makhpeilah* along with three other couples. Jacob and Leah cannot be considered the ideal monogamous couple; indeed the absence of Rachel will be felt throughout the history of Israel as symptomatic of the troubled relationships within the House of Israel right from the beginning. Moreover, Rachel's burial outside the *me'arah* will serve as a memorial to the homelessness of her exiled children following their failure to live up to the covenant. (Notwithstanding Jeremiah's later vision of "exiled" Mother Rachel eliciting from God the promise that her "children shall return to their Land!")

Abraham and Sarah are closer to the notion of official monogamy in theory — but in contrast to Isaac and Rebecca they fall short on two counts: Hagar and Ishmael are a foreign but integral part of their story; and Abraham's great moments of covenantal commitment are experienced either without Sarah present or with her in the background. Isaac and Rebecca are the exemplary couple. They are for better or worse Adam and Eve — but not in the Garden, the universalist never-never land of shattered dreams. They are an Adam and Eve for the "wilderness" of continuing struggle. They are to ready themselves and their descendants the Children of Israel to build a loving community worthy to remain rooted in the Promised Land — not as resident-aliens but as full struggling citizens of the covenant.

Toldot   תולדות

Isaac and Rebecca will walk together. In complete and total harmony? Not quite! Their marriage is monogamously exemplary. Yet, it is hardly free of turmoil. The question persists: In their relationship with one another do Isaac and Rebecca become one indivisible body-politic? Or do they appear at certain key junctures in their lives together to be so singularly separate in intention that their formal marriage is merely a decorous legal bond connecting two persons with otherwise contrary purposes?

Such a judgment is too extreme. Isaac is described as loving Rebecca. And the scene of their first meeting is redolent with romantic promise. A later scene — the only such scene described among all the relationships in the Bible except the Song of Songs — describes Isaac fondling his wife, suggestive of a natural closeness bespeaking mutuality of affection and concern. Yet at the critical moment of transfer of the "blessing," their intentions are disparate. Their focus is split — each to his/her own — mentioned specifically in the early summary description of their feelings towards their sons: Isaac loves Esau while Rebecca loves Jacob.

The preference of each parent for one of two sons is psychologically not unusual. The biblical narrative is refreshing in its candor. Yet, within this biblical narrative these uninhibited preferences are explosive. The love of Jacob for Joseph from among all his children will serve as a pernicious ground for jealousy, hatred, and attempted murder. Isaac's love for Esau and — in Rebecca's judgment — its heavily laden consequences for the future of the covenant, along with Rebecca's love for Jacob, nurture the seeds of enmity that have been sown even before birth. The childhood, adolescence, and early adulthood of the twins, we may presume, enforce the enmity.

Nevertheless, it cannot be different. There is an overriding seemingly determinative Providence deciding on yet another break between brothers. It will not be fatal such as the Cain-Abel rupture; although from Esau's point of view it could have been. It will certainly be as decisive as the severance between Ishmael and Isaac. Although unlike the latter two who will only meet at their father's funeral, Jacob and Esau will meet and dialogue at least once again in their mature years with a modicum of mutual respect! The break between Jacob and Esau following the giving of the blessings and the conspiracy precipitating it appear to be providential conditions for preparing only a later generation for unity. Yet that hoped-for unity will elude that later generation as well — whether we are referring to the early fissure, on the family plane, between Joseph and his brothers or, on the national plane, the later historic hostility between Jacob-Israel and Esau-Edom. Indeed the internal unity of later Israel will be a constant dream, rarely fulfilled. The national reconciliation of Israel with Edom-Rome will barely survive as a hope for messianic times.

Wells

It can be claimed that Isaac and Rebecca have indeed been joined as one, destined to be complementary to one another. As suggested earlier, Rebecca and Isaac coming towards each other in love has been the latter-day post-Eden reconstruction of the failed idyllic coupling of Adam and Eve. Isaac and Rebecca in Canaan, rooted in the Land as neither Abraham and Sarah have been nor Jacob and his wives will be, are a single strong unified force for grounding the next stage of the covenantal realization. They dig the wells of living waters in the Land. It is poetically significant that the episode describing the quarrels over the wells between Isaac's men and the Philistines uses labels like *"esek"* meaning "contention" and *"sitnah"* meaning "strife." But finally when the contention and the strife have ceased in favor of a new well called "Rehovoth," signifying a "broadening," there has now occurred a broadening of possibility for the covenanted Isaac. He *will* be fruitful in the Land.

His fruitfulness in the Land, however, will be short-lived. It will not survive the next generation — at least as far as the Jacob-line is concerned. Jacob will have to escape his brother Esau's wrath. He will have to regenerate wealth in Diaspora in order to re-establish his roots in the Promised Land. The history of his descendants, moreover, will continue to be a history of internal contention and bitter internal strife with only a dream of "Rehovoth" nourishing the hungry wandering exile. The archetypal Diaspora leader of the medieval Jewish community, the Ramban, will see in these early wells of living water signs of the future Temples and future Jewish Commonwealths which the Jewish people will build and then see destroyed.

The first and second wells — "contention" and "strife" — represent, according to the simple reading, the ongoing quarrel between two forces which will seek hegemony over the Land. The early negotiation of Abraham and Avimelekh leading to a treaty will have proven fruitless. Treaties will have been ignored. Wells dug by Abraham and Isaac's shepherds will be stopped-up and choked by Philistine malice. But the Ramban, suffering with his people a never-ending exile — in his case the exile of Medieval Spain — sees the history of his people as a history of *internal* rancor. Both wells, representing the future first and second Temples and Commonwealths, will be destroyed precisely because of the internal contention and strife among the Children of Israel. That a third well will be dug, a third Temple and Commonwealth built, reflects for the Ramban the millennial yearning of the scattered Children of Israel, a broad opening of possibility — Rehovoth — in the Land of Israel.

But anticipating the "contention and strife" in the history of later Israel, Jacob and Esau, children of the same father and mother, are already ushering in a thematic pattern which will not let go of Jews as a people for millennia. The seeds of fraternal strife have been sown inside of Rebecca's womb; for these have been seeds of uncertainty that have lain dormant within Isaac ever since the trauma of the *akeidah*. How else can one explain his blind adoration of Esau?

A Mélange of Blessings

Is Isaac really blind during the dramatic crisis surrounding the alleged transfer of the blessing(s)? If he is, what has caused it? Rashi through the use of three alternative interpretations puts before us, somewhat obliquely, a rich psychological portrait of a patriarch tortured by conflict going back to his relationship with his father. According to Rashi's grandson, the Rashbam, the reason for Isaac's blindness is the infirmity of old age. But this simple *peshat* explanation is a possibility unacceptable to Rashi, even though as a commentator Rashi usually prefers the *peshat*. In this case he says: "His eyes were dim because of the smoke raised by these women (Esau's Hittite wives) in offering incense to idols. Another explanation is: Isaac was bound upon the altar and his father was about to slay him. At that very moment the heavens opened and the ministering angels saw what was about to happen. They wept, and their tears flowed and fell upon Isaac's eyes which thus became dim. Another explanation is: They became dim in order that Jacob might take the blessings."

Serious questions underlie these three interpretations. They concern Isaac's attitude to Esau and to Abraham — and peripherally to Jacob. The first interpretation is based on the previous two verses which describe how Esau's wives have been "a bitterness of spirit" unto Isaac and Rebecca. These women have been idolatrous and the strange fire which they have brought into Isaac's house has caused damage to Isaac's eyes. The smoke itself is a metaphor for the idolatrous practices which Isaac has permitted to infest his home. Why has Isaac tolerated these practices, if not because he has loved Esau too much? But why should he have loved Esau to begin with?

This may be connected to the second interpretation: the trauma of the sacrifice which will forever torment Isaac. Despite the spiritual awesomeness surrounding the *akeidah*, for Isaac to have experienced his father preparing to slaughter him has marked and will forever mark the relationship of father and son. In spite of "walking together" through the experience, the relationship between Abraham and Isaac must now be ambivalent — to say the least. One cannot but indulge the thought that because of the trauma, Isaac's affections are turned subconsciously to the son whom Abraham could not and would not prefer. Perhaps there is a reluctance on Isaac's part to transfer the blessing at all, since he intuitively knows that Esau is an inappropriate recipient; yet he cannot bring himself to reject Esau. Isaac lets his dilemma be resolved by inaction. Thus we have Rashi's third interpretation: Isaac permits Jacob to step in and the two of them together — the allegedly naïve Isaac and the "Esau" who Isaac "knows" is Jacob — stage a dramatic scene which will allow Jacob to seize the blessing himself.

Yet what is this blessing? Is it the covenantal blessing of Abraham? Apparently everyone involved in the drama thinks it is. But the content of the blessing intended for Esau and given in "error" to Jacob bespeaks personal-parental well-wishes — nothing more, nothing less! And in the end, Esau *will* receive his own personal-parental blessing. Moreover, after the entire episode is concluded, Jacob will receive — in the open — the covenantal blessing of

Abraham! It is as if Isaac's old trauma is so great, so acute, that he gives initial priority to his personal-parental blessing over the covenantal blessing, unconsciously reacting to Abraham's reverse prioritization at the *akeidah*. At the *akeidah*, we remember, Abraham lets God's covenantal command override his natural parental concern. Here, with Isaac as father, the priorities are reversed. Once the drama is played out, however, Isaac will recover his sense of awe at God's larger purposes and will pass on the covenantal blessing knowingly to the chosen son Jacob.

In the meantime, what of Rebecca? She has also chosen between sons. From the beginning, she has made such an emphatic choice that eventually she will assume the additional moral burden of contriving a degrading deception of her husband. Rebecca has dug the wells of living water with Isaac. With Isaac she has invested deeply in the Land in order to "reap a hundred-fold." What then will have brought her and this husband, her beloved Isaac, her surrogate Adam, to this breach of mutual trust?

As unified as Isaac and Rebecca seem to have been in their courtship and their marriage, Rebecca's pregnancy consigns each of them to a position of solitude. In reaction to Rebecca's lengthy period of barrenness, Isaac entreats God on behalf of his wife. Hannah of a later generation of barren heroines will plead on her own behalf before God. Perhaps it is because Rebecca has come from a family and civilization of idolaters that she has felt inadequate to the task of praying on her own to God. God senses her reticence, but nevertheless chooses to speak to her directly when she is going through her writhings as the future twins struggle within her. And this will usher in her growing solitariness in the face of the future of all of them.

God's prophecy regarding the destiny of the two sons and the two nations within her is given to her and to her alone. Rebecca never shares this prophecy with Isaac. In point of biblical fact, this prophecy is the one revelatory moment which any of the matriarchs experiences. Rebecca has performed her own autonomous *lekh-lekha* in going with the servant to a land that is strange to her. Now, in the midst of her pregnancy, this prophetic prediction of God pronounced directly to her as she cries out in pain is her own second *lekh-lekha* — sentencing her to her own private unaccompanied *akeidah*. For just as labor pains are the utterly private reserve of a solitary woman enduring her internal writhings, Rebecca will endure alone the knowledge that one son will be chosen at the cost of rejecting the other. Rebecca realizes that she must keep this revelation to herself. God has intended it to be so. But Rebecca pays for it by watching her husband move precipitously towards what she believes to be spiritual disaster. For Rebecca, there is no distinction between the personal-parental blessing and the covenantal blessing of Abraham. She sees her husband Isaac ready to forfeit the covenant. How can she allow it!

At the same time it is out of her love for Isaac that she spares him the early knowledge that his beloved Esau is not the chosen one. It is out of that same revealed knowledge that Rebecca holds back on what would otherwise be a natural unconditional love on her part for Esau who is, after all, as much her son as he is Isaac's. Rebecca has sensed that what she has carried inside her with all its ramifications and portents for the future has been meant to be carried by her alone — physiologically, of course, but psychologically and theologically as well. Somehow, though unarticulated, Rebecca has been given a glimpse of the dark dread of the *Brit bein ha-Betarim* as she has maneuvered her way from pregnancy to the critical and confused trial of the transfer of blessings — personal-parental and covenantal.

Brothers in Enmity

And what of Esau and Jacob — these twins whose destinies will diverge and yet will intersect mysteriously and portentously on an international stage through the later ages? Soon enough these twins — Esau the older and Jacob the younger — become independent persons who will represent particular ways of viewing reality and acting within that reality. Later homiletical Jewish history will contrapose the two brothers — the twins — as eternal enemies. It is a tragic opposition for they are both the offspring of the covenanted Isaac and Rebecca. Nevertheless, they do emerge, and grow up to be different and separate from one another, divided by an intellectual and spiritual gap which only effectuates what God has revealed at the beginning to their mother Rebecca.

The characterization of Esau as a hunter associates him immediately — to his misfortune — with his predecessor as hunter Nimrod. Esau is predestined for rejection vis-à-vis the covenant. If Nimrod's sin has been the building of a totalitarian civilization based on the worship of the all-powerful hunter, then whatever attractive attributes Esau may have, he cannot be trusted because he cannot be given the opportunity for Godly empowerment. He will sooner or later rebel against God and violate human beings created in God's image.

The Torah compromises with the necessity of hunting for food. It accepts that beast or fowl will be hunted, killed, and will be eaten. The Written Torah legislates that as long as the blood is poured out and covered with dust, it will be permitted halakhically to serve as food. By the rabbinic period, a fully detailed prescription for sanctifying the necessary acts of animal-slaughter and eating will have been established. But hunting-for-sport will never be tolerated, let alone endorsed, by the covenant. The association of hunting-for-sport with Esau, therefore, is a repudiation of him. The association comes out of his perceived role as an early Don Juan personality, yearning for freedom from discipline, responsibility, and obligation.

Rashi and Ibn Ezra connect Esau's ridicule of the *bekhorah* ("the birthright") with a projected ridicule of his obligation to offer firstborn animal sacrifices — *bekhorot* — upon the altar. Rashi imagines Esau saying: "If the particular sacrificial ritual has associated with it the threat of capital punishment if one should allow himself to be intoxicated or unkempt generally, then I risk death if I accept the *bekhorah*. Who would want such a burden?" Ibn Ezra, on the other hand, describes Esau as perfectly willing to risk his life everyday as he goes out to hunt wild animals. He knows that his own death may precede his father's. Why then should he care about the birthright now?

The two commentators reflect respectively both sides of this impetuous self-indulgent personality. On the one hand, as Rashi sees him, he doesn't want to die. On the other hand, according to Ibn Ezra, he is willing to follow a life-style in which he risks death every day. More subtly, Esau is seen on the one hand as afraid to take risks based on his own behavior, i.e., he knows that he will not perform the ritual with appropriate respect for its required discipline. But on the other hand, he is absolutely unafraid to take risks in his daily mode of occupation as hunter. Esau has no problem living with the contradiction: he is essentially afraid to risk adopting the discipline of a covenanted way of life; yet he is recklessly unafraid to endanger himself with his own happily chosen free-fall existence.

Esau — like Nimrod — is not an unattractive personality. Nimrod, after all, draws the people to him, to the virtual worship of him, as the greatest *gibor* ("hero") of their given civilization. Esau, like Nimrod and like Don Juan, will have no trouble galvanizing advocacy for his way-of-life. He represents indulgence of the physical — not a crime per se. He has a joi de vivre which is infectious. He is not lacking in emotion. He laughs, he weeps. He is capable of affection as he is prone to bursting out in anger. He is a vital if volatile human being. As a Don Juan figure, however, he cannot and will not conform to the terms of any covenant, even if he is a partner to it, let alone if it has been imposed upon him by external standards past or present.

And like Don Juan and Nimrod Esau cannot be trusted. His unpredictability, his tempestuousness, his animal nature will fight to sustain — with delight, with lustful zest — patterns of the "wilderness." Any idea of covenantal cultivation of that "wilderness" will be sold by him for an immediate sensual gratification, e.g., selling his birthright for a lentil stew. In the end his threat to God's purposes is less formidable than Nimrod's. For Nimrod will exercise enough self-discipline to ultimately lock an entire civilization into a totalitarian machine harnessed to his whim. Esau will find eventually enough self-discipline to lead a *tribe* of formidable strength. But no more! And by then Esau is well out of the covenantal drama — even as rebel. He will appear years later to "threaten" Jacob; and his descendants — Edom reincarnated in Rome and the Medieval Church — will be seen by later descendants of Jacob — the Jewish people — as an eternal oppressive adversary. But Esau himself will agree in later years to a truce with his hated brother who has "swindled" him, not once but twice.

But has Jacob indeed swindled Esau — out of the *bekhorah* and then in collusion with their mother out of the *berakhah*? The Zohar has a pointed defense of Jacob's action in the "*bekhorah*-for-lentils" episode. Rabbi Elazar says to his father Rabbi Shimon, "Esau has protested that Jacob has swindled him." Rabbi Shimon responds, "Yes, my son, but do you believe Esau? The Bible also says that Jacob was *tam* ('honest'); yet you believe Esau? My son, what of the passage 'and Esau *despised* the *bekhorah*'? Does this statement not have any bearing on Esau's overall credibility?"

There is no doubt that the chain of stories that are told in the Book of Genesis from Abel versus Cain, Isaac versus Ishmael, Jacob versus Esau, Joseph versus Reuben (and the brothers), and Ephraim versus Manasseh, all have a younger sibling receiving preference over the older legally entitled sibling. Moreover, the single fraternal relationship noted in the Book of Exodus has Moses the younger similarly being chosen to shepherd Israel over his older brother Aaron. Jacob's story is the central link in the entire series and the most complex. He is described early as *"tam"* ("honest" or "blameless") as opposed to *"tamim,"* as if his *"tam-ness"* lacks the fullness of Abraham's or even Noah's *"tamim-ness."* But he will grow into being *tamim.*

Jacob is never meant to be the absolute antithesis of Esau as some *midrashim* make him out to be. Jacob is not physically meek. He will become *tamim* in that his range of experiences will be the most variegated of all the patriarchs and will demand of him a genuine wholeness relevant to a morally complex world. His world is one of competitiveness beginning at birth, continuing into his sojourn with Laban and the return in later years to confront his brother Esau again, culminating in the agonizing period of parenting a tribe of jealous sons vying with each other for seniority. To survive in such a world, all the while aware of the covenant that he is charged with upholding, requires Jacob to be *tamim,* wise but clever, strong but flexible, spiritually committed but materially engaged. In short, if he has "swindled" Esau, not once but twice, it has been — according to Jacob's complex sensibility — "for the sake of Heaven." The later Children of Israel will similarly be charged by Moses to be *tamim* (Deut. 18:13) in the face of God's long-term purposes for the world.

The *midrash* which sees Jacob dancing ecstatically within his mother's womb when she passes a House of Study as opposed to Esau dancing before a House of Idolatry has a value agenda suffused with later rabbinic preference. The biblical image of Jacob, however, the man who will become Israel, is not that of a sheltered *"yeshiva-bahur."* If Esau is a Don Juan, then Jacob is not a scholarly puritan nor a saintly ascetic. He is one who has been chosen to continue a line of partnership with the Creator of Heaven and Earth. As such he will struggle. His very existence, his being called Israel, will represent quintessentially "struggle," but not from inside a cloister, but in the "wilderness" that is life lived to the fullest.

Jacob as Jacob will serve as the foil for Esau's active forfeiture of the birthright. Jacob as Jacob will follow his mother Rebecca's instructions to the letter in the crucial dramatic playing-out of the transfer of parental blessing. Jacob as Jacob will again heed his mother's warnings to escape the impending attempt at revenge by his enraged brother. At this stage of Jacob's life and career as the bearer of the covenant, he is not fully active, not fully responsible for decision-making regarding policy for safeguarding the covenant. Rebecca and Isaac, after all, are still alive. And within Isaac's possession is still the very special blessing which he has preserved beyond the intrigue surrounding the giving of the personal-parental blessing.

As mentioned earlier, there has been confusion. Isaac himself has confused the two blessings and led Rebecca, Jacob, and Esau into this conspiratorial fiasco. Not that the personal-parental blessing is not important! It is a universally recognized rite of passage in which the child receives a patent of approval from the source of life as he has known it — his parent. Every child wants it, needs it, and with varying degrees of subtlety will fight for it and ache for it should it be withheld. One commentator — the Radak — builds an apologetic defense for Isaac which attempts to clarify the confusion: Isaac has known all along that Esau has needed his personal-parental blessing precisely because he is not respectable; he is unstable, unpredictable. Jacob, Isaac has determined, does not require the personal-parental blessing, since he will receive the covenantal blessing of Abraham, the blessing promising long-term survival of Abraham, Isaac, and Jacob's seed along with the gift of inheriting the Land.

Radak's view of Isaac underscores the desire of every parent to bestow upon the next generation the blessing of material sustenance. Esau comes in for his blessing, and Isaac is flustered enough to say that "your brother has taken your blessing." But he *does* give Esau a blessing of material sustenance. It may not have quite the fullness of what he has given to Jacob as a personal-parental blessing; but it is far from negligible. Isaac errs, however, in not believing that Jacob needs the blessing of material sustenance. Jacob will struggle twenty years with Laban in order to provide himself with the material resources sufficient to raise a family large enough to begin building a socioeconomic foundation in the Promised Land.

Anticipating the Prophetic Dream

What is clear is that there is a unique disquietude associated with Isaac brought on by the *akeidah*. It is unrelieved by God's revealed encouragement of his efforts in the Land. He is told not to be afraid; and yet he agrees to another treaty with the Philistines. Isaac, as described in the Torah, will always be stricken with *pahad* ("trepidation"). He among the patriarchs never leaves the Land. He digs deeply the wells of fruitfulness, yet needs Rebecca to compensate for his insecurity. And Rebecca in favoring Jacob over Esau has not contraposed an otherworldly model against an extreme this-worldly model. She is looking to nurture a Jacob who will embody *both* dimensions of God's creative process — the heavenly and the earthly.

Rebecca will anticipate a lengthy history in which the Children of Israel will struggle for covenantal survival. It will be a struggle in which a satisfactory symbiosis between the heavenly and the earthly will elude the national and religious grasp. Sovereignty in the Promised Land will surrender to the earthly with sufficient abandon to warrant prophetic condemnation. On the other hand, the lack of sovereignty in exile will ultimately unveil the hopelessness of ungrounded heavenliness in a world of real peoples with real tensions and anxieties over limited material resources. At any turn these real peoples may convert previously welcome minorities into unwelcome and utterly vulnerable "aliens."

The debate within the Children of Israel over the primacy in human existence of the heavenly and earthly, the spiritual and the material, "Torah" and "Life," will be summarized in millennially spaced evocations of rabbis and rebels. A classic rabbinic maxim will say: "He who walking along, concentrating on his Torah-studies, stops to admire a tree or a meadow, forfeits his life." With undisguised hyperbole, the talmudic author of this maxim — whose name happens to be Jacob — will be emphasizing the indispensability of a heavenly purpose and direction to life-on-earth. But a much later rebel *against* the rabbinic tradition, Micah Berdichevsky, living under the clouds of total vulnerability in exile, will turn the maxim on its head: "Whoever walks along and sees a fine tree and a fine meadow and a fine sky and leaves *them* to think on other thoughts is one who forfeits *his life!*"

It will be the biblical Jacob who will dream of the symbiosis. It will be he who will be carrying spiritual yearnings along with material strategies in his single consciousness. Will he be a schizophrenic personality unable to grasp together the two-sidedness of God's plan for creation? Or will he, at least in his dreams, be able to envision a unity of thought, feeling, and purpose? In short, will Jacob hold on to his dream — and God's dream for humankind — the persistent dream of the ladder linking heaven and earth and be able to concretize that dream in the "wilderness"?

Va-Yetze

ויצא

Jacob understands something about human life and human destiny which Nimrod — in his arrogance — had never been able to understand. Nimrod had seen himself as pulling the whole world into his orbit and climbing up the Tower in order to challenge God over sovereignty of the universe. Jacob sees life for the human being as an adventure-on-earth attuned to a perpetual dialectic between the earthly and heavenly, the material and spiritual, the real and ideal. Jacob has an image of a horizontal push-and-pull to life. It is an image of himself leaving home, settling elsewhere, then returning home and resettling in the Promised Land. But Jacob also has an image of a vertical ascent and descent in life. It is of himself — unlike Nimrod — struggling to integrate in his own life the earthly and heavenly, the material and spiritual, the real and ideal.

The image in Jacob's dream of *"sulam mutzav artzah ve-rosho magi'a ha-shamaymah"* ("a ladder set on earth with its top reaching the heavens") is not only extraordinary. It is formative, archetypal, in that it will serve as a seminal image-pattern for the House of Israel's efforts in the world thereafter. The angels ascending and descending add to the dream's potent suggestiveness. And the revealed content of God's spoken message in the dream is the necessary further endorsement of Abraham and Isaac's offspring Jacob as the rightful heir to the Promised Land. The dream serves as the beacon-call for Jacob as he is leaving the Land. It is to remind him that his search for a wife among his mother's brethren in exile is legitimized only as part of a long-term preparation to return to the Land.

Twenty years later, when Jacob does return, he will be met again by angels. Rashi sees the image of the angels in the dream and the angels greeting Jacob upon his return as the same group — integrated in function, i.e., the angels who are going up the ladder are the ones conducting Jacob on his return to Eretz Yisrael whereas the angels going down the ladder are the ones who have accompanied Jacob on his sojourn in exile. The *aliyah* and *kenisa la-aretz* are one; the *yeridah* and *yetziyah min ha-aretz* are similarly one.

The dreams and realities that heretofore have made up the life of Jacob and will continue to make up his life are the preparatory events for the transition from the pre-history and history of an individual family to the history of a people. As noted above, from the moment that Jacob chances upon this place that he will call "Beth-El" ("the House of God") and chooses a stone upon which to lay his head, his experiences — whether in dream or in reality — will become the archetypal experiences of the House of Israel.

The Ladder

There is a legend which speaks of Jacob taking twelve stones from the stones of the altar upon which his father Isaac had been bound. Jacob then reflects: "The Holy One Blessed Be He has decreed that He is to build up twelve tribes in the world. Abraham hasn't done it. Isaac hasn't done it. If these twelve stones join themselves together to become one stone, then I know that it is I who am destined to produce these twelve tribes. And these twelve tribes will become one nation." The legend records that at that moment a miracle occurs and the twelve stones indeed become one. Jacob takes the unified stone, places it under his head, and it becomes for him a pillow, a cushion — and a portent.

Jacob goes to sleep on that stone and dreams the dream of the ladder. It is at one and the same time a dream of human aspiration leading heavenward as it is a heavenly projection earthward revealing the hoped-for destiny of humankind. And the earthly destiny of humankind is to be mediated by the dream-inspired reality of a single human family turned into a nation suggesting ultimately a broader unity of human families turned into nations. For God has reiterated to Jacob what He had prophesied to Abram — that he and his descendants would be a blessing for all the families of the earth. Becoming this blessed nation which in turn is to be a blessing for all nations begins with Jacob — son of Isaac and Rebecca, grandson of Abraham and Sarah — soon to be renamed Israel.

With regard to the dream of the ladder, Israel Eldad has pointed to the difference between a psychoanalytic approach to dream interpretation and a psychosynthetic approach. Analysis is the act of resolving a compound into its smaller parts or elements in order to study each of them. Synthesis is combining separate parts or elements into a whole. Religiously speaking, when one asks what is happening when revelation or prophecy or prayer occurs, the tendency is to answer too often with a discussion which is analytical, i.e., attempting to discuss discrete aspects of the experience of revelation, prophecy, or prayer. But revelation for the Children of Israel, prophecy for Jacob, or prayer for generations of worshipers is based upon a synthesizing and resynthesizing of one's perceptions of grand purpose. It is putting together the pieces of one's experience in life, one's hopes and goals and sense of overriding purpose into a grand design — a design for living in the world as it is while dreaming of making the world better than it is.

What Jacob sees in his dream is the collective soul of Israel struggling constantly in dynamic tension between the earthly and the heavenly. Jacob sees the earth with its gravitational pull bending human beings to material needs and pursuits while the heavens above — with all that is unknown about them — drawing human beings to an investigation of their mysteries. The struggle within Jacob and later within Israel and the Children of Israel will be to attempt to find an equilibrium between the physical and the metaphysical, knowing that it is impossible to achieve such an equilibrium.

What Jacob sees in the dream is an encapsulation of all of later Jewish history — its religious thrust and its secular thrust. The *sulam mutzav artzah* ("the ladder set on earth") represents Israel's groundedness in the secular "real." But if the Children of Israel will give themselves over too much to that secular "real" they will fall prey to hedonistic materialism. Jacob thus sees the ladder reaching upwards: "ve-*rosho magi'a ha-shamaymah* ("with its top reaching the heavens") representing Israel's devotion to things spiritual, to sociomoral aspirations, to mystical enchantment. But should the Children of Israel transport themselves too far into the wafty spheres of infinity and speculation thereof, they will risk disappearing from the earth like a breeze and a shadow.

The struggle which the ladder comes to represent is — as written — superintended by God: "*ve-hinei Hashem nitzav alav.*" Two talmudic rabbis, Rabbi Hiyya and Rabbi Yanai, have a theoretical argument over the meaning of these words. One says that the image suggests that God is to be found on top of the ladder because the word *alav* means "on *it*." The other, however, insists that *alav* means "on *him*," that the Torah is suggesting that God stands over Jacob, that God is becoming at this point a fully realized Presence over-seeing Jacob's aspirations and destiny. According to either interpretation, a vivid statement is being made in confrontation with the worldview of idola-try: Israelite man does not stand over his god; Man is seen as subservient to God. Israelite Man stands outside his deeply held daydreams and perceives the Presence as superintending these daydreams. Jacob and the future Children of Jacob-Israel will be enraptured with the superintending Pres-ence. Moreover, Jacob and the future Children of Jacob-Israel will be con-fronted with the challenge to remember always that their ego — individual and collective — must act in relation to Him who is transcendent above all human egotistical conceit.

Jacob is not the first in the biblical imagination to recognize the essential spiritual and sociomoral challenge of being a created human being. Like all who have come before and who will come after, he will have to respond to the double exhortation to love God and to love his fellow human being. His immediate background has prepared him to recognize that life as he will live it will hold out before him temptations and barriers — temptations to avoid allegiance to God and barriers to relating to his fellow man in any way except through stressful suspicion and competitiveness.

Jacob has doubts regarding this heavenly-earthly enterprise symbolized by the ladder. He has always had to struggle. He has struggled from the begin-ning — even before the beginning, i.e., before his birth, in the primordial *hitrotzetzut* ("jostling"/"jousting") with Esau in the womb. He has had to per-form the "hoax" for the "sake of Heaven" in order to wheedle the birthright out of Esau. He has had to go along with Rebecca's ruse in order to gain the personal-parental blessing from Isaac. His life has been and will continue to be one of flight — flight from Esau, flight from Laban. Among the three patri-archs, only he will be described as *wrestling* with God, with God's messenger, and with himself.

As vividly real as his dream of the ladder is, he even doubts whether God has indeed been "there" for him. On the one hand, Jacob confesses: "Surely the Lord is present in this place and I did not know it!" But the Midrash reflects Jacob's self-doubts as to his ability to carry out his responsibilities in the face of God's epiphany. His doubts are transferred to the later national plane.

In the name of Rabbi Meir, God shows in Jacob's dream of the ladder a succession of empires represented by their respective angelic ministers ascending, but then descending, i.e., rising in power but then being eclipsed. First Babylonia rises and falls; then Medea; then Greece; finally Rome. They will all soar to greatness only to decline, to disintegrate and to disappear. God then urges Jacob to ascend the ladder. At that moment, Jacob shudders: "Are you indicating to me, O Lord, that just as these glorious empires have inevitably faced dissolution, so will I?" God assures Jacob that if he goes up, he will *never go down*. Nevertheless, Jacob refuses to believe and doesn't go up! In the name of God, a later sage then scolds Jacob: "Since you lacked faith, your descendants will face enslavement by all four of these empires in this world." Jacob then pleads: "Does this mean forever?" At this point, God relents and comforts Jacob with the words: "Do not fear, O Jacob, do not be dismayed, O Israel, for I will save you from afar, as well as your descendants from their captivity."

Notwithstanding his doubts and his need to flee to exile, Jacob does succeed in building an economic future for himself and his burgeoning family. He assumes the mantle of the covenant even as he must contend with a greater variety of challenges than either of his patriarchal predecessors. He may seem to lack the iron-clad conviction of Abraham. He doesn't have a determinedly resourceful Rebecca at his side, sharing the covenantal task as does Isaac. What Jacob has, however, is a keen sensitivity to the temptations and dangers of the real world, to the wily machinations of men as they show constant hospitality to the *yeitzer ra*. The very name "Ya'akov" from the root *"akev"* meaning "heel" recalls God's condemnation of the Serpent in the Garden: *"Hu yeshufkha rosh ve-ata teshufenu akev."* ("They (human beings) shall strike at your head and you (the Serpent) shall strike at their heel.")

The Serpent's bite at Jacob's heel teaches him the painful lesson which many centuries later a wily Machiavelli will attempt to teach his prince "that a man who wishes to make a profession of goodness in everything must necessarily come to grief among so many who are not good. Therefore it is necessary for a prince who wishes to maintain himself to learn how not to be good and to use his knowledge and not to use it, according to the necessity of the case." For Jacob this means that he will determine in each case, under the given circumstance, how to deal with adversaries ranging from Esau to Laban to the residents of Shekhem. The grand purpose is to survive in a world of rapaciousness in order to introduce — at the very least — finer standards of social intercourse, if not yet more elevated spiritual and moral goals for humanity. But the prerequisite for such opportunities must be initial minimal survival.

Once minimal survival is secured, then the mandate will be and must be to cultivate the means to develop enough vitality to activate purposes such as one's love for God and one's love for one's fellow human-being. These purposes will require an overall commitment to what will be spelled out later at Sinai as the detailed demands of the covenant — already envisioned in the "ladder."

Jacob's "Zionist" Vow

The history of Jacob's descendants will represent an attempt to realize in the life of a people the message inherent in the "ladder." Firstly, the message as translated into Jewish history will argue that Judaism as a religion is an ethnic or national religion. Secondly, if the Jewish people — as the Children of Israel will be called — will be an ethnos or nation, then it will be an ethnos or nation endowed with spiritual and sociomoral aspirations. The suggestive image of the ladder standing on the earth reaching heavenwards will underscore the impossibility of defining the Children of Israel or the Jewish people in any but such an integrated fashion.

Yet post-Emancipation Jewish history will argue the case for the "natural" and the "supernatural" Jew and the gap between them. The claim will be made that the prolonged exile and accompanying absence of sovereignty, i.e., the loss of the capacity to determine one's national destiny or to write one's autonomous national history will have fractured the integration. The medieval pre-Emancipation period will have spawned — perhaps out of necessity — an over-emphasis among Jewish communities on the spiritual, the metaphysical, the ideal. The post-Emancipation reaction will see the emergence of two new attempts to define Judaism and Jewishness. On the one hand there will be an aggressive secular revolution committed to redefining Jewishness in non-religious and even anti-religious nationalistic terms, e.g., secular Zionism. At the same time, various philosophical approaches to Judaism will seek to accommodate it to an optimistic belief that Jews can live a full religious life in a welcoming Diaspora situation — that Judaism as a religion neither needs a nationalistic base which is Jewish nor an ethnic-national dimension in order to consider itself Jewishly vital and relevant. In short, both post-Emancipation initiatives at re-definition of the covenant will in effect be a blatant attempt to abandon Jacob's dream-vision.

Jacob will live out his dream-vision in a life full of wrestling. He has already wrestled prodigiously before the dream. As he wakes from the dream he makes a vow, a troublesome one according to the commentators: "If God remains with me, if He protects me on this journey, gives me bread to eat and clothing to wear, and if I return to my father's house — then the Lord shall be my God." Abrabanel asks two questions about the vow. The first is how could Jacob doubt what God had already promised him, namely, that God would "be with him." Secondly how could Jacob make an unseemly vow full of conditions, demanding guaranteed rewards before committing himself to God? Would this mean, Abrabanel conjectures, that if these conditions were not fulfilled, Jacob would give up on the covenant, would not worship the one true God?

The Ramban has responded earlier to such questions. He first quotes Rashi to the effect that even though God promises, if Man does not meet the challenge from his side, if he falls short, the promise is not kept. In other words, Jacob is not doubting God; he is doubting himself and his own religious sincerity and persistence. As to the question regarding Jacob's setting conditions for his faith-commitment, the Ramban changes his homiletical direction. Focusing on the phrase *"Ve-shavti be-shalom el bet avi,"* ("I will return in peace to my father's house,") the Ramban argues that Jacob's return to the Land of Israel is not part of his conditions. It is an essential part of his vow. All his hoped-for, prayed-for blessings — material blessings, not conditions — he vows to dedicate to his return home, to Eretz Yisrael, where he will worship God in that place where he slept, having gathered together the twelve stones with which to make one stone on which to dream the great dream. To sharpen the thrust of his argument, the Ramban then quotes the radical talmudic statement from tractate Ketubbot: "He who lives in *galut* (exile) — no matter how many blessings he may experience there — is as one who has not God!"

The Ramban will become one of the great medieval articulators of the Zionist credo: that settling the Land of Israel — no matter how long the exile — is a positive commandment with priority status in any consideration of what Jewish values are considered to be. If Jacob represents for all ages the struggling Israel moving up and down the ladder, moving in and out of Israel, it is this struggle, this moving in and out, which is the "happening." Jacob's faith in the ladder's integration of the spiritual and the material, the ideal and the real, will be measured in terms of his relationship to the demand to remain in Israel or, if he has had to leave Israel, his commitment never to forget to return.

Galut Delay

The conditions surrounding Jacob's leaving the Land and returning to the Land are exceedingly complex. In contrast to Isaac who never leaves the Land and to whom Rebecca is brought — a Rebecca whose dynamic strength will support Isaac's efforts in the Land — Jacob's life is strewn with obstacles. The circumstances under which Jacob has had to leave the Land, the deceptions of Laban, and the familial stresses generated by the bigamous reality which has been forced upon him will plague Jacob throughout his life.

Emphatic is the contrast between Isaac's meeting and love for Rebecca and Jacob's meeting and love for Rachel. Rebecca is brought to Isaac and, as the text reports, he takes her as his wife and then loves her. Jacob, on the other hand, sees Rachel, falls in love with her, and then — after Laban's machinations — eventually marries her. The Bible nowhere says explicitly that if a man is attracted by a woman's beauty enough to marry her on that basis, things will necessarily turn out badly. Yet, in this case, in this particular story of romantic physical love, the attachment between Jacob and Rachel has tragic overtones for the future.

Rachel is portrayed as a tragic figure. She suffers barrenness, made even more painful in contrast to her sister Leah's fruitfulness. When Jacob and his family leave Laban's house to return to face their destiny superintended by the covenanted ethical monotheism of Jacob's forbears, it is Rachel who is weak and uncertain enough to carry along with her the *terafim* (idols) of her father Laban's household. It appears then that it is Rachel who can't quite assume the burden and responsibilities of the new vision without some vestige of the past supporting her and thus blemishing her — and along with her, Jacob and the family.

During this time what do we know of Leah? She is described as relatively plain in looks, but, as already cited, fruitful. Leah grows in importance as

Rachel's weakness becomes more apparent. For despite the initial lack of attraction which she has for her husband, it is she — Leah — who endures and produces the progeny. Not only does Leah have more sons than her sister; it is Leah who is ultimately buried with her husband, while Rachel is buried on a lonely road near Bethlehem.

Rachel is certainly not forgotten nor will her departed spirit be lost to the Israelite saga of *yeridah* and *aliyah*, exile and return. From her grave, Rachel will serve as the comforter for her exiled people in later ages, refusing to be comforted until God promises that her children will return to Israel. As history will show Leah's and Rachel's children becoming the tribes of Israel and tragically being destroyed except for the two tribes of the southern kingdom, it will be the tribe of Judah which will dominate — Judah, a son of Leah. At the same time, however, the tribe of Benjamin of Rachel's line, geographically close to Judah and eventually home to the Holy Temple, will also survive the loss of the tribes of the northern breakaway kingdom and share in the continuity of covenantal history.

In summary, both Rachel and Leah cannot match the stature of Rebecca. Yet, together they give birth — along with their maidservants — to the Children of Israel. The covenant will now be passed on to a large family. Jacob has worked for twenty years to raise the family with which he will now return to the Promised Land. He has been cheated consistently by Laban but has learned to outwit his father-in-law in order to achieve his own independence. He is now prepared to fulfill the vow which he made following his dream of the ladder. The spur for his return, however, is a second dream.

The second dream is connected to the first dream. For in the second dream God reminds Jacob of what he had promised upon waking from the first dream. God says, "I am the God of Beth-El, where you anointed a pillar and where you made a vow to me. Now, arise and leave this land and return to your native land." Within the commentaries there is general agreement that God is impatient with Jacob's delay. The Ramban, for example, sees this dream as having been repeated any number of times during Jacob's feverish attempt to outmaneuver Laban with regard to the flocks and Jacob's otherwise legitimate attempt to gain some financial wherewithal for himself and his family.

The question is asked. "Why the Godly concern over the delay?" After all, Jacob has had to work fourteen years for Leah and Rachel and another six years to accumulate his wealth — respectable reasons for remaining in *galut*. Yet, a careful reconsideration of Rebecca's farewell to Jacob twenty years earlier will shed light on God's "anxiety." She says to her son who needs a place of refuge from the wrath of Esau, "Go to my brother in Haran where you will stay *a few days*." Ibn Ezra has explained that the word *yamim* is used in the Torah to mean "a year." In any case, Ibn Ezra allows for it to mean "several years, but less than ten." Yet Jacob has delayed much longer — to the point that Isaac and Rebecca will never see their son Jacob again.

Why then has Jacob waited so long? Even with Laban's duplicitous nature, Jacob might have left with Leah and Rachel after the first seven years. There would have been a confrontation? There will be in any case after twenty years. He would have left with nothing? True! But instead Jacob has paid a heavy price in never seeing Rebecca and Isaac again. The Rabbis will see Laban's initial deception of Jacob in switching Leah for Rachel as Jacob's bride as a *middah ke-neged middah* (measure for measure) punishment of Jacob for his own similar deception of Isaac.

But there will be an additional *middah ke-neged middah* inflicted upon Jacob. Because Jacob has not been sensitive enough to Rebecca and Isaac's anguish in not seeing him over so many years, Jacob will himself experience a similar longing when his son Joseph disappears, does not die, but lives on, achieves greatness, yet "forgets" to communicate with his family. Exile from the Land — as exile — is painful enough from the vantage point of the covenant. Exile nourished by the *forgetting* of the Land — and Joseph in his rise to power in Egypt will forget much about his family and the Land — can mean the suspension if not the demise altogether of the covenant and the dream.

On a New Threshold

Jacob's dream of youth has been a dream in which the material and spiritual are seen as struggling for dominance but promising an equilibrium which is covenantally redemptive. This dream has given way within Laban's hothouse of competitiveness and greed to Jacob's dream of material achievement, which if not short-circuited can turn Jacob from his sacred vow. Granted, the vow had to include a pre-condition of material well-being: bread to eat and clothing to wear for him and his growing family. But how much material well-being is necessary before the original dream and its vow will have fallen into the well of forgotten ideals?

Jacob does come back. He will re-enter the Land with formidable wealth and a potentially sturdy tribe. He has already wrestled mightily with Man and survived, even prevailed, by means of varying strategies of resourcefulness and escape. He has, in a sense, wrestled with God as well, though hardly prevailing. To "prevail" against God could never mean "defeating" God. It could only mean eliciting from God a blessing. And this Jacob has not yet received. His own doubts and fears have prevented him from climbing the ladder decisively enough "not to come down." His own doubts and fears have delayed his return to the place where his own private revelation (the dream of the ladder) had indicated was the House of God and the Gate to Heaven.

But at long last he has returned; and angels of the Land are leading him more deeply into the Land. At this juncture, on the threshold of a new stage in his life, he will need — despite his large family — a critical moment of solitude, one in which he will finally learn the full scope of his destiny. That moment will give him a third blessing — beyond his father's personal-parental blessing and his grandfather's covenantal blessing. It will be God's blessing; and this third blessing will bestow upon Jacob a new essence, a new name — Israel.

Va-Yishlah   וישלח

At two of the most critical junctures in Jacob's life, he is utterly alone. As he begins his journey of escape from his brother Esau and moves towards the necessary *yeridah* ("departure") from Eretz Yisrael, he is alone. As a solitary traveler, lying down to rest, he dreams his revelatory dream of the ladder. And twenty years later, as he approaches the re-entry to Eretz Yisrael and a confrontation with the same brother Esau, he transfers his entire tribe of family and additional entourage over the river Yabok — intentionally — so that he may again be in solitude. Alone, all alone, he wrestles with a mysterious stranger, emerges with a blessing and a new identity.

Jacob is afraid. He knows that he has a right to be afraid, for he is preparing to meet his estranged brother. In such a mood of trepidation — or at least weighty uncertainty — the appearance of the mysterious stranger brings Jacob to the realization that he has to "wrestle it out" with three forces: with the "angel" of Esau, with the "angel" of God, and with his own "angel," i.e., himself. In wrestling with all three forces he will discover his authentic self. He will no longer be merely a Jacob snapping at others' heels, fighting for a place, for legitimacy, for primacy, in a world of serpentine turmoil without sociomoral purpose, without transcendent meaning. He will become Israel, perennially struggling with God and with Man — but prevailing in a goal-directed strategy for mending God's Creation and Man's investment as partner in that Creation.

The Wrestler

The "angel" of Esau represents for Jacob the multiple adversarial forces in life which he has already faced and will continue to face. These are forces which have the power to paralyze him but which he has learned to combat with imaginative cleverness and resourcefulness. The "angel" of God reminds

Jacob of his weakness in the presence of Transcendent Power. But at the same time this "angel" of God promises him reservoirs of strength energized by faith in that Transcendent Power. And somewhere in the available existential space between the "angel" of Esau and the "angel" of God is Jacob's own "angel," his authentic self — his ego — struggling to emerge amidst all the apprehensions, confusions, and self-contradictions in his prior life. Jacob feels intuitively that his struggles with the three angels will never cease. But to orchestrate his struggle he seeks now to move from having a patchwork identity to having what Buber will call "a united soul."

With his dream of the ladder as a younger man Jacob was mired in a plethora of complex thoughts, emotions, anxieties, and expectations. He was leaving his homeland and family against the background of the ugly reality of his brother's enmity, his father's ambivalence, and an understandable sense of insecurity regarding his future in Haran. Nevertheless, upon waking from this exotic but revelatory dream, Jacob was able to make vows with a degree of confidence. Now, twenty years later, at this more mature stage in his life one would expect him to be even more confident than heretofore. He has worked diligently in Haran and has the wealth to show for it. He has raised a family. Yet at this moment he is struck by what seems to him to be a relentless siege upon his sense of self. The wrestling at night is the quintessential symbol of the siege.

Is Jacob's wrestling *only* a dream, albeit a prophetic dream? The Rambam understands it as such; the Ramban sees the dream as real. How can it not be real when Jacob comes out of the "match" with a limp? Whichever the case, the impact of the dream is sufficiently critical for Jacob to come out of the experience with a new identity. His change of name is clearly conveyed as such. "Ya'akov" as descendant of Man in constant battle with the Serpent has been plagued by the ongoing schemes of the Serpent aiming to poison his heel, i.e., by way of pertinacious pulling of Man from the covenanted path. But the name "Yisrael" will bespeak "struggle," frontal fully conscious struggle to realize the implications of the covenant. And the struggle for realization in the Ramban's field-of-vision is to be redemptive of spirit but wounding of body. And the struggle within this new Israel who is the former Jacob will become the perennial struggle of the Children of Israel through the generations.

As cited earlier, the struggle within Jacob is on three fronts at the same time. Rashi, echoing the Midrash, sees the adversary as the ministerial lord of Esau and all the later descendants of Esau, the nations hostile to Jacob-Israel. The *peshat* (simple meaning) of the text points to such an interpretation. For Jacob has sent messengers to Esau and what does Jacob see as an apparent result of the delegation's mission: a band of four hundred men trooping ominously towards him — a situation threatening hostilities.

As noted by Nehama Leibowitz, an expansion of the description of the adversary will be articulated millennia later by Nachman Krochmal in his *More Nevukhei ha-Zeman* (*A Guide to the Perplexed of Our Time*): "The essence of a nation is not discovered or uncovered except in studying the spiritual identity of that nation. This is what is meant in the Bible by the citation 'the god of the nation' or 'ministerial angel of the nation.'" Jacob is thus seen as the nation of Israel wrestling eternally with its enemy nation Esau or other enemy nations. It is a conflict in which the nation of Israel stands alone — "*am le-vadad yishkon*," as Balaam the later Gentile prophet will see it — derived from the description of Jacob's individual existential loneliness: "*Va-yivateir Ya'akov levado*" ("And Jacob remained alone"). This nation of Israel emerges not completely victorious, for it limps; but it is never completely defeated. For its name is Israel, i.e., "you have wrestled with Man and prevailed."

The biblical verse, however, says "You have wrestled *with God* as well as with Man and prevailed." The Rashbam seeks to answer the question "What does it mean to wrestle with God?" Jacob — according to this interpretation — is confronted with an angel of God who serves as an obstacle to Jacob's running away. In case Jacob has entertained the notion of escaping from his covenanted destiny — the destiny forecast for him as the heir of Abraham and Isaac — the angel of God won't let him. Jacob will be forced to battle the angel until he realizes that there is no escape from this destiny. And once he is reconciled to his existential "entrapment" he is also brought to the realization that he has nothing to fear from a confrontation with Esau or any combination of Esau's. For what is this destiny? Jacob has learned it in the original dream of the ladder. It is to limp through history with the tension of striving to integrate the material — in this case the "Esau-ness" in life — with the spiritual, the "Jacob-ness." But all under the blessed providential concern of God!

The descendant of Jacob-Israel, the historic Jew, is to represent the determination to unify these two elements — the earthly and heavenly — into a single dedicated human purpose to share in God's Creation. This determination will serve as a model for all nations on earth who struggle to unify material need with spiritual aspiration. In short, Israel, the Jewish people, will wrestle with God, i.e., with the covenant that won't ever permit surrendering the hope of *"tikkun olam be-malkhut Shaddai"* ("mending the world in the image of the Kingship of God").

But the challenge will be daunting, frustrating, and spiritually, morally, socially, and politically exhausting. To meet the challenge, Jacob-Israel will not be able to afford not having a united soul, fully aware of his covenanted self. Wrestling with himself, therefore, or his own alter ego will encompass the ongoing struggles with his God and his external adversaries.

There will be times when as a human being he will seek to shed all personal responsibilities; but he will know what a later wise man will conclude: that one's life is "woven too tight with the thread of other lives" to abandon them. There will be times when as an Israelite, as a Jew, he will react to the destiny with which he has been burdened — wrestling with God and men and "prevailing" — as a destiny impossible to bear. A Yitzhak Lamdan poem (translated by Ruth Finer Mintz) will capture the agony of Israel — personally and collectively:

> "And so night after night, God, you come to me,
> Not to favor me do you come, but my strength to try,
> And as I prevail against you until morning — again I am alone,
> A poor strange wayfarer, limping upon my thigh.
> 'You have contended with Gods and with men and you have prevailed' —
> Is this all the blessing you apportioned me, mysterious one?
> Woe is me, I know, against all of you I have prevailed, over everything,
> But over one I could not, over myself alone —
> Your blessings weigh heavily upon me, I cannot carry them, Limping and alone over all the highways I go,
> Vanquish me once, oh You, and let me rest at morn
> the rest that all the vanquished know!
> Again it is night, I am alone. Again God descends.
> 'Israel!' — Here I am, God, here I am!
> Oh, why do You come down each night to wrestle with me,
> And as dawn rises you forsake me limping again?"

Israel will be covenanted to carrying blessings which will indeed leave him "limping and alone." There will be no respite. The wrestling will be a constant. The yearning to be vanquished, even once, in order to share the ordinariness of life with other human beings will never be satisfied. God will not grant Israel nor Israel's descendants respite. They will seek it, pursue it from time to time, in their yearning to relax from the responsibility of the burden. But the identifying name Israel will be a permanent mark, a name to be given again and again and reclaimed again and again through every "long *night's* journey into *day*."

Becoming Israel Permanently

The Torah mentions the name-change from Jacob to Israel twice. It needs to be repeated. The first time that Jacob's name is changed to Israel — along with the accompanying blessing — has occurred after Jacob's early confrontation with Esau, after the twenty years with Laban and the building of his family, and as the climax of his "wrestling match" with the mysterious "angel." The second time Jacob becomes Israel will come after three later significant incidents: after the peace agreement with Esau, after the rape of Dinah, and after the removal of the vestiges of idolatry from Jacob's family members. Jacob may become Israel after early crises in his life; but the crises never cease! They renew themselves under different circumstances, with different personalities, with new problems, challenges, and provocations. And the charge to struggle and to prevail — to be Israel — must be answered again and again.

Each of the three crises mentioned between the "naming" episodes calls for a particular degree of maturation on the part of Jacob. The first crisis which pervades the attempt at reconciliation with his brother Esau is the demand made upon a Jacob who before the fateful meeting has prayed one of the most ironically tragic prayers in all literature: *"Hatzileni na mi-yad ahi!"* ("Save me from my brother!") It is a prayer which Abel might have felt as he was on the verge of his confrontation with Cain. The Torah cannot leave Jacob with the spiritual and psychological cavity in his life that is the not entirely unjustifiable hatred Esau has for him. There must be an attempt to re-establish at least a hint of fraternal concern.

There is a traditional legend which speaks of Rebecca entreating Jacob to approach Esau with compassion, not to speak toughly to his brother. He is to bless Esau. He is to share with him all that which has befallen him over the twenty years in Haran, hiding nothing from him. In this way he is to help build up Esau's self-esteem; for, after all, as the legend reminds us, Esau is the older brother. The Netziv of Volozhin will further expand the theme of the legend with his interpretation of the verse: "Esau ran to greet him, embraced him, and falling on his neck, kissed him, and they wept." Emphasizing "they wept," the Netziv points out that they both wept, that at that moment there awakened in Jacob as well as in Esau strong feelings of love for one another. The Netziv extrapolates from this moment of fraternal reciprocity of affection and respect later historical analogies of ideal Jewish-Gentile relationships. Rabbi Yehudah the Prince, the final redactor of the Mishnah, for example, will with affection and respect accept the wisdom of Antoninus (Marcus Aurelius?) of Rome.

The simultaneous weeping is one key to the restoration of fraternal fellow-feeling. Weeping is an overtly expressed uncontrolled manifestation of vulnerability. The individual senses his incompleteness. He needs another, a significant other, to help him, to support him, to love him. But there is a more positive dimension to the joint weeping of the brothers that the Netziv notes in his illustration of the relationship between Rabbi Yehudah the Prince and Antoninus. Because there is mutual respect between them, Rabbi Yehudah has no hesitation in accepting wisdom from the non-Jew, from a Roman non-Jew no less. Antoninus asks Rabbi Yehudah "From what time does the *yeitzer-ra* hold sway over Man? From the formation of the embryo or from its issuing forth into the light of the world?" Rabbi Yehudah replies: "From the formation of the embryo." "If so," objects Antoninus, "it would rebel in its mother's womb and go forth prematurely. No, it is from the time when it issues forth, when it is fully born." And Rabbi Yehudah accepts the explanation: "Antoninus has taught me something, and the Torah supports him, for it is said, 'At the door (where the babe emerges) sin lies in wait.'"

Rabbi Yehudah has learned from Antoninus, a sage of Israel's hated enemy Rome, that whatever evil influence may capture the personality of a human being it is not conditioned in a hopelessly determined way before birth. Quoting the verse from Genesis to support Antoninus, the verse which God tries to impress upon Cain, further legitimizes the insight of the erstwhile enemy. But further to the Netziv's purpose in quoting this entire passage, Jacob must look upon Esau as an adversary whose evil tendencies are not permanently embedded in him. This time may indeed be the opportunity for genuine reconciliation.

The second crisis of Jacob's later years is brought on by the incident of the rape of Dinah. In and of itself the rape is clearly an emotional and spiritual crisis for Jacob. But the reaction of his sons, led by Simon and Levi, thrusts Jacob into a political quandary which places him in direct confrontation with what has now become a new, young, active generation of Israelites. Jacob doesn't argue the case from an abstract moral point of view. He is as distraught and as angry as his sons at the vileness of the rape. Moreover, throughout the entire meeting with Hamor, the rapist's father, and the latter's attempt at pacification by means of negotiated terms for a marriage, Jacob knows that Dinah is being held captive by Hamor, Shekhem, and the townspeople.

If there is any question among commentators as to Simon and Levi's right to do *something*, it has to do with the brutality of their attack. Do they have to slaughter them? The townspeople, after all, are weakened physically because of the collective circumcision. But then the decision of Simon and Levi becomes one of a tactical judgment call, not a moral decision made in utopia. The Shekhemites have not only countenanced abusing this Israelite girl. They are still holding her captive!

Jacob's crisis becomes one of confidence — he in his sons and they in him. He excoriates them: "You have brought me trouble, making me odious among the inhabitants of the land…we are too few to withstand a combined attack of all who will have heard of this incident. We shall be destroyed." Their answer to their father is a heavily laden emotional retort: "Shall they treat our sister as a *zonah* ('a harlot')?" And the tactical decision of the sons in the end is vindicated. For the text reports that the fear of God paralyzed the peoples around them so that they did not pursue them.

At the same time, if Jacob's authority as father and as patriarch bearing the covenant has been questioned and perhaps been found wanting tactically by the new generation, he will be uncompromising when it comes to idolatry and idolatrous traces within the fabric of his family. In this third crisis, Jacob will in no way temporize. He orders the removal of all strange gods from their midst, indicative of the fact that the incident concerning Rachel's absconding with her father Laban's *terafim* is not exceptional. And here Jacob — despite his previous vacillation over political tactics — stands firm regarding the overall transcendent truth of the monotheistic covenant. Here he will not compromise with the weaknesses of the next generation. The Midrash and Rambam will capture Jacob's firmness in the face of his sons' spiritual weakness with his later death-bed concern: "Perhaps there is among you a *paslut* ('fault'), religiously speaking." The sons at that time will respond: "*Shema Yisrael, Adonai Elohenu, Adonai Ehad* — Hear Israel — that is, hear us Jacob who has been named Israel — we assure you that the Lord *our* God — the same as *your* God — is One, Unique, the ultimate unifying purpose in Creation."

That Jacob has become Israel the night before his crucial meeting with Esau, therefore, is no guarantee that he will remain Israel in his struggle with new problems which lie in wait for him. He must constantly wrestle with his "demons," as it were, in order to discover and rediscover who he is. This will not mean that Jacob-Israel will not be able to tolerate contradictions in his personality. Buber will see Jacob-Israel's "united soul" as having the capacity of "binding the conflicting forces together, amalgamating the diverging elements." But it will be his "united soul" recognizing the transcendent One as unifying all of reality which will enable Jacob to finally claim title permanently to the name "Israel." And it will only be the unified dedication of the Children of Jacob who has become "Israel" which will deserve the blessing of the promise of the Land of Israel. This "Zionist" promise is renewed with Jacob explicitly when he is named Israel the second time.

A Tripartite Strategy for Survival

The task of covenantal survival will be more than formidable; it will be merciless. Jacob's own personal story will be summarized by himself when he meets Pharaoh in Egypt years later: "Few and hard have been the years of my life, nor do they come up to the life spans of my fathers during their sojourns." According to the Bible's esoteric scheme of measuring symbolically the years of a patriarch's life as an indication of qualitative "fulfillment," Jacob's life has been "shorter" than Abraham's and Isaac's. Jacob's life has indeed been more plagued with reversals than his father's or grandfather's. And the end of his life will find him where he will have least expected to be — outside the Land of Jacob-Israel in Mitzrayim, in the *meitzarim* ("straits") of Egypt.

But he will have survived! Survived and lived and remembered the covenant! If Abraham is the revolutionary idealist and Isaac the well-digging settler, Jacob is the clever, resourceful struggler who survives. Abraham moves to a new society inspired by an overpowering commanded insight. He is sufficiently possessed by the command to fight a war, to join in a covenant which promises little in the short run, and to be ready to sacrifice anything or anyone towards the fulfillment of his long-term vision. Isaac as a settler seems to be more passive than his father; but he is prepared to stake out vigorously his claims for water when assertiveness is required. Notwithstanding his confused understanding of priorities and preferences regarding "blessings," he does transmit the covenanted blessing to the right recipient. He has, in short, fulfilled his role as second witness to God's creative plan for a covenanted people. But Jacob as the third witness must learn to survive with the covenant through a greater variety of trials and pitfalls than either of his predecessors.

If Jacob is the wrestler it is because from the very beginning he has *writhed* in his mother's belly. He has *wrested* the birthright and initial personal-parental blessing from Esau. He has *wrung* out a family and property from Laban. His wrestling with the mysterious "man" is the melodramatic epitome of his previous and future life's pattern: struggling to survive covenantally and surviving in order to continue struggling. Symptomatic of his mode of struggle (as suggested by the Midrash, Rashi, and Nehama Leibowitz) is his preparation for the meeting with Esau in which Jacob plans three alternative strategies — prayer, gifts, and war. In this tripartite strategy Jacob-Israel presents a paradigmatic survival mechanism for any individual or group of individuals confronting a danger to existence. And the Children of Israel will employ this strategy with varying degrees of success and failure throughout its history. Indeed, the Children of Israel *will* have a history — limping through most of it, but surviving in order to keep the covenantal idea and embodiment of the covenantal idea alive to a hope-filled future.

For Jacob-Israel and the later Children of Israel, prayer will be the first line of defense. Trusting in God, appealing to God to support and help in implementing His own covenant is the initial existential posture of Israel. The firm assurance that God sides with Israel is found in the oath which God has taken following the *akeidah* ("the binding of Isaac"). God declares: "By Myself, I swear…I will bestow My blessing upon you and make your descendants as numerous as the stars of heaven and the sands on the seashore…."

No matter who the enemy, no matter how successful the enemy appears to be in the short run, the message of the prophet Obadiah will neutralize the doubts: "Liberators shall march up on Mount Zion to wreak judgment on Mount Esau."

Along with *tefilah* ("prayer") comes the *doron* ("gift"). However one translates *"doron"* — gift, bribe, economic negotiation — Jacob has learned early, as will his descendants, that the world of the "wilderness" demands various applications and concretizations of the concept of *"derekh eretz." Derekh eretz* literally means the "way of the world" and in the later rabbinic value system it will refer in a positive way to the required mode for building a civilized society, if not a sacred one. Such a society is possible providing the "way of the world" is understood to maintain agreed-to standards of reasonably ethical behavior among human beings. But should the "way of the world" be defined from time to time by enemies of Israel, by Nimrod-like foes of human civilization, then Israel must exercise sufficient cleverness to be able to maneuver among the foxes. Any ruse, i.e., "gift/bribe/negotiation" short of war — if it will save a life, a community, the nation — will be deemed permissible.

If, nevertheless, war is the only alternative, then Jacob-Israel and the later nation of Israel and the Jewish people will see its covenant as allowing even for the use of collective organized militancy in order to defend its collective organized life. There will be stages in later Jewish history when it will be understood that a King David will initiate optional wars for the sake of economic expansion. While later rabbinic legislation will frown upon such wars, they will be understood and accepted as part of the fabric and cost of political sovereignty in the "wilderness" world of nations. But even with the outlawing of optional wars in the future, defensive wars will always be permitted, nay, will be mandatory. Jacob-Israel in the face of Esau, as the sons of Jacob-Israel in the face of the townspeople of Shekhem, will never claim ideological pacifism as a moral option.

A Dream of Ultimate Unity

Jacob-Israel goes forth to meet Esau as an equal. He will seek to avoid conflict. He will not expect fraternal bonding — not as yet. He will reject cautiously but firmly Esau's offers of commonality, let alone community. But his dream of someday being witness to fraternal bonding, to experiencing a scene of brother coming together with brothers will be projected later upon his son Joseph and his other sons. In order to set such a scene, it will be Jacob-Israel who at a particularly explosive moment in the later domestic life of this covenanted family will send forth Joseph to seek his brothers, even when the father knows how much these brothers hate their younger brother. As to Obadiah's prophecy regarding Israel's ultimate victory over Esau, later Jewish liturgists will add on to the verse from Obadiah the prophetic dream of Zechariah that on that day the world will become one under the sovereignty of the Almighty. In other words, any "victory" of Israel over its enemies will be in the service of God. The struggle, the eternal wrestling of Israel will be and must be for Godly and humane purposes.

As underscored earlier, the "wrestling" image will be an image realized throughout the length and breadth of Jewish history. The Jewish people will wrestle with nations over competing claims to land, to resources, and to all the natural points of friction which characterize social living according to the "way of the world." And the Jewish people will wrestle with religions whose aspirations will justify in their own minds imperialistic crusades and jihads in order to convert all human beings to a single humanly prescribed "faith." The Children of Israel will resist these crusades and jihads, as their pristine covenantal faith will dictate that they must deny all human attempts to impose a Nimrodic totalitarianism on earth — especially a "religious" one. At the same time, Israel will have its own long-term aspirations, dreaming of a time when all nations and religions will be joined in partnership celebrating God's kingship in a chorus of multitudinous variety. A prophet of Israel will envisage a time when "Israel shall be a third partner with Egypt and Assyria as a blessing on earth."

In the meantime, Jacob-Israel "wrestles" with his estranged brother Esau. Jacob-Israel knows that in wrestling, unlike other sporting contests, victory is not recognized by one of the contestants remaining upright while the loser is down or the victor is left alone on the field of combat while the defeated is either dead or led away ignominiously. In wrestling, both participants are on the ground. The winner is on top holding the loser down in a grip which cannot be broken. But just as the "loser" is down, in the dust, pinned down for all to see, the "winner" is equally down, in the dust, locked together with his fellow antagonist, similarly for all to see. Jacob-Israel, the wrestler, has survived to continue to fulfill God's blessed covenant. The covenant demands that ultimately — in the long run, messianically speaking — Jacob-Israel's destiny is locked into a hold which in truth is an embrace that must enfold his brother Esau. And some day, it is hoped, the hold will embrace all other Esaus on earth.

Va-Yeshev   וישב

The turmoil that has characterized Jacob's life thus far gives no respite. Jacob is described in summary fashion as "settling down in the land of his father's sojournings." And so at first look all promises to be good. His family is now large enough to constitute a tribe. As a tribe it is a formidable force that can claim whatever it chooses to as it grows and expands into a settling nation. But the sins of the local Amorites-Hittites-Canaanites are not yet "full." In other words, the Land is not yet ready, morally speaking, for a new sovereignty. Worse still, the cardinal sin of Jacob's sons will emerge to wreck any chances of neutralizing the ominous predictions contained in the *Brit bein ha-Betarim*" (the Covenant of the Pieces). Fraternal hatred will short-circuit any possibility of tranquil settlement.

In the series of brother-brother relationships described in Genesis, there is a gradual evolution in the method chosen to resolve differences. Cain and Abel "differ." Solution? Murder. Ishmael and Isaac "differ." Solution? Separation — until they meet at the funeral of their father with no prior or additional meetings noted. In the next fraternal relationship, that of Esau and Jacob, there is enough justification for violence; yet instead they also separate. But unlike Ishmael and Isaac, Esau and Jacob gain the maturity to face each other in middle age and take pride in each other's achievements. They too are reluctant to settle down together; but at this stage of their mature relationship they are able to meet and to separate in an "atmosphere of approval," i.e., diplomatic courtesy with some gestures of affection.

With this next generation of the children of Jacob-Israel we should expect a further evolution in how brothers resolve differences. Yet with Joseph and his brothers there is a virtual return to the stage of Cain and Abel. It is only through the persuasive power of first Reuben and then Judah that murder is avoided, even though abandoning Joseph to an unknown fate with traveling nomads is hardly a humane solution. The prayer which Jacob had recited on the threshold of his anxiety-filled meeting with his brother Esau, *"hatzileni na mi-yad ahi"* ("save me from the hand of my brother"), could similarly be the prayer-of-affliction of Joseph in the pit.

A Familial *Akeidah*

Where has the relationship between Joseph and his brothers gone wrong? According to the *peshat* (the simple meaning of the text), we can cite three errors which most certainly would provoke resentment. First, that Jacob is seen to love Joseph more than the other sons is bound to provoke jealousy among these sons. Secondly, Jacob shows this preference with his special gift to Joseph of the *ktonet ha-pasim* (the coat of many colors). The brothers cannot be blamed for suspecting that this gift-of-preference is a hint of future leadership preference. Thirdly, Joseph confirms the brothers' suspicions by "taunting" them with his ingenuous recitation of his dreams of lordship over them. The question is: Must this series of errors lead inevitably to a degree of family dysfunction where even fratricide is possible?

Granted, the brothers have cause for enmity. Joseph — through his dreams — may have an insight into the common destiny of the entire family. But he is dangerously naïve in the manner in which he shares with his brothers the external superficial aspects of his insight, i.e., that they will someday bow down to him. Not unexpectedly they resent his "insight," his talent, his precociousness, and ultimately him! But the brothers are hardly innocent. Taking his dreams, i.e., his report of his dreams, at face value, the brothers do not trouble themselves to seek a deeper significance in Joseph's words. They abort any impulse in themselves to explain or to rationalize the boy's dreams and his haughty ways. They prefer to hate him, to think of killing him.

And so the brothers lie in wait for Joseph according to the Torah's description: *"Va-yir'u oto mei-rahok ve-terem yikrav aleihem va-yitnaklu oto le-hamito"* ("They saw him from afar, and before he could come near them, they plotted to kill him"). The *Or Hahayyim* commentary adds: "When the Torah says, 'they saw him from *afar* [Heb., *mei-rahok*]' it means '*me-rihuk ha-levavot.*' They set him 'far from their hearts.'" *"Shelo ra'uhu kire'iyat ahim le-aheihem ela ke-ish meruhak mei-hem"* ("They did not look at him as brothers should look at a brother, but rather as a man who was distant from them as a stranger"). Once the brothers, in their hearts, have disenfranchised Joseph from any relationship to them, they can with relative ease dismiss him from their lives, plot to murder him, or sell him into slavery. Essentially they wish to rid themselves of him, to condemn him to oblivion.

They may be brothers. And yet — if the rancor between them is severe enough they can change the disposition of their hearts from brotherly love to suspicion, then to hatred, then to thoughts of elimination, to liquidation of a brother who has now in effect become a stranger. That the story will not end here, of course, is a later blessing to all the brothers. For Joseph will be enabled to work towards a higher destiny, even from the depths of his slavery. And in the end, his brothers will be brought to the realization that they have wronged him; that in truth, they need him. And once they acknowledge their need for him, then Joseph will be able to say with renewed compassion and optimism from his seat as viceroy of Egypt: *"Ki le-mihya shlahani Elohim lifneihem"* ("God has given me the opportunity to help you live and thrive").

Before reaching in later life the exalted moment of fraternal reconciliation, however, the torments of familial strife will have been suffered by all of them. They will experience the pain of regret, grief, and guilt even as the mystery of the larger national destiny will be overseeing this drama of fraternal alienation and the long road to propitiation.

The pain, grief, and guilt begin with Jacob. As Rashi has noted, it will not be Jacob's destiny to find serenity on this earth. The conflicts which have plagued Jacob's family from Abraham's generation onwards have now increased with the birth and maturation of so many sons. Who will be the leader of this large family, this tribe, this family of tribes? The oldest of the sons or the most gifted? To criticize Jacob for preferring Joseph merely on the basis of his love for Joseph's mother Rachel is narrow. At stake is a larger purpose: the transmission of the covenantal blessing to twelve sons. And these twelve will need a leader.

The obligation to choose in order to better promote the fulfillment of a covenantal destiny draws Jacob-Israel into a vortex of familial tragedy which can only be described as his own familial *akeidah*. Jacob struggles like Abraham to respond to the double demand of loving God and his fellow human beings — his sons. He has a spiritual consciousness as well as a moral sensibility. And like Abraham, his awareness of God's larger vision demanding from him total commitment to that vision conflicts with his understanding of what moral obligation entails. The *akeidah*-like question arises: Jacob has himself heard Joseph's dreams and is perceptive enough to notice how much the brothers despise the youngster. Jacob himself has scolded Joseph for his lack of tact. How then can Jacob send Joseph out to seek his brothers in Shekhem at such an emotionally volatile moment, a moment of clear and present danger?

Is Jacob insensitive to the danger which awaits Joseph among these resentful brothers in Shekhem? And doesn't Jacob realize that these men, his sons, are not just jealous of this dreamer; at this stage they are enraged? Joseph is certainly aware of the danger. His *"hineini"* response to his father's call to seek his brothers in Shekhem confirms the ominous situation into which they have all fallen. Yet it is precisely this situation which requires an *akeidah*-like risk to be taken by all of them — Jacob, Joseph, and the brothers. Except that here, Jacob is in effect feeling the command to "take his sons" and to offer all of them up as the collective lamb on the altar of a covenantal destiny. Why does Jacob need to do this in this way? Why does he need to dispatch Joseph into the proverbial "lions' den"? The answer is found in a complex consideration of the confrontation between the transcendent and moral dimensions of the covenant.

A Moral-Theological Problem

On the half-verse *"Va-yishlaheihu me-emek Hevron va-yavo Shekhemah"* ("And he sent him from the valley of Hebron and he came to Shekhem"), Rashi asks a rhetorical question: "Isn't Hebron on a mountain? Why is it written 'the valley of Hebron'?" Rashi then allows himself to interpret the word *emek* (valley) as referring to a "deep" bit of advice which will be dispensed by the righteous one who is buried in Hebron — Abraham — regarding the prognosis of the "Covenant of the Pieces." Part of that prognosis, we recall, has been that the descendants of Abraham and Jacob are destined to be enslaved for four hundred years in a land not theirs. Rashi then looks at the rest of the half-verse and continues with his interpretation that Shekhem is a place which augurs calamity. It is there where the tribes will disgrace themselves, where Dinah has been raped, where the future kingdom of David and Solomon will be divided because of the prideful enmity of two stubborn men — Jeroboam the rebel and Rehoboam the arrogant king.

Rashi senses in the first part of the half-verse an expression of a hidden, comprehensive, transcendent plan, which in the "Covenant of the Pieces" has already decreed upon the descendants of Abraham enslavement for four hundred years in a strange land — in Egypt. Therefore, to fulfill the transcendent plan, something must occur which will lead the Children of Israel to go down to Egypt. And at first look, it would appear as though the scheming of the brothers to rid themselves of Joseph is the first causal element in a series of events which inexorably will bring the Children of Israel into slavery in Egypt.

But there is a problem with this assumption. It is the classic moral-philosophical-theological problem articulated in the form of a declarative statement in *Pirkei Avot* but put here in the form of a question: If everything is already foreseen or decreed above, how can free will truly be given below? A possible translation of the proposition is that free will is given to Man below to accept what has been decreed above — not as a judgment of fate but as an opportunity to fulfill a destiny. With such an attitude one can truly be fused to God's transcendent agenda while accommodating one's moral sensibility accordingly. In other words, such a view postulates that whatever occurs on earth has been decreed from on high. Presumably even something immoral like selling one's brother into slavery — in the ancient world tantamount to murder — is in the long run for good, at least according to God's long-term transcendent secret agenda. After all, will not Joseph forgive the brothers in the future, agreeing with the proposition that there is a transcendent agenda to consider — God's providential plan — which should exonerate the brothers from long-term pangs of guilt?

But the alert religio-moral consciousness is disturbed by such a thesis: If according to the Lord of the Universe the Children of Israel are fated to be enslaved in Egypt and if the sale of Joseph is part of this fateful process, why should the brothers be held guilty of a heinous act? And the Rabbis and the commentators do indeed hold the brothers guilty: there is a talmudic tradition which sees the martyrdom of the ten sages during the much later Hadrianic persecution as atonement for the sale of Joseph by his ten brothers! In other words, it is impossible to avoid a severe moral difficulty if we assume that brotherly hatred is part of some mysterious transcendent Godly agenda — an agenda which posits human actors performing on the stage of human history unaware of the high drama which transcends all their efforts.

These human actors initiate acts — even immoral acts. And after the crime is perpetrated, shortly thereafter or much later, another explanation or rationalization will be given for the moral "catastrophe." The explanation or rationalization may even be given by the victim himself. Joseph will come along years later and proclaim: "Do not be sad…for God has thus given me the opportunity to help you live and thrive." Or a much later commentator like Rashi will explain (justify?) somehow a frightful deed with the claim that the "sale" is somehow part of a secret Godly process tied up with the "Covenant of the Pieces" promulgated much earlier.

There is a certain moral-theological embarrassment with such logic. That Joseph chooses after many years to give a new rendering to what must have been the major trauma in his life cannot suggest that he welcomed or justified what his brothers had done to him years before. Moreover, even if the "Covenant of the Pieces" foresees a descent into Egypt on the part of Abraham's descendants, is the only way they can get there part of a pre-determined act of fraternal enmity leading to banishment of one who is innocent and defenseless!

It is noteworthy that the Ramban writing of the "Covenant of the Pieces" and the forewarned four-hundred-year enslavement mentions the famine which had caused Abram to leave the Promised Land and would serve as an anticipation of the later descent into Egypt by the Children of Israel. There is not a word about the sale of Joseph or the hatred of the brothers. Ramban seems to be suggesting that there can be an alternative cause for the descent into exile — other than a moral crime pre-ordained by a Godly master plan.

At the same time this is not meant to suggest that for Joseph — and Jacob, and later commentators like Rashi and the Ramban — there is not a large mysterious transcendent master plan being promulgated by the Lord of the Universe which is hidden at least in part from mortals and part of which God has permitted Abram to see at the time of the "Covenant of the Pieces." This master plan may include phenomena which are beyond simple moral comprehension such as, for example, famine which will certainly bring on natural human reactions such as *yeridah* (descent from the Land). And this may be part of what God reveals to Abram at the "Covenant of the Pieces." But not only this!

With God's help, Abram sees something which is too complicated for the simple, normal, rational, moral understanding to grasp: that according to the "way of the world" or the way of the world which is not Eden but a "wilderness," an alien population like the Children of Israel may receive permission to enter the sovereign state of Egypt in order to seek sustenance during a period of famine. But let this alien population never deceive itself into thinking that they will not suffer sooner or later from a possible change in policy by the host population. This change in policy may lead to persecution, enslavement, or worse, should the situation be judged by the sovereign population to warrant special strategies, e.g., finding scapegoats to blame for various internal social, economic, and political crises. In short, there are certain social, economic, and political problems emanating from the human predicament in the world-as-wilderness which are so complex that only a Godly intuition is capable of comprehending and resolving them. Such issues may indeed be beyond simple domestic-familial moral calculations.

But such is not the case with the problem of brotherly hatred! Brotherly hatred is dependent exclusively — as the brothers with their well-suppressed sense of guilt will learn — on the free will of human beings and on the moral sensibilities of human beings. When, as the *Or Hahayyim* commentary has argued, the brothers distance Joseph from their hearts, they do so out of free will and as a result of a scarred moral sensibility. And it is their freely initiated criminal act which brings upon all of them the family tragedy. The tragedy is not God-inflicted no matter how mysterious God's ultimate agenda may be.

Rashi is sensitive to the moral dimension necessary not only to the humane expectation within Torah aspirations; he also attributes a deep moral concern to the Godly dimension within Torah as well. After all, in Abraham's *akeidah*, God in the end does not permit the slaughter of Isaac. The explicit and implicit demands of God through Torah that Man is to love God *and* the human being lead God to prevent Abraham from culminating the test with an act of murder. Similarly here, Rashi sees in the phrase "*va-yavo Shekhemah*" ("he came to Shekhem") a morally inspired reminder of evil occurrences. Shekhem is a place where moral calamities occur, and a primary example looks ahead in Israelite history to the division of David and Solomon's kingdom set into motion in Shekhem. There because of perverse pride on both sides, i.e., a lack of fraternal love, there will be a rupture among "brothers" which will in turn lead to further national catastrophes. In other words, even according to Rashi — not just the Ramban — the hatred of the brothers towards Joseph is not the *cause* of the later enslavement in Egypt. It is a *symptom* of an inner sickness which has characterized all the relationships among the brothers in Genesis.

In the case of Joseph's brothers, the symptom reflects a lack of readiness to be a socially concerned entity, a unified nation on its land. Not only will the idea that "the sin of the Amorites is not yet full" delay the Promised Land from becoming Israel's. It is this fraternal hatred which itself will indicate the lack of responsibility among the sons of Israel to take on the obligation of genuine reciprocal trust necessary to building a nation-state.

It is clear from the thrust of Rashi's historical associations with Joseph's "mission" to Shekhem that his "seeking of his brothers" is an indispensable moral test. Jacob is obligated to test whether his children are capable of fulfilling their covenanted destiny — that which requires as an initial step familial closeness and trust as a precedent for a closeness and trust more difficult to attain: social and national cohesion. Because there *is* tension in the family, Jacob *must know* if this tension will lead to a denouement reminiscent of Cain and Abel, a precursor of the break between Rehaboam and Jeroboam, or a coming-together of brothers in close fellow-feeling for one another. Jacob himself has characterized his own fraternal relationship with Esau by the tragic prayer "Save me from my brother!" Therefore, in the face of Jacob's own sensitivity to what is at stake in passing on a national covenant to a group of sons — no longer choosing one son to exclude the other — Jacob must offer Joseph and the brothers up on the altar of fraternal expectation no matter what the risk. Replacing the tragic "*save* me from my brother" must be the hopeful "*Et ahai anokhi mevakesh*" ("I am in *search* of my brothers").

And who is the mysterious figure who directs Joseph to find the path to his brothers? Might it be the same mysterious figure with whom Jacob has wrestled through the night? Tradition names him as the angel-messenger Gabriel. This is the same Gabriel who will explain in the rabbinic generation of the ten martyrs that their sacrifice is to atone for the crime of the sale of Joseph, for the sin of fraternal hatred which appears again and again in Jewish history — most emphatically and fatally during the wars of the Second Temple and the failed Bar-Kokhba revolt.

The Necessary Moral *Yeridah*

In essence, the entire Torah and all of human history will be seen posing the question: "How do we evolve from the overly prevalent reality of 'save me from my brother' to 'I am in search of my brothers'?" The spiritual, psychological, and moral distance to be moved between the two characterizations of fraternal expectation and behavior seems out of reach. But without the aspiration to make the evolutionary move there can only be "flood-like" disasters beckoning. If the *Or Hahayyim* commentary sees the distance to be covered as a distancing of hearts, then the spiritual, psychological, and moral aspiration must be to turn the hearts from hatred to love. How if not through a therapeutic reciprocal *yeridah* (a going down)!

The *yeridah* is a going-down from the spirit of self-glorification which has dominated the attitudes of the brothers — Joseph's tactless and graceless exhibition of his visionary talents and the brothers' wrathful response that will barely stop short of fratricide. Judah saves the life of Joseph by suggesting the compromise, a compromise which the Talmud criticizes as being insufficient. If Judah had enough influence on his brothers to convince them not to kill, he could have persuaded them to return the boy to the safety of his home. In any case, both Joseph and Judah — Judah representing the brothers — must be brought down, humbilified!

Each of the protagonists who have been antagonists must be brought down to a level of humility which will allow for love, i.e., empathy for the other, to pierce their alienated hearts. Judah is described in terms of "*va-yeired*"; Joseph in terms of "*hurad.*" Both are "going down" to situations in which their personalities will face crises and will mature in turn from having coped successfully with the crises.

Judah's trial and disgrace over his mistreatment of Tamar brings him to a level of self-understanding that will enable him to assume leadership of his brothers with the appropriately requisite combination of character traits. The episode of Benjamin's predicament in Egypt when he is falsely accused of stealing the divining cup of the mysterious "stranger" (Joseph who is at that point unknown to his brothers) will bring Judah to the fore as a commanding leadership presence while exhibiting at the same time his readiness for personal self-effacement in favor of a brother.

Joseph's growth at the same time comes from a succession of descents. His whole early life is a progression of descents into various pits. He is thrown down into his first pit by his brothers; from there into the pit that is Egypt; and in Egypt into a further pit of incarceration following the episode with Potiphar's wife. But through his own precocious abilities and with the help of a providential transcendent force Joseph is given the opportunity to survive and to "succeed."

Jacob's *akeidah* has led him and especially his sons into the same *svakh* (thicket) of complexities characteristic of a life lived covenantally. In contrast to Tamar's *discreet* behavior Judah is lifted to an awareness of his own shameful conduct. In admitting publicly to Tamar's moral superiority, Judah has thus grown in ego-strength and moral responsibility. And the Bible is not hesitant to record in the Book of Ruth as a climax to the Judah-Tamar episode that out of this "sinful" liaison will come forth the future line of kingship in Israel — Peretz...Boaz...David!

Meanwhile, Joseph finds himself in exile and discovers his mature self in idolatrous Egypt, with temptations all round him. Some of these temptations will be close enough to be in his own household: Potiphar's wife. Other temptations will be comprehensive enough outside his household to beckon to him to assimilate to general Egyptian custom. Nevertheless Joseph grows to become the "provider." He saves his family from starvation, saves Egypt from social and economic chaos. That his success in exile, specifically in the sociomoral "straits of Egypt," will serve as the "welcome mat" to distant future enslavement for his people is a question on another theological plane — the transcendent mystery of God's ways. Morally, however, he will have fulfilled a familial blessing — returning to his brothers favor and largesse for rancor and hatred.

A History of Fraternal Enmity

It has been said that every war either begins or ends as a civil war. Joseph and Judah's descendants will bear out that truth. Two great national conflagrations memorialized in Jewish history will be the warfare surrounding the destructions respectively of the First and Second Temples and concomitant loss of Jewish sovereignty over the Land of Israel. In each case, civil strife will have either accompanied, precipitated, or succeeded the failed battles respectively against the Babylonians and the Romans.

From the prophetic writings of a Jeremiah and the historical description of the assassination of Gedaliah, the Jewish governor of Judaea appointed by the conquering Babylonians, one can trace the evidence of the civil strife wreaking havoc among the Israelites. This self-destruction occurs even as these Babylonians — external enemies — are prosecuting a war against Israel without hesitation and without mercy. Two prophets — Jeremiah and Hananiah son of Azzur — represent respectively the anti-war and pro-war passions among the people. The defeat of the Judaeans is inevitable. Jeremiah interprets the inevitability of the disaster as decreed by God because of the sinfulness of Israel. But in terms of realpolitik how could a fraternal division among the people hope to challenge the all-conquering Babylonian empire!

Similarly the rebellion against the Romans five hundred years later lacks the full support of the people. Because of divided opinions throughout society, various Jewish zealot groups decimate whatever power can be mustered by the undermanned Judaeans in the face of the forces of Imperial Rome. Again, the defeat of Israel — despite heroic effort — is predictable. The same can be said for the Bar-Kokhba revolt: Valiant heroics, rewarded somewhat with three years of Jewish independence, culminating bitterly in national ruin!

The most pronounced example of brotherly enmity determining national disaster is the larger story of the Maccabean dynasty. The initial victory of the Maccabees is not the only theme associated with the Festival of Lights — Hanukkah. There are other themes which tarnish the celebration of Judah the Maccabee's victory. Preceding the Hasmonean rebellion it is the competition among the Jerusalemites for control of the Temple treasury which leads to a virtual civil war among the Jews and which helps precipitate the issuance of the genocidal decrees of Antiochus. Granted, these decrees in turn force Matityahu and his Hasmonean family to step forward and lead the insurrection which will drive the Syrian Greeks out of the Temple and lead to sovereign independence. But then the later Maccabees of the period of John Hyrcanus and Alexander Yannai and their heirs will witness the gradual decay in the nation's fortunes. Essentially it will be divided loyalties among the Jews themselves — the civil strife between the brothers Hyrcanus II and Aristobolus II — that will serve to invite Rome into Jerusalem and to eventual disaster, i.e., loss of sovereignty, national humiliation and exile.

It will be an exile of two millennia in which the Children of Jacob-Israel will carry on the search for fraternal love. Jacob's *akeidah* will continue unabated, generation after generation. His descendants will find themselves either on the altar or in the thicket — searching for their brothers, pleading for an elusive fraternity before they will be deemed worthy of coming back to the Land, settling it again, and undertaking once more the onerous demands of the covenant.

Mi-Ketz מקץ

Intersecting circumstances and purposes bring the Children of Israel down to Egypt. Joseph, the first of Jacob-Israel's sons to settle in Egypt, has been brought there involuntarily — in a traumatic state. He has been a victim of fraternal ruthlessness, stopping just short of murder. Instead he has been sold into bondage in a foreign land. And Joseph will carry the burden of knowing that the perpetrators of the sale — if indirectly — have been his own brothers. In effect, his own family has intended for him to be forsaken and forgotten. His father Jacob, through some vague intuition that Joseph is not dead, refuses to be comforted when informed of the "loss" of his beloved-preferred son. But Joseph doesn't know this. And as he becomes more and more acclimated to his existence in *galut* (exile), he will accept that he has been forsaken and forgotten and will behave accordingly.

At the same time, we have argued, one cannot say that the *cause* of the future four-hundred-year enslavement of Israel in Egypt will have been the anti-Joseph animus of the brothers. Personal cause and effect play a role not easily determined in any of the stories concerned with the Patriarchs. What is clear is that famine and other natural disasters also play a role — a dominant role — in the confluence of events that will bring the Children of Israel into eventual bondage.

The Ramban has implied a reproach of Abram for having been the first *yored* even though in his day famine was afflicting the land of Canaan. As an exemplar for future generations Abram, suggests the Ramban, should have had more faith in God's power and will to give Canaan "their food when it is due." Similarly, in a later generation, the Sages will criticize Elimelech, husband of Naomi, for leaving the Land of Israel because of famine. As a leader, he should have remained. As punishment for leaving, his sons Mahlon (a name derived from the word "sickness") and Kilyon (a name derived from the word "destruction") will leave nothing enduring after their demise. And to emphasize the sin, Naomi's single goal following the loss of her husband and sons is to leave the *galut* of Moab and to return to Israel in order to reclaim her property there.

The Ramban's assertion in relation to Abram's *yeridah* that *"ma'aseh avot siman le-banim"* ("the deeds of the ancestors serve as precedent for the children"), seems to him to refer to the principal *explanation* — not *cause* — for the coming Israelite descent into Egyptian exile. The crime of the brothers is a separate moral event which will contribute, it is true, to the circumstance that Joseph will be brought into exile; but it is clearly the famine which will bring the rest of the family there.

The question arises: Is the covenant binding the God of Israel and the People of Israel with the Land of Israel meant to entail terms so severe that signatories to it are expected to endure economic disaster rather than leave the Promised Land? Yes and no! It is obvious that all three patriarchs have been economically well endowed. Moreover, the Land promised to Moses and the Children of Israel who will be taken out of Egypt is to be a land of milk and honey. Furthermore, a major part of the hortatory rhetoric surrounding the covenant will have to do with socioeconomic reward and punishment. A society obedient to God's *mitzvot* will be blessed with abundant rain in its season bringing with it successful crops. A rebellious society will be cursed with natural disaster and economic ruin.

The sociotheological problem presented by the famines in both Abram's days and Jacob's, however, is that we are not dealing with an Israelite society that is being punished. There is as yet no larger political entity called "Israelite society." In the patriarchal period famine seems to be part of the natural landscape. Later on, once the covenant is actualized by the Israelite mass settlement under Joshua, then how individual Hebrews, Israelites, and later Jews will relate to the challenge of famine and other natural disasters will be part of the ongoing tests of loyalty to the Land that they will have to face and contend with, come what may.

As the halakhic corpus within Jewish tradition will develop under the later Rabbis of the talmudic era, it will recognize economic necessity as critical under all circumstances and will not insist on an ordinary Jewish family remaining inside Israel under conditions of starvation. Where leaders are concerned, however, the halakhic assumption will be that by virtue of their superior capacities for maintaining *emunah* (faith) and inventiveness, they would find — as Joseph does in Egypt — the means for surviving and reconstructing society in such a way as to be able to cope with the specter of famine and any other "act of God" or Man.

Joseph's Psychosynthetic Power

Joseph represents the Jewish leader who through the centuries will find or be given the opportunity to find creative solutions to problems facing foreign societies and governments. From his earliest appearance on the biblical stage, Joseph has shown himself to be a leading figure among the members of this new generation succeeding Jacob. Through his dreams and reportage of these dreams, Joseph has shown that he has special gifts of imaginative insight. His brothers — and father — have focused mistakenly on the formal aspects of his dreams, i.e., that someday they will all bow down to him. Instead they should have been reflecting on the possible meaning of those dreams, i.e., why they will be in a situation of bowing down and looking up to him. True, he has been irrepressibly juvenile, and soon enough he will have been brought down literally and figuratively to a position of total vulnerability. Yet not too long after his "fall" he rises to become the provider, the sustainer, the economic savior of the Egyptian empire as well as the agent enabling that empire to feed the populations of neighboring countries like Canaan, including ironically his own family.

Joseph is described in the text as the "success." In everything he does in Egypt he is *matzli'ah* (he succeeds). There is a Providence watching over him and inspiring in him a knack for measuring a situation and seizing upon it to his own benefit and that of the larger environment about him — whether it be Potiphar's house or Pharaoh's "house," i.e., Egypt as a whole. He has the spark within him to radiate success, imagination, invention. He is built to draw attention to his physical presence, to his insights, to his ideas. Potiphar's wife finds him irresistible; but so has Potiphar in having given him supervisory control of his estate. The chief butler and the chief baker similarly look to this foreign prisoner to shed light on their most intimate and vexing anxieties. And most critically, Pharaoh himself is ready to listen to him and to follow his advice completely. For Joseph exudes the brilliant, confident light of genius.

The dreams of Pharaoh that Joseph succeeds in interpreting to the king's satisfaction serve as the basis — tradition has it — for Joseph's name change.

He is called "Zaphenath-Paneah," which is connected by tradition to the two words "hidden" and "revealer." He is thus recognized and appreciated as "revealer of that which is hidden." Nahum Sarna argues for another meaning based on the Late Egyptian word *psontenpa'anh* which means "the sustainer of life." Indeed, following his reconciliation with his brothers, Joseph will accept a Providential re-definition of his destiny in assuring them that he knows that God has sent him down to Egypt as a *mihyah* (sustenance) for all of them.

Joseph's genius is described as coming from God. Pharaoh himself attributes Joseph's analysis of the economic situation in Egypt to the *"ru'ah Elohim bo"* ("in whom is the spirit of God"). Bezalel the architect of the Tabernacle in the Wilderness will be similarly described. This spirit of God bestows on the human being so endowed *"hokhmah, tevunah, ve-da'at"* ("wisdom, understanding and knowledge"). The wisdom, understanding, and knowledge which are the ingredients of the creative imagination of a Bezalel and a Joseph — particularly Joseph — are not merely esoteric cognitions or apprehensions. In the case of Joseph they turn out to be insights into highly mundane practical matters of sociopolitical substance.

Pharaoh, sovereign of Egypt, dreams, seeks to have his dreams interpreted, and is dissatisfied until a virtually forgotten prisoner Joseph arrives on the scene. The later Rabbis are curious as to why all of Pharaoh's distinguished astrologers and soothsayers fail to give Pharaoh any kind of reasonable interpretation. Surely these highly placed advisors must make an effort to explain. Surely they must have the imagination to be able to mold the material of Pharaoh's dreams into an interpreted product which the king will buy. Yet the king doesn't buy. The nineteenth-century commentator Shadal explains that the astrologers and soothsayers fail to satisfy Pharaoh because they don't realize that he is looking beyond his own psychic needs and anxieties: "Pharaoh wants them to be able to ascertain from his dreams what the future holds for his people, so that this prior knowledge of events will enable him to prepare adequately for these events."

Pharaoh does not want personal psychoanalysis. He wants political advice. He rejects all attempts at short-range fable-telling or esoteric stargazing. He seeks middle-range and long-range sociohistorical forecasts. And in acquiring an insight into what the future holds for his people, for his economy, for his empire, he will sooner be able to prepare for that future. In short, what Pharaoh seeks and fails to receive from his Egyptian advisers, he does receive from his Hebrew slave: a historical perspective! This early Jew, living in a country foreign to him, is able to give the ruler of the mighty Egyptian empire just that historical perspective which will encompass social, economic, and political policy and which will enable Pharaoh to address resolutely those issues within his purview demanding policy decisions.

From where has Joseph derived this wisdom, understanding, and knowledge? To say that he has the spirit of God moving him, inspiring him, is fair enough — as a spontaneous biblically grounded explanation. Yet even from a biblical perspective one must probe more deeply. Bezalel the artist is not an economic planner nor does he interpret dreams. But Joseph's pedigree is precisely from a line of revelatory dreamers, reaching a particularly illuminating manifestation in Jacob's dream of the ladder — the ladder which joins the heavenly (the spiritual-ethical) and the earthly (the socioeconomic-political).

As has been discussed earlier, Israel Eldad has characterized Jacob's understanding of the ladder standing on the ground with its top reaching heavenwards as an exercise in psychosynthesis as opposed to psychoanalysis. By employing psychosynthesis, Jacob perceives a vision of human life as a constant dialectic between the physical and the metaphysical, the material and the spiritual, the real and the ideal. But Jacob's psychosynthetic capacity has been inspired by means of direct revelation from God as Isaac and Abraham have similarly been inspired. Neither Joseph nor anyone else in his generation is blessed with direct revelation. Pharaoh certainly is not. Yet both Joseph and Pharaoh dream.

Joseph dreams two dreams which are one about sheaves and stars. Pharaoh dreams two dreams which are one about cows and ears of corn. Are these sets of dreams merely expressions of personal wish-fulfillments? Are they reprogrammed metaphoric reproductions of personal anxieties? In truth, these two sets of dreams — as well as Jacob's dream of the ladder — could very well be interpreted as personal wish-fulfillments or reprogrammed metaphoric reproductions of personal anxieties. In the hands of experienced psychoanalysts such dreams could undoubtedly be interpreted in a way that would dissolve the emotional blood clots paralyzing a given patient vis-à-vis his personal life and emotional well-being. But Joseph, Joseph's Pharaoh, as well as Jacob before them are not psychiatric patients looking for explanations related to their personal state-of-being. As they struggle to understand the implications of their dreams respectively of sheaves and stars, cows and ears of corn — and the ladder connecting earth and heaven — they sense the need for a broader and deeper interpretation.

Not only does Jacob prefer psychosynthesis in interpreting his dream of the ladder; he has a psychosynthetic insight into Joseph's dreams. He may question — with a degree of personal pique — the symbolic presentation in the dreams of mother and father bowing down to their son. But he knows there is a sufficiently profound significance to Joseph's dreams beyond the personal dimension. Why else would Jacob send the boy out to Shekhem to seek out his brothers when he knows the brothers are seething with hatred? Jacob does it because he is certain that the larger covenantal purpose demands a rapprochement between the brothers. The brothers, however — and at that early stage in his life, even Joseph himself — are limited in their interpretive capacities.

But Joseph will mature and will develop the "wisdom, understanding, and knowledge" to apply his father's psychosynthetic techniques to dream interpretation. The brothers' capacity to interpret dreams psychosynthetically will only be tutored and tested later on when exposed to their long-lost brother in all their desperation and helplessness. The brothers — these children of Jacob-Israel — haven't had the capacity to see the psychosynthetic possibilities in Joseph's dreams and therefore have almost destroyed their covenantal future by truncating their interpretation and incinerating their souls thereby with resentment and hostility. They will have to go through years of trial including alienation, famine, and total dependence in a foreign land before rediscovering their brother. And they will never fully recover their political and cultural independence — certainly not in Goshen — until God and Moses will step in generations later.

As for Pharaoh and his dreams — all he has experienced are emotional terror and paralysis. Pharaoh as a leader with conscience will have been deeply concerned about his economy and the fickleness of the Nile. But his unimaginative ministers, astrologers, and soothsayers have trapped him in his dreams. He needs a master plan for his society! Not just psycho-synthesis, but socio-synthesis! Joseph realizes this and not only becomes the "provider" of the solution to the dreams but *the* "Provider," the deviser and administrator of the necessary socioeconomic program itself.

The Torah as Israel's Historic Perspective

Salo Baron among others has characterized the religion of Israel as historical monotheism. It stands on the proposition that there is a single unifying purpose to the movement of the world in time, in what we call "history," the history of humankind-on-earth. And this purpose which directs the history of humankind-on-earth is contracted between God and Israel by means of a covenant made in full consciousness of the movement of history-on-earth, to be acted out within the movement of history-on-earth by the interaction of *peoples* or *nations-on-earth*. In other words, the Bible, the Torah, sees the world as a history of nations on earth living, interacting, competing with one another. Its perspective focuses on the history of one nation — Israel — living out its destiny within itself but as well in its living, interacting, and competing with other nations.

At first look, the Book of Genesis may seem to have been telling the stories of individuals — and only individuals. But from the beginning of Genesis with the creation of universal Man until Moses' concluding song on the threshold of the Promised Land in Deuteronomy, the Torah lauds the Creator who "gave nations their homes and set the divisions of Man, who fixed the boundaries of peoples in relation to Israel's numbers." Again, what Genesis does — as the remainder of the Bible continues to do — is to tell the story of the origins of nations in general as viewed from the perspective of one emerging nation — Israel, even as it is understood that this nation Israel has itself emerged from the trial-filled adventures of exceptional individuals.

The Book of Genesis, in other words, has been telling its story on two planes at the same time — the individual and the national. The expulsion from Eden into a "wilderness" of trial and error that will move from Noah to Abraham is precisely such a story told on both the individual and the national planes. The fulcrum on which the two early narratives surrounding Noah and Abraham see-saw back and forth is the story of the Tower of Babel.

Nimrod as apotheosis of Babel challenges the Lord of the Universe who counterattacks by dividing the world into differing languages, cultures, and national identities. At this point the Torah zeroes in on one particular national identity, its progenitors, and its emergence as a family, a tribe, a nation on the world scene. Henceforth, it isn't that the Torah will not consider the history of other nations as significant. But for its covenantal purposes it will see Nimrod and Babel, Pharaoh and Egypt, as well as Assyria and Babylonia, strictly as background for the tale of Israel and the Jewish people. Babel is a society from which Abraham emigrates. The Hittites, Amorites, and Philistines are peoples who inhabit territory in which Abraham and Isaac and Jacob are building the beginnings of Israelite national settlement. And Egypt is the imperial playground in which Joseph, his brothers and father, play out their descent into the long exile which will set the stage for the great historic Exodus of the nation of Israel on their way to the Promised Land.

Because, therefore, the Torah's chief concern is with those nations whose history impinges upon the history of Israel, Joseph's Pharaoh — like Moses' Pharaoh — is perceived to play an important role in the history of Israel even as he attempts to maneuver within his own people's history. Thus Joseph warns Pharaoh that famine is coming, and that God has helped him — Joseph — to perceive the current natural and historic situation which Egypt faces and has given him insight as to how to cope with the situation. Joseph convinces Pharaoh that he, the king, must take the time to prepare, and thereby to succeed in averting national and international disaster.

For Joseph, and for his Pharaoh, the "problem" presented by Pharaoh's dreams is neither an otherworldly problem to be addressed by magical incantations nor a personal emotional problem to be interpreted in personal psychological terms. The "problem" has to be understood in psychosynthetic and sociosynthetic terms, and then explained in a framework of this-worldly socioeconomics and politics. In other words, Joseph's solution to the "problem" will be catered to Pharaoh's contemporary historical situation — within his Egyptian empire. At the same time, of course, from the Torah's perspective, Egypt's problem and Joseph's solution will impinge on the contemporary historical situation of Joseph's own family and future nation — the Children of Israel.

In summary, Egypt has its own history just as Assyria with its capital of Nineveh has its own history. In these two cases, the Bible gives us a glimpse into their "story" as seen from the ideological perspective of the Bible. But because they are stories as viewed from the biblical perspective, their situation is considered exclusively from the perspective of issues with which the Bible is concerned: national rebelliousness against Godly destiny, the possibility or impossibility of national repentance, and principally as background to the history of God's covenanted nation, the nation of Israel. In the case of Nineveh and Assyria, the pathos of its situation is summarized in the short dramatic narrative of Jonah. In the case of Egypt the script is longer, more dramatic, and ultimately tragic for Egypt while redemptive for Israel. But the messianic assumption of the Bible is that at some future "end-of-days" all nations including Assyria and Egypt will come together to pray in harmony in God's House in Jerusalem as all nations will come to acknowledge the God of Israel as the One Unique Creator, Revealer, and Redeemer of all humanity-on-earth.

The Book of Genesis — and the first half of the Book of Exodus — includes, therefore, Israel's narrative of this piece of Egyptian history and relates to the socioeconomic crisis during the time of Joseph with narrative sympathy. Its view is that Joseph's Pharaoh is an enlightened monarch prepared to recognize ability wherever and in whomever he finds it. His successors — unfortunately for Israel *and* Egypt — the Pharaoh or Pharaohs of the enslavement, the plagues, and the Exodus — will be tragic Nimrod-like engines of fate fighting a lost cause against a transcendent Providence. Whatever this Providence may otherwise have in store for that later Egypt, the hard-heartedness of the later Pharaoh or Pharaohs will, from a human point of view, doom Egypt to historical decline.

In the meantime, Joseph's Pharaoh represents the antithesis of hard-heartedness. He is secure enough in his own mind and heart to reject the tried-and-true channels of thinking and analysis of his Egyptian advisers. He opens himself up to an outsider. Because Joseph is an outsider he will bring a fresh, original perspective to the Egyptian socioeconomic crisis. His perspective and recommended socioeconomic policy will save Egypt. It will "redeem" Egypt. This Israelite slave, rejected, ostracized, exiled by his family, from his land — *the Land* — will unknowingly set the stage for his family's short-term economic rescue. Also its long-term *yeridah*!

Joseph the Outsider

Joseph is the quintessential outsider. In a sense he has always been an outsider. His brothers consider him alien from the moment he tells tales about the transgressions of those of his brothers who are the sons of the concubines, not to mention the explosive fallout which he provokes with his dreams. In Egypt he is — at the beginning and through the episode with Potiphar's wife — the *ivri* (the Hebrew), which can also be translated as the one from the outside or from the other side. But Joseph is an outsider in another critical respect. He becomes fundamentally — even though paradoxically — an outsider vis-à-vis the covenant.

Joseph is not a *yored*. He is unlike Abraham who "goes down" to Egypt during a famine. Abraham reestablishes his commitment to his original *lekh lekha*, his renewed *aliyah*, as soon as he can. Joseph is unlike Jacob his father who doesn't leave the Promised Land because of famine but because of the need to flee from his brother, and to find a wife and make his fortune. Jacob is a *yored*. Jacob remains in his state of *yeridah* for twenty years, guilty perhaps of even delaying his return. Nevertheless Jacob always intends reversing his *yeridah* and going back on *aliyah*. Joseph, on the other hand, "goes down"; but as opposed to going back up like Abraham and Jacob, Joseph is determined to settle where he is — in *galut*, in exile. In this sense, if *yeridah* — as modeled after Abraham and Jacob — is defined as a temporary state, alternative to *aliyah*, Joseph's *yeridah* is more a *berihah*, an escape from *aliyah*.

Joseph has been referred to above as an outsider, *the* outsider essentially, but paradoxically. The paradox lies in Joseph only being able to perform as the uniquely gifted individual that he is — outside the covenanted circle of his brothers, and, as it turns out, outside the Promised Land. As far as his fulfilling his own personal potential, he succeeds and in the short run even helps his family — not at home, but in a strange place. At the same time, this place which in the short run will be hospitable to him and his family, in the long run will enslave them and then attempt to annihilate them.

Elohim, the God of the Universe, as opposed to Adonai, the God who has a unique covenanted relationship with Israel, is described as helping Joseph to succeed in all his endeavors. But Elohim will guide and direct and superintend all good-intentioned people such as the Egyptian midwives who save the Hebrew males from death during the later oppression. Elohim does not reveal Himself to Joseph in a personal-revelatory mode as He has done with Abraham, Isaac, and Jacob. It may be because Joseph is in Egypt, in *galut*. But the principal reason is because God's personal-revelatory mode is reserved for covenantal affirmation. And Joseph, at least at this stage in his life and career, in deciding positively and without regret to remain in Egypt and to build a family there cannot participate — certainly not as a leader — in the covenantal future.

Joseph's marriage to Asenath the daughter of Poti-phera, priest of On, cannot be condemned in the tones of later Judaism as a case of intermarriage any more than Judah marrying the Canaanite Shua or Moses marrying the Midianite Zipporah. These events all transpire before Sinai. But the explicit reasons that Joseph gives for the names he bestows upon his sons reveal how he feels about his family and the Land from which he has been cruelly expelled. He gives the name "Menashe" to his older son because *"ki* nashani *Elohim et kol amali ve'et kol beiti"* ("God has made me *forget all* my hardship and my parental home"). Joseph is thanking God for the largesse shown to him in allowing him to rise to power in Egypt which has so compensated for the loss of parental home that he has forgotten it completely. To his second son he gives the name "Ephraim," thanking God for having made him *fertile* and *fruitful* in his new home. For he is overwhelmed with the prosperity that he has achieved to the extent that it, too, compensates for the suffering he has earlier endured in Egypt.

The full depth of the irony is to be appreciated when Joseph in *galut* saves not only Egypt but the entire Middle East including his own family — that family which exiled him in the first place. The emerging picture is of a vast Providential agenda that has the ladder bespeaking among other things "going up" to Israel and "going down" to exile as being much more complicated on an individual personal basis than would appear from the initial impression one receives from God's portentous call of *"lekh lekha"* to Abram. The covenant is oriented to *aliyah* clearly and unequivocally. And true, God doesn't reveal His covenantal will in exile, although the central revelation, the fundamental revelation will be given not in Israel but in the no-man's land of the Wilderness. But Joseph's efforts in exile — whatever their personal motivations — provide Jacob and his children, the Children of Israel, with their necessary material sustenance. Without such sustenance, there can be no thought, no dream, of future *aliyah*.

Exile

Exile in all its bitter manifestations along with all its blandishments becomes in the generation of Joseph a key element in the ongoing attempt of the House of Israel to fulfill the covenant. The introduction of exile as a reality and as a concept so close to the beginning of the covenantal adventure bespeaks its critical importance. As a counterpoise to the image and reality of a Promised

Land which represents if never full redemption but always the possibility of future redemption, there is and will always continue to be exile as a temptation and as a threat.

In the case of Joseph and his brothers, in order for the covenant to be transferred to them as a unified family, there must be a reconciliation. Jacob has realized this years previously when sending Joseph to Shekhem into a highly precarious situation. From Jacob's point of view, the disaster as reported to him by the brothers has aborted for him any forward progress of the covenant. Joseph is no more. And Jacob is certain that if the stain of family disunity will remain with him and the brothers indefinitely, it will possibly spell the end of any covenantal hope for these children of Jacob-Israel.

Unless the children of Jacob-Israel can rediscover themselves as family, i.e., making possible again the fulfillment of the injunction to "love the other as oneself," there is no point to the covenant. Jacob in his stubborn refusal to come to terms with Joseph's "death," senses what is at stake for the covenant and the Land when he instructs his sons to take with them to Egypt *"mi-zimrat ha-aretz."* They are to take to the mysterious stranger who is to be their provider samples of the *choice products of the Land of Israel* which is temporarily impoverished. Or is it the *zemirah* (the song) which they are taking, keeping alive in *galut* a *melodic* reminder of redemptive purpose?

Thus, exile becomes at one and the same time the punishment for the brothers as well as their opportunity to atone for their earlier sin — although they don't know it yet. They can't know it yet for they can't know that their brother is still alive. Joseph the vizier of Egypt sees his brothers and while he recognizes them, it is written *"va-yitnakeir aleihem."* And Rashi translates the word *va-yitnakeir* as "he made himself strange to them so that he could speak harshly to them." As a form of measure for measure, just as many years before they had distanced *him* from *their* hearts in order to plot to destroy him, *he* is now purposely alienating himself from *them*. Their inexcusable sin vis-à-vis Joseph must be requited. There is no alternative. They must be tested and Joseph's feigned alienation from them, the cruel games he plays with them, will be the vehicle for ultimately restoring the necessary family unity. It will all happen in a strange land, a land of alienation for a covenanted Israel. Yet in the short term it is a land chosen for reconciliation — as in the long term, however, it has also been chosen for national temptation and entrapment, national suffocation and near-extinction.

Va-Yigash   וַיִּגַּשׁ

What must happen to move from fraternal hatred to reconciliation? The abstract answer is relatively clear and simple: each side in the dispute which has led to the hatred must be willing to move towards the adversarial other. The pride of the brothers which couldn't tolerate the superior gifts of Joseph and the cruelty of these brothers in expelling him from home and family have to be neutralized and transformed. Their pride will now be neutralized by their having fallen into a situation of total dependence on this mysterious vizier in Egypt who is in charge of the distribution of food. And their cruelty will have been so dissipated that when Benjamin is implicated in the alleged "theft" of the vizier's divining cup, they will now show total empathy for their youngest brother who at this stage has become in effect the surrogate Joseph.

On Joseph's side, his youthful arrogance and lack of tact will now give way before his understanding that if indeed he has been called to greatness, it is because God was delegating him to be the vehicle for saving his family. Moreover, as great as his achievement in Egypt, as stellar a personality as he has become in Egypt, he has now reached a point where he realizes how important his family is to him. He will not suffer his family from Canaan to be shamed in any way here in Egypt. His own empathy for them will override any vestigial feelings of resentment towards them for what they did to him years before. He will see to it that they settle in the highly fertile region of Goshen, so that they may be "fruitful and multiply."

A Three-Fold Weeping

In short, each side's maturation into empathy with the other is the sine qua non for true reconciliation. But to describe each side's maturation as a "short" process is to deny the excruciatingly painful reversal of attitude required when resentment gives way to empathy. Benno Jacob and Nahum Sarna note the three stages of weeping which Joseph endures while he continues to perpetrate the masquerade in which his brothers are participating unwittingly. As painful as Joseph's staged intrigue is for the hapless brothers, it must be carried out to its denouement to test whether or not there has truly been a change in the fraternal attitudes of these brothers.

The intrigue will not be pleasant for Joseph either. He weeps first when he hears the words of mutual recrimination of the brothers who are now standing accused and helpless before this regal stranger: "Alas, we are being punished on account of our brother, because we looked on at his anguish, yet paid no heed as he pleaded with us." And Reuben reminds them: "Did I not tell you, 'Do no wrong to the boy'? But you paid no heed." Joseph weeps out of legitimate self-pity, recalling his agony, his sense of total rejection and abandonment. He has learned to "forget" his past, his home, his family, as he has emerged from the various "pits" in his later career in Egypt. But all the repressed memories — the denials, the blotting out of those lurid events of years past — have now exploded to the surface, returning him to a vivid adolescent consciousness while standing over these men, "lording it over" these strangers, his own brothers who were ready to cast him out of their lives, and did!

Joseph weeps again after fully realizing who the young man Benjamin is — his full brother, son of Rachel. He blesses Benjamin and then hurries out, unable to restrain his tears of joy and love. On a factual evidential level, Benjamin was too young to be implicated in the original crime. In Joseph's mind there is no way his "full brother" would have collaborated in such an act had he been of age. But beyond the objective aspects of Benjamin *not* being one of them, to Joseph he is special. He is the beloved remnant of the beloved Rachel — Joseph's mother — who was buried (abandoned?) on the road home. And so these two remnant sons joined together now — on Joseph's terms, i.e., Benjamin is to be made to belong to him, to Joseph, not to Judah and the brothers — releases in Joseph a wellspring of grateful tears, genuine uninhibited fellow-feeling for "another," *the other* whom one wants to love, whom Joseph must love.

The drama is reaching a climax. Joseph weeps a third time when after Judah's emotionally wrenching appeal on behalf of Benjamin — and on behalf of their father Jacob — the estranged vizier of Egypt cannot restrain himself. But the weeping at this stage of Joseph's tortured reawakening to the past broadens to empathetically include his brothers: "Do not be distressed or reproach yourselves because you sold me hither; it was to save life that God sent me ahead of you." This is a weeping of awe in the face of an emerging appreciation of Jacob his father's covenanted destiny and the Children of Israel's special role in a plan that is much beyond the early conceits of an adolescent boy. Joseph now understands that the dreams of his adolescence have heralded a destiny that dare not suggest that the Children of Jacob-Israel will bow down to Joseph in worship. On the contrary, Joseph's entire being, he now realizes, is to have been granted the privilege of providing saving sustenance to his brothers, to his family who are destined to become the Children of Israel.

From Enmity to Empathy

Joseph's weeping represents emotional outpourings of what for both sides of the fraternal divide must be a radical change in attitude. Everyone must have moved from enmity to empathy! Judah and the brothers are ready to rediscover their excommunicated brother only after the years have deflated their arrogance, their high notions of fraternal primacy. If one judges the content of those years for the brothers by the amount of space given to them in the Torah account, then those years have been drab and denuded of significance. During the time of Joseph's rise to prominence in Egypt, the brothers in Canaan are apparently doing nothing of note — nothing worthy of being recorded. The single episode to be included from this period in Canaan is the one concerning Judah and Tamar. And it is precisely this episode that most emphatically underscores the radical moral comeuppance which Judah must suffer if he is to assume a necessary leadership role in his family.

A brief review of the story is in order. As noted earlier, the Midrash cites the word used to open the story: "*va*-yered *Yehudah me'et ehav*" ("and Judah *went down* from the midst of his brothers") as indicative of his debasement and humiliation. He has placed his daughter-in-law Tamar in an impossibly dependent situation waiting for a levirate marriage that will not happen. And Judah in any case forgets about her.

Resourcefully, she lays a trap for him through his libido as she will for his conscience in discreetly reminding him later as to who is the gentleman who has impregnated her. He has conveniently chosen to forget Tamar twice — first as his daughter-in-law, then as his harlot-for-hire. In the shocking climax to the story, Judah is exposed to himself as a moral hypocrite. Tamar is brought before the community in public disgrace. She is pregnant, having violated the ancient law of the levirate. And only she — and Judah — know that the father is Judah. With moral restraint she will not reveal the truth but is prepared to be executed. Judah could choose to keep his sin hidden from the community. Instead he is shamed into responding to his private predicament by assuming a mature repentant posture *in public*: "She is more in the right than I!" His admission of guilt is the first step in Judah's self-rehabilitation and by extension the rehabilitation of his brothers in their own eyes. They can thus begin to conceive the possibility of bridging the gap between enmity and empathy.

The brothers — including Judah — learn what it means to find themselves in a pit of uncertainty, total vulnerability, bald fear, when they find themselves totally at the mercy of the Egyptian vizier. Subject to the whims of the vizier, they learn what it means to be victimized. But more! They will transcend the level of subjugation and victimization to so empathize with their brother Benjamin in his adversity, and with their father Jacob left alone in Canaan, that the morally eloquent offer which Judah makes to become a slave in Benjamin's place is the final straw that shatters Joseph's masquerade. Judah, representing the brothers, now understands the implications of "loving one's brother" perhaps *more* than oneself, whether he be Benjamin or Joseph.

To Joseph the tears symptomize a similar change of attitude. He is ready to accept his forgotten brothers only after the years have tempered his own narcissism. Like Judah, he has also been "brought down." Thomas Mann among others will extend the symbolism of the pit into which an arrogant obstreperous youth has been thrown to include the descent from Potiphar's house into the pit that is prison, and into the larger pit that is Mitzrayim — Egypt itself. A proverb will state that no matter how low one may find himself on the ladder of life, he can be brought yet lower. "*Yosef* hurad *Mitzraymah.*" Joseph has been brought down literally and symbolically when sold into the "straits of Egypt." He will learn humility. He will realize that any special gifts with which he has been blessed have been essentially to "provide" for the well-being of others as dictated by the Providential Force who is the true object of worship. And finally, Joseph himself bridges the gap from enmity to empathy with all the brothers when he removes the Egyptians from their presence at the moment of self-revealment. Rashi says: "He couldn't bear that Egyptians would be standing there witnessing the brothers' shame at his uncovering himself to them."

What are the parameters of feeling and intentional will that bring one to the threshold of reconciliation, of full empathy with the "other"? Empathy involves a degree of identification with the "other" that has been expressed in *Pirkei Avot*: "Don't judge a person until you're in his situation." Empathy means placing oneself in the "other's" existential predicament. If this involves a suspension — at least temporarily — of one's own ego-stance, so be it. For humility is the conceptual bedfellow of empathy. Rabbi Israel Salanter will build an edifice of moral education on the summary conclusion: "On my way to studying *'musar'* ('morality') I used to consider the world guilty and myself innocent. Once I started studying *'musar'* I considered both myself and the world guilty. But now I have reached a point in my studies of *'musar'* when I consider only myself guilty; to the rest of the world I give the benefit of the doubt."

All the brothers who are the Children of Israel are brought to reconciliation only when their empathy for one another has become total, perhaps even beyond to the point of self-denial in favor of "the other." The purpose of the reconciliation, after all, has not just been to reward Judah and Joseph as individuals. It is not merely to relieve Judah and the brothers' guilty conscience; nor is it to provide a stable loving Jewish community in Egypt to allow Joseph's children and the brothers' children to be nurtured. The reconciliation is the sine qua non for the continued growth of a unified covenanted family into a nation. Unity will be the indispensable pre-condition for any future hope of redemption. This reconciliation is the central theme of the later Ezekiel's vision of the broken branches of fragmented Israel coming together to be one, just as the dry disconnected bones of a later Israel in exile will be resurrected into a unified vital organism ready to rebuild an Israelite sovereignty in Eretz Yisrael.

The series of disasters which have characterized the fraternal relationships in the Book of Genesis beginning with Cain and Abel have come full circle and beyond with the reconciliation of Joseph and the brothers. Murder (Cain and Abel) and separation (Isaac and Ishmael, Jacob and Esau) have been the recorded "solutions" to fraternal enmity. With Joseph and the brothers, we have retrogressed to thoughts of murder again. But now the reconciliation and determination to live together is a new stage in the evolution of the fraternity dreamed of for "Eden" but thus far inaccessible in the "wilderness."

The story of Joseph's sons Manasseh and Ephraim will come as a striking postscript to the achievement of Joseph and Judah. The giving of the blessing to these grandchildren of Jacob-Israel will remind us of the fraternal tension which has characterized previous similar "transfers-of-blessings" throughout Genesis. For Ephraim and Manasseh it becomes a mere ceremony. At least it is treated that way by the grandsons. Joseph may very well question Jacob-Israel's procedure in placing his right hand on the younger grandson; but the reaction of Ephraim and Manasseh is not recorded at all. It would appear that the grandsons have accepted the covenantal bond that binds them together inextricably regardless which one of them is promised greater future blessing.

Jacob's Fear

And so the covenanted Children of Israel are reconciled. Hoping to reconstruct their fraternal community, they find themselves in Egypt. Paradoxically they have had to wind their way down to Mizrayim in order to rediscover each other. And does the fact that they couldn't live and build together in Canaan cause them no anxiety? The question echoes a bit differently for Jacob who is Israel. Nehama Leibowitz raises the question as follows: "To each of the forefathers of Israel — and even to Moses — God gives assurance that they needn't be afraid. The text quotes God even though the same text never says explicitly that they were afraid." It is as if the Torah wishes to emphasize that nothing is hidden from God: "That there is fear even within the strong personality, within him who is confident of himself and calm in that confidence; but that this fear which resides deep in the heart is known to Him who knows all."

Jacob-Israel is afraid to go down to Egypt. Otherwise the Lord would not need to assure him: "I am God, the God of your father. Fear not to go down to Egypt, for I will make you there into a great nation. I myself will go down with you to Egypt, and I myself will bring you back, and Joseph's hand shall close your eyes." Jacob-Israel, we may presume, has been aware of the tradition which recalls God telling his grandfather Abraham that the latter's descendants will spend a significant period of time in a land not theirs but that they will be brought back to the "homeland" eventually. Why then should Jacob be afraid?

The nineteenth-century commentator the Netziv of Volozhin will answer the question: "Jacob-Israel is afraid lest his seed become assimilated into the Egyptian nation. For only in the Promised Land, the Land of Israel, will the central pointed essence of Israelite identity be protected from generation to generation. It cannot be protected in Egypt."

It is not surprising that a late nineteenth-century supporter of the Hovevei Zion precursors of the Zionist Movement will superimpose his own historically fed anxieties back on to Jacob-Israel, who in his day is contemplating his son's invitation to join him in exile. The Netziv will have been witness to centuries of lamentations over exile. He will have continued a long medieval tradition energized particularly by Yehudah Halevi in whose *Kuzari* there is underscored prominently the theme of the centrality and indispensability of Eretz Yisrael. But in both the *Kuzari* and the Netziv's *Ha'amek Davar* there is the vitriolic tone of why does the *galut* (exile) continue if the Jewish people love Israel so much?

In the *Kuzari*, the King of the Khazars longs to understand the Jewish dream of return to Eretz Yisrael, the prayers entreating God to restore Jerusalem and Zion, when they — the Jewish people, heirs of ancient Israel — persist in remaining in *galut*. And the bitter response of the *haver*, the rabbinic spokesman for Judaism is: "Prayers such as 'restoring God's Indwelling Presence in Zion' and other similar invocations of love for Zion are like the twittering of the starling-bird in which we don't think about what we are saying." In the *Ha'amek Davar*, the Netziv sees the beginning of the Zionist return happening; but he also sees the majority of Jews remaining in *galut*. And so he wants them to at least be *metzuyanim* (distinguishable) in their *galut*.

The Netziv is referring to the noteworthy passage in the Midrash *Sifre* on the Deuteronomic portion of *Ekev*: "My children, be *metzuyanim* [distinguished] in the commandments' (in exile) so that when you return they will not seem new and strange to you." This in turn has been based on the celebrated passage in Jeremiah 31 which speaks of the return of the exiles to Israel with the urgent call *"hatzivi lakh tziyunim"* ("erect markers"). The interpretive liberty taken with the word *tziyunim* points to the overall strategy for retaining the memory of Eretz Yisrael while enduring the exile!

In the same passage from Jeremiah 31 Mother Rachel is pictured as weeping for her children, refusing to be comforted over her children who are "absent," i.e., in exile. It is Rachel who will implore God to bring them back from exile even as it has been her son Joseph who has pioneered the first exile in Egypt. It has been Joseph who has invited his family to "come down" and join him in settling in Goshen. Jacob's fears regarding future assimilation are not groundless. Yet again, there is a master plan which God in His prescience has shared with Abraham regarding future lengthy servitude in a land not theirs; but this doesn't suggest that Jacob's descendants are meant to disappear in Egypt. On the contrary, being "distinguished" in exile while waiting for redemption is to be the programmatic agenda for the Children of Israel, their religio-cultural strategy for maintaining themselves as a separate nation wherever they are forced to live — while waiting.

Jacob has gone on *yeridah* before. But under the spell of his revelatory dream of the ladder and the vow that he made at Bethel as a result of the dream, he never had any doubt at that time that he was coming back to Eretz Yisrael. His certainty was born of his confidence in his own sincerity of purpose and will power. He *knew* what he *intended* doing, if not tomorrow, then in seven years; if not in seven years, then in twenty years. But here, going down to Egypt as the senior member of a new tribe of vigorous younger men who are being brought into what looks like a permanent settlement situation presents Jacob with an entirely new predicament — and presentiment.

God calls to him: "Jacob, Jacob" and elicits from him a *"hineini,"* the response always redolent with portent, with awe-filled readiness for ultimate challenge. Jacob could have been addressed in this revelatory moment as "Israel." Or if he had to be called twice, he could have been addressed as both "Jacob" and "Israel." Instead, it is "Jacob, Jacob." Jacob is being called into a situation — exile — where the temptation for his descendants to forget the covenant will be multiplied exceedingly in correlation with the fruitfulness of their settlement there. And they *will* be fruitful and they *will* multiply there. Joseph will see to it. But the Serpent of temptation and illusion which ever since Adam has been biting at Jacob's heel will sharpen his sting. Jacob has good reason to be afraid. He is afraid for his sons; he fears for himself.

So the God of Israel, knowing full well that the name-change from Jacob to Israel has not obliterated totally from Jacob's psyche the serpentine doubts, anxieties, and foreboding regarding the new *galut* situation, calls out "Jacob,

Jacob." God is saying, as it were: "I know the 'Jacob' in you, Israel. I know that you are sensitive to the ambiguities, to the paradoxes in life. And to cope with these ambiguities and paradoxes, you will need the clever 'Jacob' in you as well as the 'Israel-wrestler' in you. Do not be afraid!"

Nevertheless, Jacob-Israel will persist in his fear. The Talmud says about Jacob's descent to Egypt: "It was fitting for our father Jacob to go down into Egypt in iron chains, but that his merit saved him. He went down as Joseph's guest!" The Talmud's supporting verse is from Hosea: "I drew them with the cords of a man, with bands of love; But I seemed to them as one who imposed a yoke on their jaws, though I was offering them food." There is in the interpretive intermingling of these passages a summary description of what will become the fundamental theological-national-moral neurosis of Israel: its rebellion against God's largesse summarized in Hosea's following lament: "They return to the land of Egypt!" They yearn for the blandishments of Egypt when God offers them love and the food of humaneness where they are — in their own land, the Promised Land. Jacob-Israel foresees the ambiguities, the paradoxes — and the neurosis — as his Joseph, now ruler of Egypt beckons to him: *Redah eilai* ("Come down to me"). Down, down, down to the golden pit of Rameses-Goshen.

The neurosis of exile will manifest itself in the frustrating search for identity which every generation of Israelite-Jews will experience as it dreams of theological-national-moral redemption even as it persists in remaining in a state of *yeridah*. Wherever Jacob's future descendants will live they will, given the opportunity, succeed like Joseph. They will rise to positions of power and to the political, social, cultural, and economic opportunities for influence which accompany that power. But they will always suffer from a malaise — even when finding themselves in a benignly ordered exile like Joseph's Egypt. They will sense that the mask of accommodation that they must wear to appear as though they really belong may be torn away at any time to reveal the raw Israelite stranger who does not belong. This will be true — sooner or later — in every country where Jews will settle: from Persia to Spain; from Poland to France; from England to Germany.

The *Galut* Syndrome

The seed of the *galut* neurosis or syndrome is reflected in a *midrash* which turns the *peshat* (the simple meaning) of Judah's appeal to Joseph on behalf of Benjamin inside out, so to speak, in that both Joseph's breakdown and the tone of Judah's entreaty are not what they seem. Judah — in the part of his appeal unrecorded in the Torah but enlarged upon in the *midrash* — is imagined as threatening Joseph: "The fire of Shekhem is burning in my heart. If you do not respond positively to my entreaty, I will unsheathe my sword and I will fill all of Egypt with corpses." The *midrash* then explains Joseph's additional reason for finally ending the charade: Lest his brothers destroy Egypt!

There is an ambivalence in this *midrash* which bespeaks the confused identity inevitably spawned by national exile. Will Jacob's children and grandchildren see themselves as Israelites living temporarily in Egypt, as Egyptian Israelites residing permanently there, or as fully acculturated/assimilated Israelite Egyptians barely distinguishable from native Egyptians? Will Jacob's descendants living after the European Emancipation see themselves as Jews living in Germany, as German Jews, as Jewish Germans, or will they drop their Jewish identity entirely in their craving to be "pure" Germans! Gabriel Riesser, a leading German Jewish political figure in the 19th century, claiming legitimacy for his fellow Jews as Germans, will argue: "To claim that our forefathers came here (to Germany) thousands or hundreds of years ago is an inhuman and tasteless charge. We did not come; we were born here and we have no claim to any other homeland. If we are not Germans then we have no homeland."

Even a Shakespeare who will barely know Jews, yet will not be free of ingrained biases towards Jews, shows in his *The Merchant of Venice* a keen understanding of what living with a mask does to the personality — any such personality — let alone a Jew living and having to compete for survival in *galut*, in a world of overt and covert anti-Semitism:

> I am a Jew. Hath not a Jew eyes? Hath not a Jew hands, organs, dimensions, senses, affections, passions? Fed with the same food, hurt with the same weapons, subject to the same diseases, healed by the same food, hurt with the same means, warmed and cooled by the same winter and summer as a Christian is? If you prick us, do we not bleed? if you tickle us, do we not laugh? if you poison us, do we not die? and if you wrong us, shall we not revenge? if we are like you in

the rest, we will resemble you in that… The villainy you teach me, I
will execute; and it shall go hard but I will better the instruction.

What Shakespeare sees in Shylock is a bitter but poignantly proud and keenly
aware person. Shylock not only removes his own mask of accommodation
when provoked but has a criterion for unmasking the moral hypocrites who
surround him. In Judah's dialogue with Joseph as understood by the unusual
midrash, Joseph is pictured as the classical *shtadlan* who is primarily
concerned with keeping the Jewish profile visible enough to survive — if not
to gain materially — within a Gentile community, but not visible enough to
elicit overt hostility. Shylock — at the particular stage in the play where he
uncovers his true feelings — is much less sanguine than Joseph about the
possibility of maintaining the appropriate balance of visibility and anonymity.

But there is no way that Joseph can maintain — assuming he would wish
to maintain — his invisibility and anonymity in Egypt. He is the most visibly
active official in the empire as he executes his program of administrative centralization. To save Egypt, its economy, and its people, as well as the foreigners including his own family who have come for succor, Joseph has had to
centralize all the wealth of the empire in Pharaoh's hands. This child of Israel,
Joseph, turns out to be the unwitting instrument for laying the foundation of
a state so centralized that it will have the capacity, given appropriate circumstances, to turn itself easily into a totalitarian prison, reminiscent of Nimrod
and antecedent to the much later Hitler and Stalin. And there will most assuredly be a change in circumstance, given a new Pharaoh who with his "native"
Egyptians will have forgotten that Joseph did what he did for the benefit of
Egypt and how and why Joseph's family — the Children of Israel — arrived in
Egypt. But by then the Children of Israel will themselves have forgotten…to
their dismay, to their despair.

Va-Yehi   ויחי

Over and over again the Book of Genesis has related to the transfer of blessings — blessings of material good fortune and blessings signifying covenantal purpose and continuity. As the Book comes to an end, father and grandfather Jacob-Israel will continue to give blessings.

Structurally speaking, Jacob-Israel, who has been backstage for several portions of the Torah, returns to dominate the scene. He does it by looking back and looking ahead. He reviews the past and predicts the future. He reviews the covenant of Abraham and Isaac and predicts the future of the twelve sons or tribes. Not that he sees the entire future! The Zohar comments: "Whatever Jacob wanted to say, he said, but in a way that combined the revealed and the hidden." But what Jacob-Israel seeks to do on his deathbed is to give his children and grandchildren a lesson in history — a lesson that there is a history, their history, their story. And it is a story that must continue to be told and to be lived.

Jacob and Joseph in Egypt

Jacob blesses Joseph saying: "God before whom my ancestors Abraham and Isaac walked." There is an immediate echo in this blessing of the majestic phrase which punctuated God's covenant with Abraham: *"Hithalekh le-fanai ve-heyei tamim."* ("Walk before me and be wholehearted.") But the transfer of blessings, which heretofore has been suffused with tension, jealousy, and threats of violence, will now have Jacob saying what he has to say in an atmosphere of awe-filled silence. For there has been a reconciliation among the sons. And so the sons and grandsons will listen, will apparently accept, and will see themselves as Jacob wishes to see them — a single, dedicated confederation of tribes, ready to grow into a nation.

Jacob's general blessing will be ritualized in later Jewish tradition as one of the blessings for the onset of a new week: "The Angel who redeems me from all evil — may he bless the young…" And the Midrash cites the analogy between *ge'ulah* (redemption) and *parnasah* (sustenance or livelihood.) The image of the ladder, which has served as Jacob's ensign throughout his mature life, continues to juxtapose heaven and earth, the ideal and the real — heavenly salvation and earthly livelihood.

Whatever Jacob has struggled to achieve in his life — notwithstanding his trials, his agonies, his losses — has deepened his faith that God has shepherded him. There is a midrashic debate as to the meaning of the "shepherding" image. Rabbi Yohanan sees God as Providence casting his caring eye over his flock. Resh Lakish, on the other hand, compares God to a prince who walks while a group of elders precede him, heralding Him, as it were. The dialectic represented by Rabbi Yohanan and Resh Lakish focuses alternatively on Israel's need for God and God's need for Israel. Jacob's understanding of the covenant bespeaks the emphasis on the reciprocal responsibility that falls on both "partners."

Intrinsic to the concept of "walking before God," as has been pointed out to Abraham, is the full participation of the human partner. Just as Abraham has been described as the disciple who lights up the dark alleyway for the King, so Jacob reminds his sons that their task is similar, albeit more difficult in a land of darkness — Egypt.

There is a special urgency to Jacob's reminder: for his sons are now more and more deeply ensconced in Egypt. And God's plan is for the light of human redemption to shine forth from Eretz Yisrael. Eretz Yisrael is the chosen place for the Children of Israel to turn back the "wilderness." And Jacob, foreseeing the long-term darkness that will envelop Israel in Egypt, is in effect anticipating a much later appeal to Israel when they are afflicted over many centuries in *galut*. Rabbi Nahman of Bratzlav will call out to his fellow Jews: "*Gevalt Yiden, zeit zich nit meya'esh*" ("Alas fellow Jews, do not dare to despair"). Jacob is urging his children never to stop believing that God is their shepherd, "we shall not want," and the Children of Israel are His heralds, He shall never be abandoned!

Jacob is deeply concerned about his sons' loyalty to the covenant. He questions them directly, according to the Midrash, and is assured by their collective response: "*Shema Yisrael Adonai Elohenu Adonai Ehad; Barukh Shem Kevod Malkhuto le-Olam va-Ed*" ("Listen, our Father Israel; The Lord — that is, your Lord, is our Lord; that Lord is One; Praised be His glorious Sovereignty for All Time"). In other words, the Midrash presents the sons as understanding the full implications of the covenant: that God is to be considered enthroned as Creator, Revealer, and Redeemer of the Children of Israel and through them ultimately all of humanity.

But Jacob is especially concerned about Joseph. As he nears death, he entreats his son Joseph not to bury him in Egypt but to carry him back to his homeland so that he may be buried with his family. Joseph agrees immediately. But Jacob insists that Joseph take an oath on it — which Joseph does. Why, it may be asked, does Jacob demand the extra confirmation of an oath?

The answer is found in the two parts of Jacob's monologue, which at first look do not appear to be connected. But Rashi senses the connection. First, regarding Jacob's referral to Joseph's two sons "who were born to you in the land of Egypt before I came to you in Egypt," Rashi adds "that is to say, those who were born from the time that you departed from me...." Rashi sees Jacob as imagining Joseph's maelstrom of negative emotions that had to have overwhelmed the boy years before when rejected by his family.

The very names which Joseph had given his Egyptian-born sons must haunt Jacob: As mentioned earlier, the name "Menashe" [Mannaseh], reminding Joseph that "God has made me forget completely my hardship and my parental home"; and the name "Ephraim", expressing Joseph's thanksgiving that "God has made me fertile in the land of my affliction." Jacob now reminds Joseph that these two Egyptian-born grandsons may be the natural progeny of Joseph ruler of Egypt. But more importantly, Ephraim and Menashe are his, Jacob's, "that is, they belong to me in their right and obligation to share in the covenant which must be implemented not in Egypt but in Eretz Yisrael." Indeed, Jacob fears, is it possible that Joseph has forgotten the covenant, the Zionist destiny, in the flush of the success which he has achieved in exile?

There is an additional personal anxiety that haunts Jacob as he imposes an oath on Joseph to bring his father's bones back for burial in the *me'arat hamakhpeilah* in Eretz Yisrael. In the *peshat* Jacob seems to be confessing guilt over not having taken Rachel, Joseph's mother, back for burial in the family plot. Instead he had her buried on the road to Ephrath. As cited earlier, Rashi has Jacob defend his actions by citing an instruction that he had received from God. As the Rabbis will see it, God wants her buried precisely there on the road to Ephrath so that when, in the future, the Children of Israel will be exiled and will pass her grave, her cry will elicit from God the comforting promise that there is hope for the future, that her children will someday return to Eretz Yisrael.

In other words, whatever guilt feelings Jacob may have regarding Rachel's burial, he also fears that Joseph's having been cut off so early and so abruptly from any connection to family and place will have severed for him any appreciation of the "story" of the family. And so here, both to neutralize Joseph's sensitivity to his mother's "burial," and to remind him of the long-term vanity of his "success" in Egypt, Jacob has thrust before Joseph the "Zionist" dimension of the covenant, the hoped-for "Zionist" fulfillment of Israel's story in the Land of Israel. In short, Jacob has a defense against Joseph's not illegitimate personal resentments, be they his mother's burial or his having been rejected early in his life by his family and sent thereby to his "success" in Egypt. Jacob's defense is a variation of the patriarchal defense of Abraham and Isaac at the *akeidah* or Jacob's own "family *akeidah*" in which a "cruel" father Jacob sent out a vulnerable Joseph to seek his resentful brothers in Shekhem. The defense is the *primacy of the larger covenantal demand*!

Continuing the Story

Joseph's success in Egypt has been unparalleled. He has saved Egypt and its surrounding neighbors from economic collapse and catastrophe. As such his glory as the Provider is deserved and presumably immortalized in the ancient chronicles of Egypt which record such achievements. But, of course, it is not recorded; he is not remembered. There will arise a new leadership in Egypt that will no longer "know" Joseph. He and his efforts will not have been considered an intrinsic part of the Egyptian "story." He will be as he has always been — a stranger, a "foreigner." He is to be forgotten even before the notorious Pharaoh of the enslavement will have expunged him and his family officially from the national consciousness and conscience.

In any case, the blessing which Jacob must transmit to his children — including Joseph — is not an Egyptian blessing. It is the recollection of the narrative of the *lekh lekha* of an individual and then a family that is decidedly not Egyptian. There is a way of life to be continued — if necessary, in Egypt, but with a clear direction to leave Egypt eventually for somewhere else. In essence the general blessing of Jacob to his sons and grandsons is the gift of historic awareness, of narrative awareness, i.e., a sense that there is a unique story which must be continued. And the continuation of the story is to move towards an exodus from Egypt, a reliving of Abram's *lekh lekha*.

Later rabbinic tradition will argue for two modes of preserving the story in memory and in practice. It may be God instructing Abraham on what lies ahead of him and his descendants during the vision of the "Covenant of the Pieces." It may be Moses throughout his Deuteronomic lectures reviewing whence Israel has come and to where they are going. It is Jacob blessing his sons connecting past and future. They all speak in the mode of *aggadah* — telling and retelling the saga of beginnings and continuity in narrative form — keeping alive the emotional identification of later generations with the "story." The second mode for keeping alive the Israelites' memory of the covenant is *halakhah*; i.e., maintaining Jewish normative practice as codified by the Rabbis.

When Jacob says to Joseph, "Don't bury me in Egypt," he is pleading with Joseph and his other sons not to bury the Israelite future in Egypt — its "aggadic" and "halakhic" future. As pointed out before, the seminal pedagogic strategy for remembering "halakhically" is found in the midrashic passage in *Sifre Ekev*: "Even though I am exiling you from the Land, be *distinguished* in the commandments so that when you return to the Land they will not be new to you." "Aggadically," God was telling Abraham: "You're here at present in the Land of Canaan. The story is going to take you elsewhere; but eventually you're coming back." "Halakhically," the Godly instruction to "walk before me wholeheartedly" will flower into a comprehensive system of private and public behavioral patterns catered to preserving in memory through active behavior a covenant-in-detail, a culture, a civilization.

Jacob could have chosen to look upon the settling-down in Egypt as not only fortuitous but desirable. In his meeting with Joseph's Pharaoh, Jacob describes his previous years in Canaan as "few and hard." In contrast, the remaining seventeen years in Egypt for Jacob are stable and peaceful. Yet Jacob's message not to be buried in Egypt is a cry-in-protest that this stability, this peace is not meant to be the end. Halakhically speaking, the message of the *Sifre* is similar. Speaking to any group of Jews going into exile or already living in exile, it is that this is not the end. The story must continue; every Jewish community no matter how distant, no matter how self-sufficient, is charged to remember through the performance of a network of *mitzvot* that the story must continue and it must continue with the aspiration to return to the Land.

Every ritual practice beginning with the circumcision of the newborn male-child will be associated with the covenant; and the covenant will be a "Zionistically inspired" covenant recalling God's words to Abraham in Genesis 17:7–8: "I will maintain My covenant between Me and you, and your offspring to come, as an everlasting covenant throughout the ages, to be God to you and to your offspring to come. I assign the land you sojourn in to you and your offspring to come, all the land of Canaan, as an everlasting holding. I will be their God." Daily prayer will allude regularly and often to the Promised Land and dreams of redemption *there*. The celebration of Holy Days through laws, customs, and liturgy will be focused on the Land and its seasons. A calendar of Torah readings will institutionalize the memory of the story of *"lekh lekha"* and *"aliyah"* — going forward and going up to the Land.

Jacob is not ungrateful — not to Joseph and not to Pharaoh. Later Jewish tradition will explain a certain altruism towards Egyptians in contrast with the legislated Israelite attitude towards Moabites and Ammonites as due to the hospitality shown by Egypt towards Jacob's family and the immediately succeeding generations. But the story — if it is to be an Israelite story — must touch base sooner or later with the Land of Israel. If it is to be a Jewish story, it must return to take up residence and achieve sovereignty in the Land of Israel.

For this reason, it cannot be said that the Book of Genesis ends on a happy note — despite all the blessings that dominate its concluding chapters. True it is that Joseph is able to comfort his brothers in their anxiety: "[A]lthough you intended me harm, God intended it for good, so as to bring about the present result — the survival of my people, and so fear not, I will sustain you and your children." True it is that Joseph *and* the brothers have found peace, security, and serenity in Goshen. But as Joseph himself gets older, his own words — these words are now not just Jacob's — resonate in a tone of blessing mixed with a mood which is ominous: "I am about to die. God will surely take notice of you and bring you up from this land to the Land which He has promised."

Fraternal Peace and Unity

At the end Joseph has digested Jacob-Israel's covenantal blessing. Joseph's plea to have his own bones taken up to the Land of Israel as part of the process of redemption is an anticipatory objection to the last verse in Genesis: "So Joseph died...and they embalmed him, and he was put in a coffin in Egypt." Joseph in essence is begging not to be left embalmed in a coffin in Egypt, not to be left embalmed in the coffin that *is* Egypt and *will be* Egypt — certainly for the Children of Israel. The last word of the book of *Bereishit* is the antithesis of creation, hope and covenantal redemption. It is the word *Be-mitzrayim* or *Be-Meitzarim!* In straits!

It is significant that at the end of Joseph's eventful life, the straits that close about him, embalming him, attempting to petrify his memory, are those of the foreign empire which he has served. They are no longer the daggers of resentment aimed at him by his brothers. For there has truly been a reconciliation among the brothers. There has been a complete turning from the summary comment following the early episode of the dreams *"ve-lo yakhlu dabro le-shalom"* ("the brothers could not speak a friendly word to him"). Their attitude to Joseph had been more than hostile; it had been homicidal. And now — by whatever circuitous route they have been brought to this point — they are again one with him. Joseph's bones will be taken up to the Land of Israel and buried appropriately under Joshua's leadership in Shekhem. It must be Shekhem — the place where Joseph sought his brothers, but found instead a brotherhood of blood bent on murder. Joseph's burial in Shekhem will close the circle as the fraternal bond has now been knit together firmly and resolutely.

Not that the brothers will forget their guilt completely! Nor will they ever feel completely at ease with him, their erstwhile victim. But Jacob's sending out Joseph to seek the "peace" with his brothers — that necessary mission, the indispensable element in proving the Children of Israel's worthiness to carry on with the covenant — has now been vindicated. This "peace" is so crucial that the later rabbinic tradition will hold that lies may be told in order to achieve it.

The *Midrash Tanhuma* relates: "The power of 'shalom' ('peace') is so great that the text may record words of complete fiction for the sake of achieving peace. When Jacob our father died the tribes were afraid lest Joseph take revenge for all the evil that had been done to him. And so they told Joseph that their father had commanded them on his deathbed to beg Joseph to forgive them for their sin against him. But Jacob had not spoken those words. The brothers fabricated them. The Sages said; 'How many pens were broken and how much ink was poured out in order to write these words — in the *Torah*, no less — and yet these words were never said. All for the sake of peace.'"

Shalom (peace) within Israel as mutual fulfillment will be felt by the Rabbis to override truth. The Rabbis will interpret the destruction of the Second Temple and the concomitant loss of sovereignty as a result of *sinat hinam* (gratuitous hatred) within the fellowship of Israel. They will understand what Jacob understood at the beginning, that the children of Israel would have to pursue *shalom* among themselves as their incontestable priority. The covenant would never challenge Israel to discover absolute "truth." For essentially the tradition would insist that only God knows the full and absolute truth. The Rabbis would argue that human beings are charged principally with *being* together, *communing* together, and *building* together. Moses would be drawn out of the water to become a redeemer of Israel not because he possessed some overriding "truth." Only God had the "truth." Moses' chief attribute, the attribute that led him out of the Egyptian palace and into the arms of the Hebrew slaves was his intuitive empathy, identification, and love for this people.

As underscored earlier, the later Rabbis, suffering through the degradation of the loss of their sovereign Israel, would express their own certainty as to the indispensability of *ahavat hinam* (gratuitous love) within the House of Israel by connecting the martyrdom of their colleagues during the Hadrianic persecution with the original crime of Joseph's brothers. Fraternal hatred had to be expiated. There would be no hope for a reconstructed Jewish sovereignty over the Land of Israel without fraternal love and peace. As also underscored earlier, obsessed with the yearning for peace within Israel, the Rabbis would even use pedagogically the biblical character of Moses as a foil for Aaron, the lover of peace. They would contrast Moses and Aaron as archetypal representatives of truth-law-justice versus compromise-for-purposes-of-peace. The Rabbis would have Moses represent the motto "let the law cut through a mountain." Aaron, on the other hand, would be described as loving peace, pursuing peace, and making peace between man and man.

According to this particular rabbinic picture of Moses, if Moses' position was correct — that the truth, the law, justice, must be permitted to cut through a mountain uncompromised in any way — it could only be because the ultimate true judgment would indeed be God's. It would have to have the absolute Sinai-stamp of God on it. Aaron's predicament — the human predicament — was that he lived not on Sinai with God but at the foot of Sinai with men. Because he would have to apply the law and God's truth among men, he would not be able to avoid tempering justice with peace-seeking mercy. Granted, Aaron's mercy could so compromise the redemptive truth of Sinai that a "golden calf" of human idolatry could emerge to blemish the truth irredeemably. But, on the other hand, according to this midrashic model, Moses' inability to compromise would lead to his smashing the tablets of "truth" and instigating a civil war within Israel. Who was right therefore?

The rabbinic answer would be clear: In an unredeemed world where men must live with men, arbitration leading to peace would have to be the preferred way. To strengthen this rabbinic answer, many other *midrashim* would base themselves on those Torah passages where Moses shows his own compassionate side when defending Israel before God's attribute-of-justice. In other words, Moses and *his* "attribute-of-mercy" in these *midrashim* — superseding Aaron's — would be cast as the preeminent *ohev Yisrael* (lover of Israel). Moses would love the Children of Israel unconditionally — in spite of their weaknesses, their transgressions, their stiff-neckedness in the face of the demands of the covenant.

Anticipating then the *ahavat Yisrael* (the love for Israel) of both Moses and Aaron and the later Rabbis, Joseph and his brothers have now come together. And their being together serves as a later manifestation of a response to the primordial question addressed to Cain, "Where is your brother?" It is the only response acceptable to God the Creator, Revealer, and Redeemer. It is a response that overrides truth. It is underscored in an astounding comment in the same *midrash* quoted earlier: "So great is the power of peace that at a time when Israel comes together as a group *even to perform avodah zara* ('idolatry') God's attribute of justice will not injure them, as it is said in Hosea 4:17: '*Havur atzabim Ephraim hanah-lo*' ('Ephraim is addicted to images, but let him be')" — for in their sinning, Ephraim (Israel) are at least standing together!

The corollary of peace is pluralism. What Joseph, Judah, and the others have suffered through is an evolution in temperaments which have brought them to the realization that other views exist in the persons of other people and that a strongly held view must always be tempered by the knowledge that because only God has the whole truth, other views must be given their due. The notability of pluralism will be associated with a much later sociocultural reality within an advanced Western Civilization. But the vision of pluralism goes back to Eden or at least as far back as the failure of Cain and Abel to live together. In his *A Far Glory*, Peter Berger will argue: "It is a challenge to hold convictions without either dissolving them in utter relativity or encasing them in the false absolutes of fanaticism." Cain and Joseph's brothers in their early confrontation with the "otherness" of Joseph are fanatics and therefore, sooner or later, fratricides. For the uncompromised certainty of their sense of "right" leaves no room for "the other." But now the brothers have learned what many a wise man has known: that a person with never a sense of uncertainty is surely a madman.

And so Jacob-Israel has gathered about him his children — and his "adopted" children Ephraim and Menashe — in order to place in their charge the covenantal blessing of Abraham and Isaac. This blessing is a blessing that Jacob-Israel has wrestled with through a lifetime of spiritual, moral, political, economic, and psychological conflicts. He himself is now prepared to be gathered in to his forefathers. He prays that his children, the Children of Israel, will be up to the task of covenantal continuity. They will be led — not by Joseph, nor by Joseph's children Menashe or Ephraim. The scepter of leadership will be given to Judah and will not depart from Judah. He may not have been Jacob's beloved, but he has turned out to be the strongest of the sons. Jacob's individual blessing to Judah will reflect the father's appreciation of Judah's strength and future vitality.

The content of the other individual "blessings" to the sons is a confluence of feelings, expressions, and articulations based on prophetic prescience. There are poetic plays on words, unequal in space devoted, but reflecting a high sensitivity to the dynamics of history. Principally the blessings show an awareness of the variegated, even disparate personal qualities (destinies?) of the sons. How will they be able to live in peace as brothers? Reuben's impetuosity, Simon and Levi's contentiousness, Issachar the timid, Zebulun the ambitious traveler, Dan the viper, Gad the warrior, Asher the prosperous,

Naphtali the swift, Benjamin the fierce — and Joseph perennially the crown of material success despite the arrows of misfortune.

Is there a conceptual coherence to Jacob's recitation beyond his implicit prayer that these sons will find their fraternal peace? There cannot be, for to the end, Jacob is honest in his affections; and his affections are mixed. But to the end Jacob knows what is required to survive as a nation in the world. To that end, the tribes will represent in combination the requisite variety of skills, talents, and attributes necessary to make survival promising.

Judah, David, and the Messianic Promise

In a later generation King David, an heir of the tribe of Judah, will also pass on an ethical will to his son and successor Solomon. David's will will be an explicit integration of two messages: the sublime instruction to keep the *mitzvot* (commandments) of the Torah; but also "realpolitik" advice regarding adversaries and the need to confront them and neutralize them. The nineteenth-century commentator the Malbim will see the key word *ve-gam* (and also, or furthermore) followed by the tactical warning "you know what Joab son of Zeruiah did to me" as the transition word between the two types of instruction. David will know — and must instruct Solomon to know — that there are subjects that must be dealt with by the king which will not easily be legislated for him by Torah law. He will have to use his own clever political intuition and at times arbitrarily ruthless authority to safeguard his rule and the polity he is charged to protect. Jacob has willed the same message implicitly generations earlier to his sons.

David will speak in prose to his son Solomon. Jacob-Israel speaks in poetry to his sons. But Jacob's grasp of the kind of resourcefulness that will be required from each of the tribes is alluded to with varying degrees of clarity. Granted, his anger with Reuben, Simeon, and Levi cuts short his words to them. But Jacob's "prophecy" to Judah — with all its hidden meanings — is a testament to strong assertive leadership: "Your hand shall be on the nape of your foes even as your father's sons shall bow low to you." Judah is a lion's whelp, having grown on prey, alluding to the expansion of the later kingdom of Judah by David. The messianic hint associated with Judah and Shiloh makes its later claim on David as the ideal king, but a king who will owe tribute nevertheless in equal measure to Moses and Machiavelli.

Jacob is gathered to his fathers, having now left the scene to a new generation. These Israelites will now find themselves in a situation of short-term economic opportunity. But this will be followed by a middle-term deterioration in their relationship with the ruling government leading to long-term subjugation. The most critical achievement at this juncture following Jacob-Israel's passing must focus on the brothers who at long last have come together. A nation will be born out of the coming together of the Children of Jacob-Israel. It will be a nation that — like the midrashic Abraham — will have to be brought out of the fires of servitude and idolatry. But even in their servitude they will survive as a nation prepared as a nation to be redeemed. A promise, after all, had been made by the God of Israel at the *akeidah*. More than a promise! God had taken an oath: *"Bi Nishbati!"* (I have sworn by Myself!) It had been an oath sworn by the God of Israel guaranteed by God's own very Essence!

SHEMOT

שְׁמוֹת

From Human Enslavement to Covenantal Freedom

The long-predicted darkness has arrived and blanketed the Children of Israel in Egypt. The plan of the oppressor is genocidal in scope. The despair among the Israelites will be epitomized in the decision of a mother to abandon her three-month-old child to the caprice of the Nile River. In total despair she challenges God — or the Fates — to decide on the future of this child. In effect this child represents all of Israel. Redemption will come. It has been promised in the *Brit bein ha-Betarim*. But the enslavement has also been promised. And it is intended by Pharaoh to be a proto-Holocaust.

The Zohar will speak of two kinds of luminaries created by God. Those which ascend to the realm of the "above" are called "luminaries of light"; those which descend to the realm of the "below" are called "luminaries of fire." Once the redemption begins with the punishment of Egypt through the ten plagues, Israel will be blessed with "light-from-above." But before God's revelation to Moses in the "burning-bush-below," Egypt for the Israelites will be an inferno.

What is this "burning bush" if not the "burning bush" in the heart of a human being like Moses — saved from the Nile by a Gentile "daughter-of-God" (Batya in the Midrash)? Pulled out of the reeds and raised to be a prince in Egypt, Moses — despite his lofty station — will bear in his heart and soul a sociomoral ache. God's light from above and fire from below will be fused together in Moses well before his epiphany that special day in Midian. But once the epiphany occurs, and Moses' destiny and mission are made explicit, he will become not only the human redeemer of Israel working with God the Redeemer of Israel. Forever after Moses will be known as the supreme teacher of Israel — Moshe Rabbenu.

❦   ❦   ❦

In Gaston Bachelard's *The Psychoanalysis of Fire*, he studies Man's primeval fascination with the phenomenon of fire — from primitive Man's preoccupation with the life and death forces that fire represents to modern Man's use of fire in its many technical applications and metaphorical allusions. He says, "Among all phenomena fire is really the only one to which there can be so definitely attributed the opposing values of good and evil." Fire energizes; it also incinerates. Fire warms and in so doing enables otherwise cold creatures to survive; but fire also devours indiscriminately. As a metaphor, fire serves good and evil: the holy fire of love; the profane fire of hatred. Bachelard calls the man who studies the fire "man in reverie" and the man who thinks as he stands before the fire is a man "centralizing his reverie." We have suggested earlier the Hebrew phrase *"yirat shamayim"* as the equivalent of such a centralized reverie. Such a man projects images out of his conscious and unconscious being, transcendent and immanent images and ideas born out of his yearnings, hopes, and anxieties.

Long before Bachelard's phenomenological description, the biblical Moses fits the archetype of a human being centralizing his reverie before a fire. His people Israel will similarly confront the fire that burns and burns and beckons to it as it burns throughout its history. But Moses first! Already a man who has shown his humaneness, defending a slave, mediating a quarrel between ungrateful disputants, taking the part of disadvantaged women! But Moses in Midian is now a man alone in the wilderness, a shepherd removed from human conflict and misery, separated from worldly concerns. But is he, can he be?

Moses sees a fire in a lowly thorn bush. The perennial intellectual and emotional ambivalences associated with fire in general and the irrational "behavior" of this particular fire that burns but is not consumed stir Moses' sociomoral imagination. For a long time Moses has had a creeping sense of intellectual and emotional malaise. All the ideas which he had in Egypt and which led him to begin his fight to help his fellow man have been submerged while he has led his calm bucolic life as a shepherd in Midian.

But the fire in the *sneh* (burning bush) now arouses in him conscious intimations, vapors of fantasy. Is it fantasy? Moses has seen the reality about him in Egypt — a reality of hedonistic pleasure, yet suffering, of human wealth and high culture, yet humanly engineered oppression and degradation. And so Moses rebels. He rebels against the ambiguity of the fire of life, against the "acceptability" of the mixed conditions of aesthetic glory and moral decay characterizing the Egyptian empire and afflicting in particular his people the Children of Israel. Moses' consciousness becomes possessed, fully and sharply honed to project a vision of his loftiest hopes for humanity in general, but through his people Israel in particular.

This heightened moral imagination is now ready to hear God's voice. It will be a commanding, demanding, uncompromising voice — but a voice representing the weak, the enslaved, the dispossessed, the forgotten. It will be the God of Abraham, the God of Isaac, and the God of Jacob-Israel calling to him. And Moses will respond *"hineini"* — the only acceptable response — to a call to revolution. Moses will be God's prophet to this people, a people who God will remind Moses is henceforth to be known as God's children, God's Children of Israel. Moses will learn that this people is ready; yet not quite ready to be redeemed. It is ready; yet not quite ready to receive the Torah. It is ready; yet not quite ready for the journey to a new covenantal existence in a new/old Land.

Redemption will come nevertheless. Israel as a people has endured as a people its collective *akeidah* as slaves in Egypt. Notwithstanding the suffering of many individuals and families, Israel as a people has survived enough to cry out. And the "*ze'akah*," the cry, has been heard. The redemption is at hand. It has been ordered; it has been promised — a vow by the God of Israel at the original *akeidah* on Mount Moriah. A vow by the God of Israel ratified by His very own Essence!

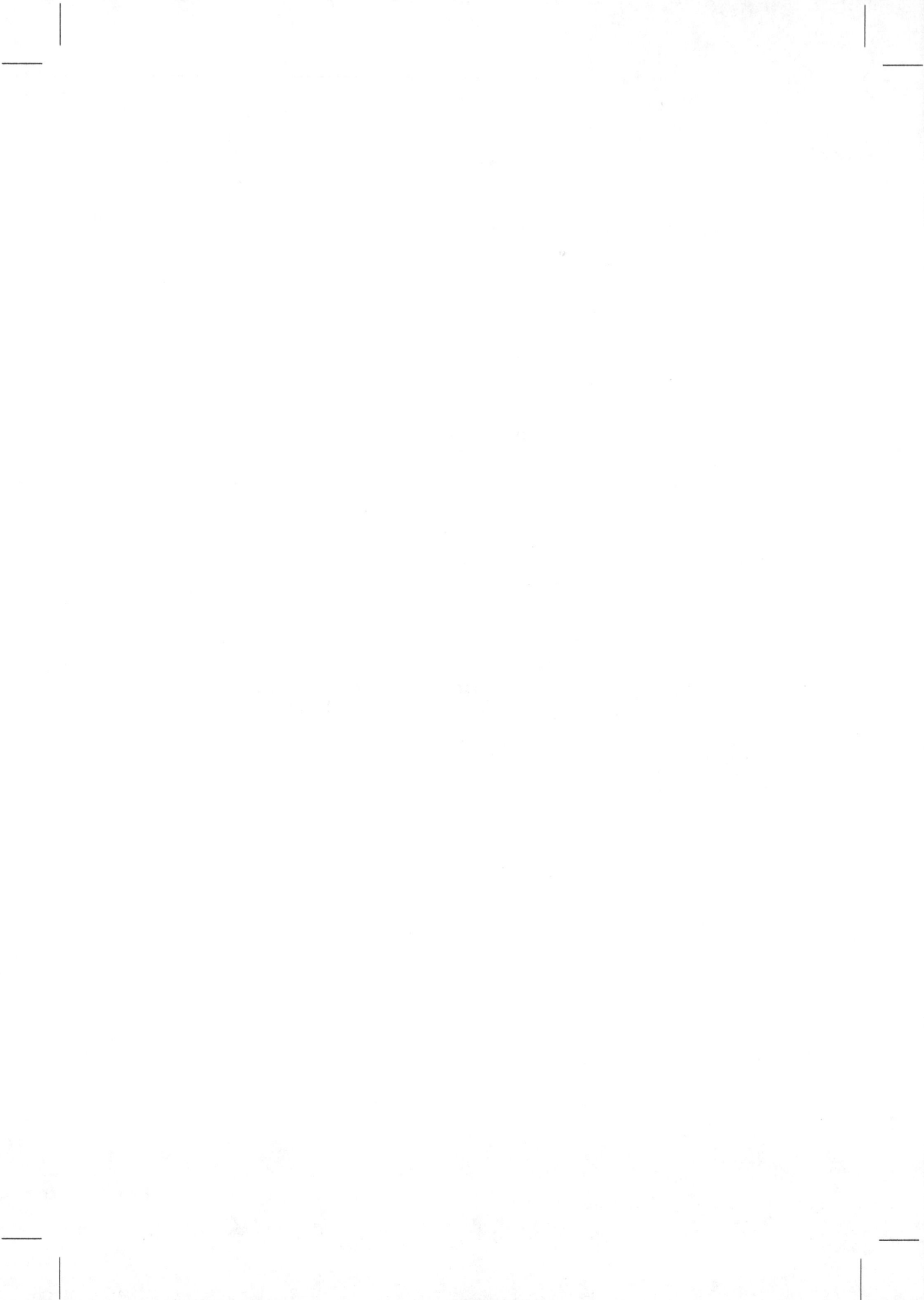

Shemot   שמות

In his classic essay "Moses" Ahad Ha'am points to Heine's characterization of Yehudah Halevi, the great Hebrew poet, as having been born with a kiss. Ahad Ha'am then criticizes Heine's image: "This concept is foreign to the spirit of Judaism. When the national tradition sought to describe the greatness of its greatest prophet Moses, it described him as *dying* with a kiss. Moses died with a kiss after he concluded the task that had been placed upon him, after he bore the burden of life and stood all his life as a sturdy rock in the heart of the sea of turmoil."

Heine's description of Yehudah Halevi the poet envisions a child; Ahad Ha'am's description of Moses the redeemer-prophet envisions a mature proven adult. Underscored here is the difference between being a poet who is a brilliant spectator, and a prophet who is an involved participant.

There are two kinds of seeing: the seeing of the spectator and the seeing of the participant. There is aesthetic seeing which is childlike in its openness, distanced, and cathartic; and there is moral seeing which is engaged, responsible, and reactive. Moses sees the suffering of the Israelites (2:11). But it is not a distanced seeing. Rashi says: "He set his eyes and his heart to be grieved for them." Consequently, Moses acts. He punishes the Egyptian taskmaster who is brutalizing a Hebrew slave. God is described similarly as seeing the situation of the Israelites (2:25). Again, it is not a distanced seeing. Rashi says: "God set his heart upon Israel." And God's empathetic seeing leads Him to act to save this beleaguered people.

Enslavement and the Seeds of Revolution

But there's more to the story. Moses has escaped to Midian following his initial "engaged" behavior. This involved killing the Egyptian taskmaster who was beating an Israelite slave. Moses tried in vain to mediate between two quarreling Israelites — and was forced to run for his life in fear of his "criminal" act being uncovered. In Midian he has distanced himself from the fate and destiny of these Israelites. He has married well and settled into the peaceful and predictable life of a shepherd. But reflecting on this stage of his life in Midian, Ahad Ha'am criticizes him: "He worshiped God with faith in universal justice; but in the meantime had forgotten the God of his fathers and his people." Ahad Ha'am is extreme in his criticism. A fairer presumption would be that Moses has never forgotten the pain of his people — even in the stillness of Midian, but he has repressed it. The memory will lie dormant until he is ready spiritually, psychologically, and morally to meet the all-consuming challenge of his mature life.

On that fateful day on which Moses is drawn to a particular thorn bush, attracted by the peculiar phenomenon of its burning and not being extinguished, he experiences first a "seeing" of aesthetic curiosity. God Himself responds to Moses' curiosity with His own attention that may be described similarly as "aesthetic." But God then calls to Moses from within the bush. And now Moses moves to the threshold of an engaged attention as he responds with the ever-portentous *hineini*. God then reminds Moses of the appropriate way to see — not with mere aesthetic curiosity, which at best can only be cathartic, i.e., emotionally inflamed at first and quickly defused — but in a fully responsible, morally committed manner: to do everything that will be necessary to free his people, to redeem his people, Moses' people, God's people. God reminds Moses *to see* in order *to remember* in order *to act*. A later talmudic sage will "canonize" the proposition: "You shall see and remember all the *mitzvot* of Hashem and do them; *seeing* leads one to *remembering* and *remembering* leads one to *doing*" (Menahot 43b).

Ahad Ha'am describes Moses as bearing the "burden of life" and standing all his life "as a sturdy rock in the heart of the sea of turmoil." The Torah portion in which we are introduced to Moses contains within it in miniature the drama depicted throughout the Bible and throughout Jewish history: on the one hand, enslavement and suffering at the hands of an enemy; on the other hand, the beginning of redemption — but with the hesitant, often reluctant, participation of Am Yisrael, the People of Israel. In the center of this maelstrom of human conflict stands the figure Moses, energized into receiving a message from God. This covenanted message will give him enough strength (1) to do battle with the enemies of his people Israel who are bent on their enslavement and ultimate annihilation; and (2) to do battle as well with the Children of Israel themselves, or at least with large sectors of them who are not yet prepared — and who must be prepared — to be mobilized for their own redemption.

As foreseen, the enslavement has been severe. The commentators understand certain general truths about nations and political circumstances that determine national policies. Later sophisticated historians will summarize these truths as follows: In the course of human events an erstwhile peaceful, reasonably tolerant society will find itself beset with social, economic, cultural, and religious stresses. As conditions deteriorate, as internal pressures become more and more heated, formerly tolerated minorities within the society will become increasingly delegitimized in the eyes of the majority population. In such situations the governmental leadership will find it expedient to take steps towards legal and extra-legal disenfranchisement of these minorities. And most of the ordinary population will acquiesce actively or passively to the new policies of the leadership.

A second truth has been confirmed time and again in the history of multi-cultural polities — but this time regarding the internal dynamic of the minority community! The very sources of minority power and influence, which the minority community has sought to exploit to its legitimate advantage in its relations with the majority, contribute to the eventual disintegration of the minority community. For the more power, influence, and success achieved on a personal basis by individual members of the minority community, the more vested the interest of these same individuals will be in saving their own individual selves at the cost of community solidarity in the face of the coming disenfranchisement.

It is reasonable to assume that at a given juncture in the history of ancient Egypt — the period preceding the enslavement that eventually would precipitate the Exodus — there was a sociopolitical crisis fracturing the unity of the empire. A severe Egyptian nationalist reaction was ignited against what was perceived as an over-dominance of the foreign Hyksos and other foreign ethnic groups in positions of influence. This reaction led inevitably to the persecution of all minorities including the Israelites. These Israelites in particular had become visible due to the success of Joseph and, we may presume, the continued success of his brothers in the Goshen area.

The Israelites must have become a particularly inviting target. *"Hava nithakma*" ("let us be wise in our planning"), says the new Pharaoh. He means this in two ways referring respectively to the Egyptian population and to the Israelites. The masses of conventionally "moral" Egyptians may not tolerate too abrupt a change in policy towards the Israelites. At the same time, too immediate a change may alarm the ordinary Israelites prematurely into an undesired organized violent reaction. And so Pharaoh makes his moves cleverly and gradually. But his long-term plan is clear: genocide!

Into this turmoil steps Moses even before his revelatory experience at the "burning bush." As already mentioned, an Egyptian overseer is beating a Hebrew slave and the Torah describes Moses' reaction *"Va-yifen ko va-kho va-yar ki ein ish"* ("He looked here and there and saw that there was no man"). Two representative commentators focus respectively on the Egyptians and the Israelites to explain the circumstances that would have led this prince of Egypt to perpetrate what turns out to be a justifiable but personally dangerous act — an act that will lead this prince Moses to abandoning his station in life for an unknown future. The *Ha'amek Davar* commentary sees Moses looking everywhere for an Egyptian authority to deal with what Moses perceives to be a gross injustice — namely the gratuitous bludgeoning of a slave. But there is no seat of justice; for all of Egypt has become an "assembly of the treacherous, all despisers of Israel." The commentary *Ha-Ketav ve-ha-Kabbalah*, on the other hand, has Moses expecting at least someone among the Israelites who is viewing the atrocity along with him and who one might expect to become sufficiently outraged to protest, to attempt to save or to stand alongside his fellow tribesman. But to Moses' chagrin there is no "man" sufficiently empathetic to the plight of his brother.

That Egypt has plummeted to a state of moral decay worthy of Babel or Sodom is part of the inevitable fate of any autocratic society that, untrammeled by any legal "checks and balances," must beat down its subjects, must turn them all into slaves. Ironically, as underscored earlier, it was Joseph the Israelite who had been responsible in his day for fashioning a new socioeconomic order for his Pharaoh. It was Joseph and his Pharoah's policy of centralization-of-power that in the period of extreme economic distress had saved Egypt, including its mixed multitudes of peoples and the entire Middle East. But now a demonic new order has emerged which, whatever its particular sociopolitical problems, has decided among other things to use its centralized power to destroy the descendants of Joseph — the Children of Israel!

This will be a scenario repeated many times in later Jewish history. For the Bible is describing the birth of the nation of Israel as a birth conceived, born, and brought forth within the storm-driven crucible of this-worldly politics. The religion of Israel — the Jewish religion — will be a religion directed to the political "jungle" or "wilderness." And as such it will not be a religion offering escape to an Eden-like utopia no matter how inviting, but a religion demanding total social and political engagement in the post-Eden "wilderness" of human striving.

Thus, no matter how deeply mired in bondage Israel finds itself — predicted in the *Brit bein ha-Betarim* — it is also inevitable that Israel will be freed. And the freedom will be, must be socially and politically overt, a freedom visible on earth. Moses from within the oppressive Egyptian system will be the seed for destroying the system in order to represent a higher unity — not that of Pharaonic dictatorship — but of God's kingship-on-earth, a vision of human betterment realized not in heaven, but on earth.

Thus a revolution is promised. It will be a never-ending revolution against the forces of Babel and Sodom and Pharaoh's Egypt. And Moses the prophet of this revolution will learn that being engaged in the pulsating rhythms and chaotic dissonances of human life means that there will be unceasing "trouble." Among the *midrashim* concerned with God's assurance to Moses that He is eternally bound up with Israel, God says: "Go tell Israel that just as I will have been with them through this servitude, I will be with them through every other servitude which awaits them." Moses protests: *"Dayah le-tzarah be-sha'atah."* ("It's enough to refer to a later trouble when it is upon us — not before.") But the ground of the *midrash's* insight is the acknowledgment that as long as there is a dynamic ebb and flow to human existence and society, there is trouble. And if there is an attempt at perfect order imposed by Man in order to control the ebb and flow, then there is also trouble because there is always a festering Sturm-und-Drang below the apparent order.

Moses' Early Struggles

Moses — guided by God — will inspire Israel to break out of the "slave order" into a freedom with which to move to a Godly order at Sinai. But Israel — even with the Torah — will also fail at achieving perfection. It is for that reason that God — in the Midrash — predicts that Israel will someday lose its independence, even after having achieved sovereignty. When Moses protests *"Dayah le-tzarah be-sha'atah"* he is in essence saying: "Perhaps Israel will not fail!" In this he is already anticipating a role which he will play countless times as *sheli'ah tzibbur* (representative of the community) and as *meilitz yosher* (righteous advocate) for his people Israel. He will often stand in the breach before God as Israel's sole representative and honest advocate pleading their case.

Standing in the breach had been an attribute of Moses right from the beginning of his adulthood. Not quite knowing or appreciating who he was, he had ventured forth to defend the Hebrew slave against the overseer. He surely knew that as an Egyptian prince he had to respect aristocratic convention — that convention which would preclude his identifying with the plight of the slave. Yet Ahad Ha'am points to Moses' "categorical postulate for righteousness" translated into live actions. It is this that distinguished Moses with prophetic traits from the beginning, even if it meant flouting convention and denying his Egyptian identity, his noble position in the Egyptian hierarchy. And so Moses threw himself into the sociomoral breach in Egypt by standing with the slave. Later as a stranger in Midian, he would again expose himself to personal risk by defending strange women at the well.

While in Egypt he had asserted himself as well as an uninvited mediator in a quarrel between two Hebrews. And it would be this tragic incident that would portend another role which Moses would have to play throughout his prophetic life. He would need to administer the lives of people who might be covenanted descendants of Abraham, Isaac, and Jacob-Israel; but they would be a people bent on internecine strife. If Moses — before the epiphany at the "bush" — shows a reluctance to accept the *shelihut* (assignment) for which God has chosen him, it is less from being awestruck by God's revealed Presence and more the recalling of the precedent of the two Hebrews quarrelling with each other and precipitating Moses' flight to Midian in the first place.

The extent of Moses' concern for righteousness and his shock at the behavior of the two Hebrews is brought out in a statement by Resh Lakish in the tractate *Sanhedrin* on the verse *"Lama takeh rei'ekha?"* ("Why are you about to strike your brother?") The Torah has described the potential assailant as *rasha* (wicked). Resh Lakish says: "He who raises his hand against his fellow human being even though he has not yet struck him is already called 'wicked.'" In other words, there is a form, a level, a style of discourse which is already called *rish'ut* (wickedness) — a style of discourse that will most certainly lead to physical violence. And it is this very pattern of verbal behavior, let alone its physically violent consequence which goes a long way to breaking Moses' naïvely idealistic spirit even then, early in the game — even before the revelation at the "burning bush."

The assailant taunts Moses: "Who made you chief and ruler over us? Do you mean to kill me as you killed the Egyptian?" The text then notes Moses' fright and conclusion: *"Akhen noda ha-davar!"* ("Then the matter is known!") What is the "matter" that is known? Rashi offers the literal meaning, but then offers a shockingly unembarrassed critique of the Israelite community in Egypt: "That *matter* which is now known to me astonishes me, i.e., the sin which Israel must have committed among the nations to warrant such enslavement. I see that they *deserve* it."

Moses must flee — but not only because his life is in danger because of the homicide which he has committed. Moses' pain at the reaction of the quarreling Hebrews is symptomatic of his lack of preparedness to undertake the role of human shepherd and redeemer of this apparently stiff-necked people. Moses will need the time away from Egypt and away from the Israelites in order to let his ideas gestate. He will need the years away to temper his impatience, to soften his prophetic zeal with moral compassion. Most of all, he will have to cultivate an unconditional love for this people, his people — whether they meet his standards of righteousness or not.

During his years in Midian, Moses will appear to have lost some of his passion for righteousness. He will settle down after getting married. He will have children. He will begin approximating the external life of Abraham, Isaac, and Jacob as semi-nomads. He must sense in himself, however, a lack of covenantal purpose and drive. The "burning bush" epiphany will thereupon awaken him from his bucolic lethargy. It will remind him that he has brethren in Egypt; that God — *"Ehyeh asher Ehyeh"* — is no longer just the God of Abraham, Isaac, Jacob, *or* Moses, that keeping and applying a universalistic moral norm in an idealized socially corrigible situation is not sufficient. The nation of Israel — as they are, stiff-necked and all — must become the focus of Moses' moral concern, as it is God's special covenantal concern. God says to Moses: "I have seen the suffering of *My people*; take *My people Israel* out of Egypt."

The two signs that God gives Moses to illustrate His power to change reality have a scolding function as well. Moses' complaint about his inadequacy to cope with Israel's stubborn lack of faith is parried by God's characterization of such arguments as serpentine and leprous: the first vivified by the staff turning into a snake, and the second — Moses' hand momentarily afflicted with leprosy, a disease associated by the later rabbis with slander. This slave people may be in the moral doldrums. It is their current predicament. But it is precisely this slave people which God has determined long before to be destined for freedom and moral modelship. Moses dare not slander them. On the contrary, he is to be the human agent for leading the political revolution to bring freedom to Israel. He is also to be the inspired tutor for turning a slave rabble into a people with spiritual and sociomoral aspirations.

What has happened cognitively, spiritually, and morally to awaken Moses to a new broadened awareness and readiness? Bahya ben Asher will call it a three-stage experience at the "burning bush" of moving from the vision of the fire, to the presence of the *Malakh Hashem* (the Angel of God), to the sound of the Overwhelming Voice of God Himself addressing him: "Moses!" He, Moses, is to be the chosen one to stand before the elders of Israel and then before Pharaoh. Moses has passed by many thorn bushes during his days as a shepherd in Midian. On this particular day there is a confluence of a "marvelous sight" and a spiritually restless searcher. The burning thorn bush with its flames dancing upward and outward, yet centralized in its brightness, not consuming itself, enraptures the shepherd who today cannot pass it by.

Moses cannot help but begin to visualize and reconstruct ideas that have been submerged — repressed — ever since he fled Egypt. The *Malakh Hashem*, as opposed to the "Voice of God Himself," represents intimations of thoughts and feelings, intuitions and premonitions, "signals of transcendence" — to use Peter Berger's phrase — not yet clearly articulated.

Moses is the kind of man whose *yirat shamayim* or centralized reverie is as yet generalized, universalized — appropriately so. He has been raised in the culture and civilization of Egypt. There are in Egypt "God-fearing" individuals like the midwives who are described as such and whose moral sensitivities can be extended to any human beings who happen to come into their charge.

It has been out of that generalized reverie and "categorical postulate for righteousness" that Moses has gone out to see and to defend the people who happen to be slaves and who only later will be revealed to him as his own flesh-and-blood. But the focused particularistic revelation has not yet occurred where Moses is concerned. He is not Abraham who is challenged to initiate a radical departure from the enclosure of Nimrod's Babel and to originate an entirely new way of "walking wholeheartedly" in the "wilderness" of God's earth. Moses — after acting out his personal protest in slaying the Egyptian and saving the Israelite — has had to run for his life at the sign of personal danger. He has not yet realized that a larger destiny will return him to Egypt for a much more comprehensive spiritual-moral purpose than he could have imagined. His return to Egypt will enable all of Israel to follow in Abraham's footsteps, to obey the Commanding Voice of God calling *"Lekh Lekha!"* Once Moses agrees to return to Egypt as God's human emancipator he will never run away again.

Moses' reverie brings him to a much more focused perception not only of a structured sociomoral ideal that is God. Enraptured by the bush, by its vividly suggestive flames, Moses' imagination has now become alert, charged, and ready. His innermost psychic recesses have never ceased burning with concern for his fellow man in general. But he has now been brought to the threshold of knowing that his most immediate "fellow man" is his fellow Israelite, no matter who the Israelite is — righteous or less than righteous. His love will be universal — in potential. To actualize this universal love, however, he understands now that he must begin with a particularistic focus — a total loving commitment to one people, his newly found Children of Israel.

"Ehyeh asher Ehyeh"

The first part of the Book of Exodus tells a story of another man besides Moses. It describes what it means for this other man to have his human heart hardened. Pharaoh is represented as fighting God in his elemental refusal to *know* Him. Pharaoh refuses to appreciate God's unlimited power. He fails to realize until it is too late the hopelessness of his attempt to dethrone the King of Kings, the true Sovereign of the universe. Unlike Joseph's Pharaoh, this Pharaoh will lack a humane imagination. He will be so possessed with *himself* as an idol, as a perfect, finished product, that he will not be capable of allowing for anything beyond him to enter his perceptual field.

The story of this Pharaoh — on its own — could serve as the plot of a classic tragic drama where the tragic hero — Pharaoh — is doomed from the start by Fate to bring destruction upon his Empire. In the Torah, this "plot" serves as the backdrop for Moses and his story, the story of God and His covenanted people of Israel. Moses — the antithesis of Pharaoh, spiritually, morally, and politically — has looked beyond himself from the day he left the palace in order to involve himself in the just cause of another. As Abram has argued against Nimrod, Moses will argue against Pharaoh. This self-extension of Abram and Moses can be experienced — the Torah will claim — by any human being provided he is not self-idolatrous. Because Pharaoh — like the pristine Serpent in the Garden of Eden — cannot admit that he is only a pitifully mortal creature, he is fated as is his people to drown in the "Yam Suf" or as Israel Eldad has called it: the *"Yam Sof"* (Sea of Extinction).

With Moses, this reaching out of self to others, this going beyond oneself towards others is idealized. And this idealized force has become Moses' alter-ego, the *Malakh-Hashem* preparing him within the flames of the "burning bush" to hear the Voice of God calling "Moshe, Moshe." By now Moses knows who calls and what the purpose of the call is. It is the all-demanding call to Moses to reach as high as a human being can reach in the search for human betterment-on-earth. Moses, the Jew, this utterly and incomparably humane being answers: *"Hineini!"* ("I am ready!")

God announces Himself as *"Ehyeh asher Ehyeh"* — positive affirmative Being. To Israel in slavery Hamlet's question is vividly real: "To be or not to be, that is the question." To live or not to live, that is indeed the question. "Whether 'tis nobler in the mind to suffer the slings and arrows of outrageous fortune, or to take arms against a sea of troubles and by opposing, end them." To opt for a choice of active opposition to the adversary in one's life or to suffer passively what fate appears to have decreed "to die; to sleep; no more...."

The readiness of the slave population — particularly their Elders — to accept their servitude as an unrelieved "given" must be neutralized by the call of the God of Israel thundering forth: *"Ehyeh!"* ("I will be!") — then stressed again — *"asher Ehyeh!"* ("I will be!") The "I will be that I will be..." must and will erase the paralyzing doubt expressed in the question "To be or not to be...." A proclamation has been made that no matter what the "slings and arrows" may bring at any time in the history of a nation, God is eternal and His eternal covenant with Israel bestows upon every member of the House of Israel a spark of eternity and therefore a patent for endurance and a spur to action.

Not only is Israel destined to yearn to cling to God; God announces His own readiness to adopt Israel as His truly firstborn "son." There is a play on the words in the Song of Songs: *"Pithi li Ahoti Ra'ayati, Yonati, Tamati* (Interpret: *Te'omati)"* ("Open to me, my sister, my love, my dove, my twin"). God expresses his empathetic concern for Israel through identifying totally with the pain of the "other," as it is written in Psalm 91: *"Imo anokhi be-tzarah"* ("I am with him/them in their trouble"). The Holy One Blessed Be He says to Moses: "Do you not sense that I am immersed in sorrow just as Israel is; know whence I speak to you, from the thorns. I am a partner in their sorrow."

God shares the suffering; and Man to be a man must likewise share the suffering of his fellow man. Will Moses be up to bearing the burden of a people who will rebel at every turn? Will the people have the moral strength to maintain their loyalty to the covenant through their suffering? Through later eons of "messianic" delay? In Moses' case, he will be called upon to lead the Children of Israel out of bondage to what will be for them an unknown destination. The vision of the Promised Land for Moses — etched into his imagination by God Himself — may be as real as Egypt. But for the Children of Israel who have not had an epiphany, and who, with a slave sensibility, are psychologically and spiritually incapable of exercising the imaginative skills necessary to envision a *real* Promised Land, the march into the unknown will seem at times starker than the enslavement.

Even Moses himself will need reminding, especially at the beginning, that the Exodus has as its goal the entrance into and settlement of the Promised Land. In a mysterious episode recorded briefly in the Torah text Moses forgets to circumcise his sons. His wife Ziporah saves his life by performing *the* ritual act which signifies the covenantal commitment to Eretz Yisrael (see Genesis 17:7-14). In short, all of Israel — including Moses — are to be schooled in the seriousness of the entire "exile to freedom to redemption" enterprise. It is not to be casually attended to. As Moses is to learn again and again, the enterprise demands a total *"akeidah*-like" sacrificial commitment.

A Tragic Pattern for the Ages

The march of Israel into history following the first conquest and settlement of the Land of Israel will continue to be marked by further enslavements, persecutions, expulsions, and even exterminations. Israel will be called upon to believe in a messianic denouement to the suffering. They will yearn for apocalyptic reversals of fortune. They will seek to define nationalism in humane terms, to counteract the pristine definition of Pharaoh who will see nationalism as an imposed uniformity within all aspects of society.

Later generations of the Children of Israel will be forced to learn bitter lessons of realpolitik: that according to the Pharaohs of history, an ethnic or religious minority within a given polity may be productive, and may have shown itself to be loyal to the overall principles and way of life of the majority. The minority, nevertheless, doesn't stop being characterized by the majority as a stranger. And the stranger — given appropriate circumstances — may be ostracized, expunged, eliminated. The idea and policies spawned by Pharaonic nationalism will not drown at the Sea of Reeds. This notion will serve as the foreign and domestic policy of imperial nations in all the world since the Exodus. Every great power in the world will sooner or later seek to mold a society where there are no "strangers," because ultimately every citizen will be expected to lose or at least to accommodate his strange ways in order to assimilate into the majority. In especially lethal terms for historic Jewry — and millions of others — it will be the way with the imperialisms of Greece, Rome, the Medieval Church, Jihad-driven Islam, Nazi Germany, and the Communist Soviet Union.

Judaism will argue that God protects not only the widow and the orphan — but especially the stranger. It will preach equality for the stranger, self-determination for the stranger. It will insist that if every man is to be made like every other man, then Man is in effect worshiping himself. Whether intentionally or not, the Jew will make himself eternally different and in effect will be putting the society in which he chooses to live to the test. The Jew will be asking of any society in which he lives: "Will you respect my human dignity even though I am different?" The answer to the Jew will all too often be the answer of Pharaoh, the answer of Hitler. For the Jew, the answer even offered by democracies will too often be as Ahad Ha'am will describe it: "When our majority population is concerned with humaneness, we shall forget the Jews; and when we are concerned with the Jews, we shall forget humaneness."

Nevertheless, the surviving Jewish remnant will have understood and accepted its marked destiny to be different. For the prayer of the covenant since Abram and Nimrod will have been that Man must learn to live with individual differences, that Man must appreciate that the fact of individual difference is what convinces humankind that they are only *creatures* of God, not God. But in Moses' Egypt this question has now become academic. It is too late for Egypt to serve as a laboratory for human tolerance. Pharaoh with his genocidal machinations has forfeited his future and the future of his people. For Moses and Israel the strategy can only be "Let us go!" Our *"lekh lekha"* must take us to our own sovereignty — out of the incarceration of exile.

Va-Era　　　　　　　　　וארא

It is Moses who more than any other human being dominates the Torah. It is he who more than anyone else creates the people known as the Jewish people; and it is he who more poignantly than anyone else bridges the gap between the demands of a demanding God and the sins of a sinful people. Yet it is ironic that in so many of the rituals associated with holidays, and prayer in particular, Moses receives at best, if at all, a secondary place behind the three patriarchs, Abraham, Isaac, and Jacob. Jews begin the *Amidah* — *the prayer* — with the invocation *"Elohei Avraham, Elohei Yitzhak, vei-Elohei Ya'akov."* Nowhere does the phrase *"Elohei Moshe"* appear! Is Moshe less a hero in the pantheon of Jewish faith-heroes than Abraham, Isaac, and Jacob? Hardly! Yet in at least one aspect of religious experience — prayer — he apparently is!

Where Is the Liturgical God of Moses?

God informs Moses that He revealed Himself to Abraham, Isaac, and Jacob as *El Shaddai*, calling Himself by the more general term "Almighty God." And that only now in response to Moses' demand has He revealed Himself to Moses by His more intimate name of *Adonai*. Moses is presented as one who all along seeks to know more and more about the innermost qualities of God, i.e., *Adonai*, whereas Abraham, Isaac, and Jacob were content to relate to the awesome external attributes of God, i.e., *El Shaddai*. The Midrash explores this subtle difference in religious temperaments: God, as it were, says to Moses: "You don't have the faith — the blind unquestioning faith — which Abraham, Isaac, and Jacob had. I revealed to Abraham, Isaac, and Jacob My Almighty Presence, My concern, and My demands, and they did not question My attributes. They did not insist on knowing more about Me before performing their appointed tasks. They did not look to question Me when problems faced them, when barrenness, for example, seemed to obstruct their efforts. They did not attempt to explore ever more insistently My essence, searching, complaining, doubting."

The Midrash contrasts the faith of Abraham, Isaac, and Jacob with Moses' need to be shown. The Midrash has God saying: "I promised each of the Fathers that the Land would be theirs. Yet Abraham in order to bury his wife Sarah had to *buy* a plot of that Land. Nevertheless he didn't question My long-term agenda. Isaac found no water in the Land, forcing him to dig and maintain wells while confronting persistent problems with security. Yet he never challenged My assurances that the Land would be his eventually, and would prove to be fruitful. Jacob in order to settle the Land had to *buy* land at Shekhem; yet he never balked at having to invest himself and his means in what had been sworn to him as a gift. In short, none of them doubted My promise that all the Land would be theirs. Yet you, Moses, before barely beginning your task have probed Me and My purposes. You wish to know My essence! Granted, following upon your first confrontation with Pharaoh, you — representing Me — failed to improve the lot of your people. In fact, you — representing Me — made it worse for your people. Yet where was your patience, where was your faith? You questioned Me, you doubted Me, you blamed Me for the short-term worsening of Israel's situation."

The Midrash is clearly unfair to Moses. Its bias comes out of its interest in stressing the difference in attitude engendered by long-term faith as opposed to short-term and middle-term agendas for concretizing visions of faith. Abraham, Isaac, and Jacob are identified with dimensions of *emunah* (faith) in long-term processes to be actualized in God's "good time." This redemptive process that God has promised He will undertake requires a loyalty to a long-term covenanted vision which the three patriarchs embody, notwithstanding the reality which each has to face — a reality of conflict and temptation. But in defense of Moses, there is no denying that Moses is burdened heavily and relentlessly with short-term and middle-term responsibilities.

He is charged with leading and teaching a horde of erstwhile slaves who are not ready for the kind of covenanted freedom God has in mind. Such a people need an impassioned, impatient leader like Moses. It is this impatience to see fulfilled what God has promised that makes Moses not only a more effective shepherd of a recalcitrant people but a more effective pleader for this people before Him who has chosen them. God may have chosen these

Children of Israel as His long-term beneficiaries, but they will need to withstand frustration and disappointment at every turn. They will need the ministry of a concerned and committed soul-on-fire like Moses who will pull and push them along through every short-term crisis. The long-term visions of the three patriarchs will be subjects for discourse here and there during the forty-year sojourn in the Wilderness. But Moses will be their leader and teacher in the real-time challenges of day-to-day survival.

Thus the later Jewish worshiper may be seeking in his prayer — in the *Amidah* — the God of the three patriarchs as the God of long-term salvation. But Moses and his Torah will provide the later Jewish people with ongoing day-to-day person-to-person salvational observances and moment-to-moment hope.

Knowing and Not Knowing God

The discouragement following his first meeting with Pharaoh has brought Moses back to God. Moses is baffled and disillusioned. God thereupon reiterates His covenantal promise that the enslavement is coming to an end. As a preamble to His review, God says to Moses: "I appeared to Abraham, Isaac, and Jacob as *El Shaddai*; but *I did not make Myself known* to them by My name *Adonai*." Already quoted above, this phrase "*I did not make Myself known*" — in Hebrew "*lo nodati*" — is explained by M. D. Cassuto. The Hebrew word *nodati* is an odd form of the verb. It relates respectively to the generations of the Patriarchs and to Moses in its emphasis on the difference between long-term "theoretical" faith and short-term and middle-term "actualized" faith. But *nodati*, argues Cassuto, cannot mean "make myself known," for then the word *hodati* should have been used. What then does the form of the verb *ve-nodati* mean? Cassuto explains that in the ancient Middle East it is normal for peoples to attribute to their gods different names for different traits.

Israel similarly tends to use the name *El Shaddai* in association with God's rule over nature and His gift to Man of the capacity to reproduce. God as *El Shaddai* has made Abraham, Isaac, and Jacob fruitful, has blessed them with offspring. With the attribute which is best concretized by the name *Adonai*, however, "*lo nodati lahem*" ("I was not known to them"), that is, "they did not know Me (nor could they know Me at that juncture in our relationship) as

One who will fulfill My long-term promises." The name *Adonai* then is associated with dimensions of God which Moses and the Children of Israel will now witness graphically. They will experience God being with them in "real time." How? They will witness God fulfilling the promises of His covenant!

First, the Children of Israel will experience God's active involvement in their short-term destiny, which is to be taken out of bondage. Their knowledge of God will be an entirely different knowledge than the knowledge associated with faith in some future event, situation, culmination. When God promises Moses and Israel *"Ve-hotzeiti, ve-hitzalti, ve-ga'alti, ve-lakahti, ve-heveiti"* ("I will take you out, I will save you, I will redeem you, I will take you to me, I will bring you into Eretz Yisrael"), the promise is to be fulfilled clearly, decisively, and imminently.

The Children of Israel will learn an additional even more pristine distinction between two types of knowing as they stand on the threshold of "redemption" from slavery. They will learn that there is an essential difference between knowing God conceptually and experiencing His Presence as vividly active in one's life. There is a difference between having an idea of God no matter how vividly imagined and actually experiencing God as a living Force who is "taking me out, saving me, redeeming me, taking me to Him, and bringing me to the Promised Land."

The difference clarifies a statement of Rabbi Akiva in *Pirkei Avot*: "Beloved is the human being who has been created in the image of God; but it is a greater manifestation of love for the human being to *know*, i.e., to vividly experience that he has been created in the image of God. Beloved is Israel who are called the children of God; but it is a greater manifestation of love for Israel to *know*, i.e., to vividly experience that they are called the Children of God."

Rabbi Akiva in the first half of each of his statements is stating his own third-person faith-proposition: (1) that the human being is beloved because he has been created in the image of God; and (2) that Israel is beloved because it is called the Children of God. It is in the second half of each of Akiva's statements that he tries to imagine what the beloved human being and the beloved Israel must feel in the first-person. Here Rabbi Akiva cannot be referring to any kind of conceptual "knowing," but the deeply felt conscious conviction and appreciation of (1) God's loving power in having created the human being and (2) His love for Israel in having chosen this people to serve as His special partner. It is "feeling" with certainty the empathy of God's Presence in human history and in particular His empathetic involvement with Israel's destiny within that history.

At this juncture in the history of Israel, however, its destiny is locked into the uncompromising grasp of Pharaoh. Pharaoh does not "know" Moses' God. He neither knows Him conceptually nor does he feel His Presence experientially. He has chosen not to "know" Joseph, i.e., he has blocked out of his consciousness Joseph's contributions to the welfare of the Empire which he, the Pharaoh of the Exodus, has inherited. This Pharaoh will join the Serpent of the Garden and Nimrod of the Tower in becoming the archetypal rebel against God's double redemptive instruction for humankind: to love God and to love Man. Pharaoh cannot love God, cannot "know" Him, or acknowledge Him. Pharaoh cannot love his fellow Man, cannot "know" a Joseph or a Moses or even his Egyptian subjects. He is foolish and stubborn in refusing to accept his own intellectual and moral limitations. He should consider his authentic human freedom as enough of a blessing to allow him to admit his human limitations; but he cannot or will not. He is trapped or traps himself by his lust for absolute power. He thus sacrifices himself — and his people — to his self-inflicted fate: social, economic, and political decay, disintegration, and destruction.

Pharaoh's predicament is an extension of the predicament of the Serpent of Eden and Nimrod of Babel. Pharaoh, like the Serpent and like Nimrod, represents the result of an arrogant refusal to doubt his own infallibility. The image of hard-heartedness by which Pharaoh is trapped not only won't permit him to see other creatures as human beings instead of slave-objects, it won't permit him to relax his guard, even privately before himself, in order to allow himself the human luxury of self-doubt. He dare not listen to the advice of his chief ministers who warn him that his policy is leading him and his people to ruin. He is certain that any openness to advice on his part will show him to be weak, hesitant, indecisive. Worse, he dare not allow even his own inner voice to dialogue with him. And so, he has in effect truncated his own capacities for addressing his problems with freshness and imagination.

Pharaoh reaches a point where he cannot change even if he might wish to do so. The plagues, one after the other, afflict him and his people; and one after the other, the plagues offer him the opportunity to change policy. But time after time he refuses to do so. God has had good reason to punish

Pharaoh by removing his power to change after his early policy of liquidating the male children of the Israelites. But God waits until Pharaoh won't relent even when his own people are suffering. He then hardens Pharaoh into a petrified stubbornness which itself is an unrelieved punishment. In addition, God will punish the Egyptians as well as their Pharaoh because these Egyptians themselves have been willing accessories to the blind dictatorial obtuseness of their mortal master whom they have helped to deify.

Arthur Koestler's *Darkness at Noon* will give a twentieth-century perspective on how the hard-heartedness of a Pharaoh feeds on the insecurities of weak-willed people around him. Koestler records the success which a latter-day Pharaoh like Stalin was able to achieve precisely because he was the most hard-hearted, the most "secure," the least plagued by doubt within the Soviet communist hierarchy. He could therefore be the most single-minded, and, when necessary, the most ruthless. For in his universe, and the universe of tyrants like him, there was no God above Stalin. Worse, all those around him, because they had normal human doubts, lacked the "courage" and "conviction" born of certainty to stand up to him. They worshiped him in their need for some force beyond themselves to provide them with certainty. The tragedy for them was in not realizing that no mere mortal, not even a Stalin (or a Pharaoh) could provide them with the certainty they longed for. All they succeeded in doing was to place themselves in a position of such idolatrous dependence that a totalitarian trap with no exit was inevitable.

Pharaoh and his subjects reach the "no exit" point in their socio-economic-political existence when their capacity for repentance has been taken from them. They have lost the capacity to entertain any notion of change. Maimonides in his Laws of Repentance will focus on the sinner looking to open himself up to new possibilities. He places into the mouth of the sinner the prayer that it not be too late, that his sins not prevent him from doing *teshuvah* (repentance), that he never lose the will to learn, to know, and to change. Pharaoh has afflicted himself essentially, and, through idolization of himself as an autocrat with absolute infallibility, has closed off any portals of possibility for his people.

And so the Book of Shemot tells the story of slave-objects, the Children of Israel, who get to *know* God and who become free, covenanted human beings because Moses was given the privilege of *knowing* God. It will be Moses who — unlike Pharaoh — will be described as the most humble of men ready for a change of destiny. At the same time the Book of Shemot also tells the story of Pharaoh who refuses to *know* God, and, in his arrogance will condemn himself and his people, therefore, to spiritless, stony immutability.

"Shortness of Breath"

The destiny of Israel — contrasted with that of Pharaoh's Egypt — should not be perceived as being simply and easily fulfilled. Perhaps the Egyptian side of the parallel study of ancient national destinies as seen by the Bible has a certain uncomplicated inevitability about it. The Israelite side, however, has many vacillations including most prominently episodes where the hard-heartedness or stiff-neckedness of Israel is almost as reprehensible in God's and Moses' eyes as that of Egypt. The tragedy of the Egyptian masses is that within their tyrannical autocracy they barely have a choice to make on any issue of vital concern to them. The Israelite masses, on the other hand, are often all too eager to exploit their newly granted power to choose by breaking what they see as Moses' unifying yoke from over their minds and bodies in order to give sway to their fickle and volatile spirit.

Not that the doubts and the hesitations of the Children of Israel cannot be understood! A leader — Moses — who is to them a stranger has appeared with grandiose predictions and promises. In his first foray into the oppressor's court, he has failed utterly and miserably. And the misery for the people is not abstract; it is real and immediate. They must now provide their own material for the filling of their brick quotas. What kind of mockery has brought them to believe in this pretender, in this clown of a redeemer! And this redeemer himself continues to manifest before God his own insecurity. "I am of impeded speech," pleads Moses before being sent back by God to try again.

And so the "jester-prophet" returns to the slaves with a particularly majestic message. In later Jewish history, the descendants of these enslaved Israelites will celebrate the pulsating percussive ring of the message over four or five cups of wine. Indeed, God will perform all these acts: "*Ve-hotzeiti, ve-hitzalti, ve-ga'alti, ve-lakahti, ve-heveiti!*" But *now* after Moses' colossal first failure, the Israelites are not ready to listen. The reason given is not just the burden of their severe labor but *mi-kotzer ru'ah* (shortness of breath).

What is meant by *kotzer ru'ah*? Rashi gives the simple *peshat* interpretation:

an asthmatic shortness of breath magnified when one is under severe physical stress. Deep breathing requires the security of steady relaxed attention to what one is doing. Under the conditions of hard, unrelieved, thankless, servile work, any pause for even minimal physical relief will be met with the lash of the overseer or the sword of the executioner. To be attentive to a redemptive message, one must already have had enough "relaxed" moments for contemplation, reflection, for daydreaming about alternatives.

An erstwhile slave who doesn't appreciate the gift of freedom is described as plagued by a "slave-mentality." Rashi's interpretation suggests an even more basic state which would blunt a slave's sensibility to promises of alternatives to his existential-physical condition. A slave's reality is a particular state that should properly be called a "slave-physicality." To be in such a state is to be chained to the moment-to-moment fight to retain enough physical wherewithal to be able to continue to breathe for another moment, to haul and to lift again and yet again, without respite. Only the physically ill can fully comprehend the existential reality of the slave's "shortness of breath" according to Rashi.

The Ramban moves up one level from Rashi's pre-occupation with the slave's most primitive physical needs to a generalized fear associated with the slave's total psycho-physical situation. The slave according to the Ramban is not only physically beaten down; he is psychologically broken in his labor; it demeans him, it denies him any dimension of dignity. His soul is in pain and his spirit full of woe. Rashi's slave is instinctively afraid of injury, pain, and death as an animal would run from danger. Ramban's slave — because he sees somewhat beyond the next creaturely breath — is in even greater spiritual and psychological disarray. He is fully aware of what his slave condition has brought him to as a human being. Because he has enough creaturely breath to know what an alternative to his condition could be, his emotional pain and sorrow are greater. His *kotzer ru'ah* vis-à-vis the renewed appearance of the prophet — after Moses' initial failure — is an uncontrollable traumatic fear of arousing himself again to believe that his situation can find relief. Can he afford the emotional price to believe again when his "slave-mentality" is not irrational but only too rational in his understanding that Moses' task is overwhelming, if not impossible? Why should he believe?

Ibn Ezra moves to the sociopolitical plane in his understanding of *kotzer ru'ah*. He interprets *kotzer ru'ah* as the inevitable corollary to the *galut* (exile) situation. Others will refer to the particular "*galut*-mentality" which will plague the collective Jewish psyche for many generations following the two major destructions of Jewish sovereignty over Eretz Yisrael. What is the "*galut*-mentality" in Ibn Ezra's sense? The *kotzer ru'ah* is a short-circuiting of "spirit" in that Moses' message of freedom associated with an entirely different, moral, social, and political reality is too much for the enslaved community in Egypt to comprehend, let alone absorb. This community can only be "short-sighted" spiritually and imaginatively. It is too downtrodden to think of itself in sufficiently aristocratic terms to imagine a situation of sovereignty.

Here the emphasis is not on the low-level status of the slave, physically and psychologically speaking, as Rashi and Ramban have chosen to emphasize. There is an assumption with Ibn Ezra (associating it with his medieval reality) that there is a formal organized community. There are, after all, elders. But just as the elders have abandoned Moses on the threshold of his first audience with Pharaoh, the people at large cannot be expected to have the moral strength and political sagacity required for what Moses is asking. It is not just the physical labor which drags them down. It is the dependent status which characterizes *galut*, the vulnerability of a disenfranchised alien group that paralyzes the Children of Israel who have forgotten that Jacob-Israel also had to wrestle — but that in the end he prevailed!

Finally, basing itself on the principle that "*ein mukdam u-me'uhar ba-Torah*," ("there's no chronology where Torah is concerned"), that is, even though, historically speaking, the events in Egypt are pre-Sinaitic, the *Or Hahayyim* commentary argues: "Because they were not students of Torah, they did not listen and could not be receptive to Moses' message. This is the meaning of '*kotzer ru'ah*' because the Torah broadens the heart of Man." If, in other words, the *galut* bespeaks an intrinsic sociocultural-political timidity, the *Or Hahayyim* blames the Jewish community in Egypt for a narrowness of vision, a moral-intellectual limitedness of perspective which a fundamental understanding of Torah would have long rectified. Instead, as the *Yalkut Shimoni* claims, they were idolaters and preferred remaining tied to their idolatrous ways.

The slave mentality pictured by Ibn Ezra and the *Or Hahayyim* and the idolatrous mentality pictured by the *Yalkut Shimoni* have in common that the Israelites will search for truth to a certain superficial depth but no further. They have not matured to a level of patience and passion sufficient to drive beyond the shallow to a new point of departure in thinking and in acting. The slave wants simple solutions. The idolater cannot live with paradoxes. Moses appears before the Children of Israel in the name of a Force called *"Ehyeh-Adonai"* whom no one can see and yet who promises that He will activate a sociopolitical revolution. This *Ehyeh-Adonai* promises that He will destroy an oppressive regime and that He will hurl an entire slave people into an entirely unprecedented situation — socially, morally, politically, economically, spiritually. How can Israel's current servile and idolatrous mentality digest such an agenda!

The Historic Neurosis of Israel

The *kotzer ru'ah* of the Children of Israel will "mature" later into a stiff-neckedness which will compete for insolence in God's eyes with the hard-heartedness of Pharaoh. Except that God will feel Himself bound by the *zekhut avot* (the merit of the Patriarchs), i.e., the covenant, and so will not reject Israel whereas ancient Egypt will be doomed to destruction.

The focus simultaneously on the hard-heartedness of the Children of Israel along with the hard-heartedness of Pharaoh is underscored in an insight of Israel Eldad who laments that the Bible never puts into the collective mouth of the slaves the plea to be redeemed from Egypt. Their only concern is to have the burden of labor lightened. Similarly there is not one word of support and encouragement on the part of the slaves for Moses and his efforts. Therefore God must increase the pressure on Pharaoh — and on Israel — by hardening Pharaoh's will in his cruelty to the slaves. Only escalating cruelty will bring Israel to so sufficient a level of desperation as to be ready for emancipation. As such the nation will be redeemed despite itself and Pharaoh will be the instrument.

This harsh critique of the enslaved generation summarized in the brutal comment that they themselves didn't seek redemption will be echoed by commentators throughout the centuries of repeated exile living. The modern Israeli novelist A. B. Yehoshua will describe Israel's reluctance to be redeemed as a neurosis: "Our people detest *galut* and dream of Eretz Yisrael. Our people negate exile in every phase of our authentic spiritual experience. At the very same time, every historical sequence of the last two thousand years and even before, consisted of but one aspiration, how to survive within *galut* and how to ensure the continued existence of this despised condition. If we had a friend who detested his fiancée and continually suffered because of her, yet continually resisted a breakup, would we not be obliged to consider him a neurotic!"

It is a devastating critique — perhaps unfair to the beleaguered and bedeviled generation of the Egyptian enslavement. Nevertheless the critique will explode millennia later when the exile will truly become intolerable, when the ancient Pharaoh's genocidal program will be advanced with exponential devastation by Hitler. But in the meantime the critique has its origins in the ancient Egyptian experience: Israel isn't zealous about redemption, does not approve of Moses, but will be redeemed anyway as a result of the merit of the Fathers and the wickedness of Pharaoh. Moral history and God's vision of a national-moral covenant with the Children of Israel are dictating a process and a destiny that override any Israelite/Jewish hesitation or reluctance to go beyond perceived capacities.

The modern post-Emancipation supportive analysis of Jewish Diaspora history will be animating the critique of thinkers such as Eldad and Yehoshua. The critique will have energized the modern Zionist movement and its radical negators of the Diaspora. It will see Diaspora Jews living in that part of Europe which has experienced emancipation frightened by radical Zionist messages which ask a comfortable and complacent community for too much. These Diaspora communities will prefer stifling those radical voices in favor of their own sundry plans for attainable programs and projects. The aim will be to build communities and institutions for Jewish survival — in Diaspora. The moderate negators of Diaspora like Ahad Ha'am will understand that stable Jewish communities unthreatened by virulent anti-Semitism will need a lengthy educational process in order to be brought to the threshold of *lekh-lekha*. The extreme negators of Diaspora like Pinsker and Klatzkin will see no other way but a radical cure for the "neurosis," i.e., an immediate end to *galut*! There can be no moderate solution, the extreme negators warn; the fires that are already burning will not be consumed until the anti-Semites actualize their "final solution"!

The bitterest irony of all in the modern saga of Jewry seeking emancipation within a European Diaspora setting will be that individual Jews way beyond per-capita percentages will be in the forefront of all liberal, socialist, and revolutionary efforts. Together with their non-Jewish compatriots they will be aiming to overthrow peacefully or otherwise autocratic systems of government. Yet all these efforts will be mounted for universal sociopolitical causes. Not that Jews as individuals will not benefit from the hoped-for success of these efforts! But Jews with parliamentary influence — direct or indirect — will for the most part be submerging any parochial Jewish interests motivating their campaigns.

The modern Jewish experience in nineteenth- and twentieth-century Germany will be the most ironic, the most bitter, the most tragic of all. Once the European Emancipation will be in full force in Germany, energized by the revolutions of 1830 and 1848, Jewish liberals in the German Reichstag will fight for the betterment of human rights in Germany as a whole. Later in the first quarter of the twentieth century, with the madness of World War I engulfing all of Europe and beyond, it will be Jews like Walter Rathenau who, among many other German Jews on the political and industrial scene, will organize the strategy for insuring access to raw materials and building an economic framework for conducting the war. Jewish socialists will have joined the liberals in reaching positions of political influence, lending further credence to the optimistic hopes of Jews to integrate/assimilate into their beloved Germany as well as into the rest of "enlightened" Europe. Following the German defeat in World War I, German Jews will achieve full civic emancipation and equality in the idealistic years of the Weimar Republic. The victory over German and European anti-Semitism, however, will be short-lived.

Melodramatic portents of what will follow for German Jews and European Jewry as a whole by the middle of the twentieth century will be the murders after the war by German nationalists of Jewish political personalities as different on the political spectrum as the socialist Kurt Eisner, the revolutionary Rosa Luxemburg, and the aforementioned Rathenau who had become German foreign minister. These extreme acts will only dramatize what the radical negators of Diaspora had been predicting — that with all the civic and humanitarian gains of the emancipation, anti-Semitism had never been eradicated in modern post-Emancipation Germany (and Europe, for that matter). At any pretext it would cast its poisonous clouds over any hopes European Jewry had for a lustrous future.

Eastern Europe in the modern era will present its own blood-drenched irony where Jewish collective fate is concerned. One literary example will suffice to illustrate the tragedy: In one of Tchernichowsky's narrative poems,

Resele will fight the good fight on behalf of the enslaved masses in Czarist Russia. Her "reward" will be imprisonment for the "cause." She will represent in her incarceration the tragic collective fate — and despair of a latter-day generation of the descendants of Moses. These latter-day revolutionaries will be seeking to arouse the masses of disenfranchised non-Jews and Jews to overthrow the traditional effete and oppressive authority. The Czarist oppressor will fall — only to be replaced by a Communist totalitarianism as cruel and as relentless as Pharaoh's. The particular Jewish irony will see these Jewish revolutionaries ready for universal revolution, ready for redemption from physical servitude at any price — while surrendering any thoughts, let alone actions, aimed at fulfilling a particularistic Jewish destiny.

Before World War II could anyone imagine a Holocaust for the Jewish people? There would be radical Zionists who had been predicting "fires" in Europe with a magnitude beyond "traditional" pogroms. There had also been the ancient satanic precedent of Pharaoh's genocidal program. But Ahad Ha'am's essay *"Avdut be-tokh Herut"* ("Slavery within Freedom") would summarize the irony underscoring the emancipation of the modern Jew in Diaspora — certainly in the case of the European experience. Jews would lust after physical emancipation at the risk of spiritual enslavement within that emancipated condition. Ironically, they would be suffering through a plague of darkness, the worst kind of darkness imaginable; for it would have appeared so bright with promise. No, Jews in post-Emancipation Europe could not imagine a Shoah. They were blinded by the brightness of their illusions.

In ancient Egypt the enslaved Israelites have no such illusions. They may not be prepared by themselves to initiate a revolution. Their "shortness of breath" requires an outer force to propel them into the struggle for political freedom. This outer force, the God of Israel — though unseen — is assuredly not an illusion. The God of Israel "neither slumbers nor sleeps." He has promised. The fulfillment of that promise is at hand.

Bo　　　　　　　　　　　　בא

The ninth plague, *hoshekh* (darkness), which God brings upon Egypt is so all encompassing that it "can be touched." The text continues: "People could not see one another, and for three days no one could get up from where he was; *but all the Israelites enjoyed light in their dwellings.*" At the same time, according to rabbinic tradition, it is the only plague among the ten in which some Israelites suffered too. The Midrash has it that those Israelites who opposed the plan of the "Exodus" were slain during the three-day plague of darkness so that the Egyptians would not see this Israelite "disgrace."

In the eyes of God it was indeed a disgrace. For by this time it should have been clear to Israel as it was to Pharaoh's advisors and most of the Egyptian people that an overwhelming force was bringing Egypt to heel on behalf of the Israelites. Still, there were Israelites who persisted in their blindness. As a corollary to the continued punishment of the Egyptians, therefore, the plague of a generalized blindness or darkness would punish these Israelite recalcitrants as well.

The Midrash asks the question: "Whence came such a darkness?" Rabbi Yehudah says that it came from above as quoted in Psalms 18:12: "He made darkness His screen: dark thunderbolts, dense clouds of the sky were His pavilion round about Him." Rabbi Nehemiah, as opposed to Rabbi Yehudah, says that the darkness came from below as quoted in Job 10:22: "A land whose light is darkness, all gloom and disarray." Rabbi Yehudah sees God's redemptive spirit as manifesting its destructive power over Egypt's destiny as it redeems the enslaved Israel. Rabbi Yehudah's view reflects the theocentric concern and hope that the blessing of authentic "light" for Israel will emerge out of the "darkness." Rabbi Nehemiah's view, on the other hand, leans to the anthropocentric as a causal explanation for the darkness with a horrific Kafkaesque description of hell — a society where its "very light" is "darkness."

Night and Day

Rabbi Nehemiah's use of the verse from Job — "a land whose light is darkness, all gloom and disarray" — echoes a truth that pervades the biblical view of history from Nimrod onwards. The generations past and future will have experienced many attempts to build splendiferous cultures, enlightened empires, which sooner or later will turn the sunny expectations of their supporters into utter darkness, a hellish darkness. Egypt serves as the archetypal example of a world power which in its period of glory casts a rich cultural effulgence throughout the ancient Near East. Yet it declines, deteriorates, and degenerates into a massive political and cultural prison not only for its slave populations but ultimately for its own citizens — including the royal house. Throughout later Jewish history there will be a variety of imperial giants that will present themselves as fulfillments of the most optimistic dreams of humanity-on-earth. International religious movements such as Christianity and Islam and revolutionary political movements such as Fascism and Communism will all promise a new light for humankind only to bring disappointment, frustration, and worse — fires of destruction, wholesale shedding of blood, immeasurable suffering, and darkness!

The deceptive darkness characterizing much of the history of the nations as experienced by a beleaguered Jewish people will inspire in Jewish tradition a strange phenomenological imagery. The concept *layla* (night) usually associated with *hoshekh* — naturally and phenomenologically — will contain within itself for the Children of Israel a positive assurance that will awaken expectations of redemption. Not that the Jewish tradition doesn't recognize the usual association of "night" with "darkness"! There is the *Havdalah* prayer separating the Shabbat from the coming weekdays: "Who separates between the holy and profane, between light and darkness...." There are other examples in the liturgy, e.g., "May God have mercy on them and take them out from misfortune to relief, from darkness to light, from enslavement to redemption, etc."

But precisely on the holy day which will commemorate the Exodus from Egypt and the celebration of national liberation — *Pesah* — it will be "night" which will signify the redemption, as it is written, *"Va-yehi ba-hatzi ha-layla"* ("and it was at about midnight"). The *Haggadah* of *Pesah* will recall the redemptive study of the five sages at Bnei Brak all night long until they are interrupted by students calling their attention to the threat which daybreak with its morning light portends. For these sages — rebels against Rome which for them is the latter-day Egypt — fear the light of day. They fear discovery.

In short, for the Jews there will be nights that notwithstanding their natural condition of darkness promise spiritual and sociomoral *light*. And there will be brightnesses that in truth mask a murkiness in sociopolitical relationships, a clouding of the human spirit, not to mention sheer physical oppressiveness that cripples and blackens all hope for human betterment.

The traditional *Pesah Seder* will focus on the questions to be asked by the youngest child: *"Ma nishtanah* ha-layla ha-zeh mi-kol ha-leilot" ("How is this *night* different from all other nights")? In essence what is being asked is "How is this *people* different from all other *peoples*?" Is this people ready to call "night" the false "Egyptian day"? Is this people ready to demand a truly new "day" from the hopeless gloom of whichever contemporary "Egypt" is oppressing the Children of Israel? Near the end of the *Seder* a poem will be recited reminding everyone of the prophet Zechariah's vision of a coming day *"asher hu lo yom ve-lo layla"* ("which will be neither day nor night"). This vision will inspire an echo in a much later description by Rabbi A.I. Kook who will see his pre-Messianic age as one in which *"or ve-hoshekh me-shamshin be-irbuviah"* ("light and darkness are intermixed"). In other words, the true hell of human political existence is when one cannot distinguish between social and cultural "night" and "day," between "darkness" and "light."

When the text says, "but all the Israelites enjoyed light in their dwellings," it is referring to a special "light" — the primordial light of God's creation, that light which at God's first words *"yehi or"* ("let there be light") sparked the creation of the world. Much has happened since that original *"yehi or"* that has plunged the world, including the Children of Israel, into an unrelieved darkness. But now Israel is to be redeemed. Is Israel ready, is it alert to the signals of redemption? Will it be ready in the future for such signals?

In the Jerusalem Talmud tractate *Ta'anit* there is a dialogue imagined between Isaiah the prophet and the Jewish people who are in exile. In this dialogue the view of "night" is the normal phenomenological view associated with apprehension, anxiety, fear. It is a dialogue which emerges out of a mysterious passage in the Book of Isaiah: "A voice calls to me from the wilderness saying: 'Watchman, what of the night?' The watchman replies: 'Morning has come and so has night; if you would inquire, inquire; respond and come!'" In the Jerusalem Talmud this mysterious Hebrew-Aramaic passage from the Book of Isaiah serves as the basis for an interchange in which Isaiah says to Israel: "My God calls from the wilderness, saying 'Watchman, what of the night?'" Israel says to Isaiah: "What is coming towards us out of this night?" Isaiah says to Israel: "Wait for me to find out." After asking God, Isaiah returns to Israel and Israel asks: "What did the Watchman say?" Isaiah answers: "The Watchman has said, 'Morning is coming and also night.'"

Israel finds the last response to be ominous and reacts with fright, "Another night is coming!" Here, the images have indeed reverted to their natural phenomenological representations. The morning represents redemption, but night represents another exile, and the Jewish people upon being informed by their prophet Isaiah that morning — redemption — is coming, but also night, protest: "Another exile, another persecution!" But Isaiah says: "Not as you think — but morning is coming for the righteous and night for the wicked; morning for Israel and night for the idolaters. When? Respond and come!"

There is no doubt that on the basis of the passage Israel wants redemption. They seem to be starving for it; they're longing to know when it is coming! But Isaiah responds to this "agonized" yearning by pulling the rhetorical rug out from under their obsessive curiosity as if to say to them, "You want to know when the redemption is coming? You asked me to ask God? God says, 'Don't ask me, it's up to you, My Children of Israel, to give the response; you decide!'" The original redemption from Egypt will have come on a night of *leil shimurim* (a night of watchfulness), that is, a night on which the *Shomer Yisrael* (the Watchman of Israel) will have fulfilled His promise. But the Children of Israel will themselves have to be ready to participate in the "watch." They will have to be ready themselves to respond, to react. Similarly, in later Jewish history, Israel themselves will have to be on guard, to be ready to advance their own redemptive agenda.

This talmudic passage from *Ta'anit* reflects the period shortly after the destruction of the Second Commonwealth and the resulting Second Exile. It is based on a mysterious piece of imagery of the prophet Isaiah written about the destruction of the First Commonwealth and the resulting First Exile. It reflects a people who are down, battered, defeated, crying out to be helped, to be redeemed by their Creator, Revealer, and *Redeemer*. And what does God through His prophet say to them — in any generation, at any time, present and future? You want redemption, you want the morning sun, *not* the night, then seize the day! Respond yourselves fully to your intolerable situation and seize the day!

Ritual Weapons against Idolatry

The collective hesitation in the face of the opportunity for national emancipation will thus be traced back to Egypt and the midrashic note on the Israelite casualties during the plague of darkness. It will continue through the periods following the destruction of both Temples and will become as A.B. Yehoshua will diagnose it: the great neurosis plaguing Jewish history, the neurosis nourished by *galut*. In prayer as in philosophic concern the question will be: Is the darkness of *galut* to be endured until the Messiah comes? Or is it a darkness to be actively rejected by the Children of Israel themselves in pursuit of the Promised Land?

Following the destruction of the Second Temple and the onset of the long exile, the spiritual leadership of world Jewry will be forced by circumstances into cultivating an ideational strategy for dealing with the reality of this exile, with the darkness of it. In Rambam's *Mishne Torah*, the Laws of Talmud Torah 3:3 there is an odd *halakhah* (rabbinic law): "Even though it is a *mitzvah* to study day and night, a man doesn't achieve his chiefest wisdom except at night. Therefore, he who wishes to earn the crown of Torah should be careful not to waste even one night in eating, drinking, and casual conversation, but should rather study Torah and words of wisdom. The Sages have said that there is no song of Torah except at night, as it is said, 'Arise and sing at night.'"

The Rambam goes on to quote the talmudic source from which he has formulated the *halakhah*. In *Avodah Zarah* 3b Resh Lakish says: "To him who is engaged in the study of the Torah by night, the Holy One extends a thread of grace by day, as it is said, 'By day the Lord will command His lovingkindness, and in the night His song shall be with me (Psalms 42:9)!' For what reason will the Lord command His lovingkindness by day? Because His song shall be with me in the night. Some report the exposition of Resh Lakish thus: To him who is engaged in the study of the Torah in this world, which is likened unto the night, the Holy One, blessed be He, extends the thread of grace in the future world, which is likened unto the day...."

Resh Lakish's comparison of this world to the night sheds light on the thrust of Rambam's formulation. Surely the Rambam is not limiting his concern for the phenomenon of "night" to the normal feelings of anxiety which most people have at night. Based on Resh Lakish's comment in the Talmud, "night" for the Rambam suggests a whole complex of spiritual, moral, and historical associations which frighten the Jew even more than the empirical reality of darkness. This non-empirical complex of associations with "night" reflects the collective experience of the Jewish people connected to and following religious, national, and moral *hurban* or catastrophe. In the case of the rabbinic-talmudic period we are referring to the destruction of the Second Jewish Commonwealth in Eretz Yisrael.

The study of Torah as the overriding *mitzvah*, the *mitzvah* which is to be considered *ke-neged kulam* (equal to all the other *mitzvot* combined), will have to sustain a Jewish community-in-exile for an indefinite period. It will serve as *the* spiritual resource binding the Children of Israel to the God of Israel through whatever afflictions and idolatrous temptations they will face. But the study of Torah will not be restricted to a mere spiritual binding. It will keep alive the memory of Egypt and the *physical* Exodus from Egypt. It will inspire Israel to push themselves constantly towards the threshold of a new redemption. Remembering the Exodus from Egypt will become a central theme in Jewish liturgy. But again, like the study of Torah, the experience of prayer will not be intended "merely" as a spiritual binding with the Transcendent One. It will remind the worshiper of the proto-exile experience of Israel in Egypt and the destiny of Israel to be redeemed from exile in order to again achieve sovereignty in the Promised Land.

In other words, the study of Torah and the regimen of prayer — as regularly ordered rituals — will serve as a spur to dreaming and working towards physical redemption, no matter how long it will take. To say that all Jews who studied and prayed while in *galut* were thinking in terms of physical, i.e., political redemption, would be patently incorrect. The precedent of ancient Egypt would be a less than optimistic reminder of the Israelite/Jewish ambivalence towards *galut* and sovereignty. Jews-in-exile through the ages would be reminded by the Midrash that there were Israelites in Egypt who were "criminal" in their serving of Egyptian patrons who in turn helped them achieve wealth and honor. These Israelites in no way wished to leave Egypt. It was they who yearned for "the fish of Egypt...for the cucumbers and melons and leeks and onions and garlic" once they were subjected to the meager diet of the Wilderness. Like blind locusts, in their own darkness, unable to see beyond satisfying their immediate appetites, these Israelites were not ready for the symbolically limited fare of redemption — *matzah* (unleavened wafers), *maror* (bitter herbs), and the *Pesah* (the paschal lamb), the latter especially offered up boldly in the eyes of the Egyptians.

The study of Torah and the regimen of prayer as pedagogic tools for remembering the spiritual, sociomoral, *and political* terms of the covenant would be reinforced by other rituals — none more vivid than those associated with the *Seder* of *Pesah* itself: the aforementioned *matzah, maror,* and the *korban-Pesah*. Jews through the ages would be asked to recall purposefully the slaughtering of the lamb in Egypt.

In the Midrash God instructs Moses on the slaughtering of the lamb and Moses protests: "How can we dare to slaughter publicly the gods of Egypt?" The Lord replies: "Precisely! Israel will not leave their condition of slavery until they've indeed destroyed the idols of Egypt before their very eyes. Thus all — the Egyptians and the Israelites — will learn of the vanity of idolatry." The blood of the paschal lamb on the doorposts of the Israelites' homes would thus not be interpreted simply as put there in order to ward off demons. It was meant to serve as a combination of three provocative acts ridiculing Egyptian idolatry: setting aside a lamb for sacrifice in public; actually slaughtering it; and then publicizing the entire procedure without fear. This entire ritual would not just give the Israelites mystical protection; it would be a manifestation of devotion to the one true God and national courage in the face of their erstwhile "human" lords and masters.

This example of the blood on the doorpost, representing an integrated purpose of praying for protection by the Almighty on the one hand while joining it to the very down-to-earth purpose of reflecting before enemies the courage of independence, will become the model for the major ritual observances of classical Jewish *halakhah*. The *mezuzah* (doorpost), identifying a household as Jewish from the Egyptian experience onwards, will no longer have the blood of the paschal lamb on it. Instead it will hold a piece of parchment. The outer side of the parchment will have one of God's names, Shaddai, written on it — interpreted as initials spelling out *"Shomer Delatot Yisrael"* ("God as Protector of the Doors of Israel"). But the *mezuzah* according to the biblical passages on the inner side of the parchment will also proclaim to the surrounding environment that the gods of idolaters are vanity, nullities. For only God is One and Unique and the People of Israel are free and independent witnesses to His Oneness and Uniqueness.

The Children of Israel will discover and rediscover throughout their history that the world about them is hungry for gods; and that among the greatest virtues of the Jew as a witness to the One True God of humankind is to be an iconoclast. But how? Not as philosophically sophisticated but marginal uncommitted skeptics! On the contrary, the Jew is mandated to serve as witness to God's Presence with religious acts, gestures, symbols, modes of behavior in every walk of life that reflect spiritual and ethical pride as well as iconoclastic defiance when necessary. The Jewish people will assume a historic role that will at times require them to sacrifice their very beings in order to maintain rituals connected, for example, to Shabbat observance or dietary laws or modes of worship — all in the name of sanctifying God's covenant while rejecting sundry idolatries. The Jewish rationale to themselves, to enemies, and to curious spectators will be that to lose the ability to say "no" to a faceless mob led by an autocratic self-proclaimed demi-god — whoever the demi-god may be and whoever the mob may be — is to lose not only one's national identity but one's humanity, thereby denying the true God.

Pesah, Tefillin, and the Zionist Dream

The collective "coming-of-age" of the People of Israel with their liberation as a nation from the chains of Egypt will be recognized moment-to-moment, day-by-day, with a regimen of *mitzvot* (commandments to be performed) that will become the encapsulations of group memory, spiritual devotion, and national self-annunciation. Turning all behavioral patterns into *mitzvot* will raise the mundane acts of human survival, expressiveness, and social utility to transcendent spiritual and moral significance. And all the *mitzvot* together will remind Israel and the non-Jewish world that may be watching that the Jewish people is independent as a nation and loyal to its covenant with God.

Rashi will begin his classic commentary on the Torah by quoting a certain Rabbi Isaac who will have said: "It was not necessary to begin the Torah whose main object is to teach *mitzvot* with the account of the creation of the world. It could have begun with the religious instructions of chapter 12 of the Book of Exodus, the first *mitzvah* given to collective Israel." Why then, Rashi asks, did the Almighty begin with Genesis? To show the power of His works, for if the nations of the world should say to Israel: "You have seized the land of Canaan," then Israel may respond: "The entire world belongs to the Holy One, blessed be He. He created it — Canaan — and gave it to whomever it was right to give it in His eyes." Rabbi Isaac's allusion to the first collective *mitzvah* in chapter 12 of the Book of Exodus, however, bears closer scrutiny. It is the *mitzvah* of keeping *Pesah*. Indeed, in Rabbi Isaac's view, all of Genesis and the first eleven chapters of Exodus are to be considered an introduction to that first collective *mitzvah* of *Pesah*.

But it is shortsighted to interpret Rabbi Isaac's comment as less "Zionistically" motivated than Rashi's. For Rabbi Isaac has in mind at least two pedagogic goals with nationalistic implications: first, he seeks to argue as does Yehudah Halevi in his *Kuzari* that the Ten Commandments purposely begin with an identification of God as the redeemer of Israel from bondage rather than as creator of the Universe — so as to underscore the critical covenantal relationship between God and His people Israel. Secondly, Rabbi Isaac hopes to memorialize the event of the Exodus on daily, weekly, monthly, and annually observed occasions. Certainly at the annual *Seder*, not to mention regular monthly, weekly, and daily liturgical reminders of the Exodus! What Rabbi Isaac is suggesting is that *Pesah* is to pervade and condition the consciousness of the Jew every day.

The *mitzvah* of *tefillin* will be another powerful example of the importance of daily memorials to seminal events in the living history of Israel. The Ramban explains the purpose of *tefillin*: "that you should inscribe on your arm and between your eyes the Exodus so as to remember it always; and so that God's Torah shall be felt as your responsibility to keep because it is God who has redeemed you from bondage." The *tefillin* as a symbol will encompass the reality of freedom from slavery and the observance of God's commandments. It will be the covenantal reminder of the double love which God intends as a goal for all humankind — the two commanded "*ve-ahavtas*" of the Torah! The *Seder* may be perceived as expressing the same double idea; but the *tefillin* will be more vivid because they are to be worn every day — and if they are not worn on the Shabbat and the Holy Days it is only because these days in turn exemplify the reality of freedom from slavery and the observance of God's *mitzvot*.

Abraham Joshua Heschel will describe symbols as "substitutes cherished whenever the object we are interested in is momentarily or permanently beyond our reach." The *tefillin* as such a symbol will become the badge of the Jew no matter what his situation — or his predicament.

A vivid characterization of what the *tefillin* will represent to the Jew in the face of his enemies will be brought out in Bernard Malamud's *The Fixer*. Yakov Bok is a Jew who is not only non-religious but whatever flirtation he may rarely have with higher thought is through the spectacles of his reading of Spinoza. He goes out of his way to remain non-political in the sunless world of Czarist Russia between two revolutions. He is a person who is uncommitted to any cause, to any ideal, to any vision of human betterment. And yet once he is falsely accused of a crime — the arch-crime of the absurd blood libel traditionally associated by anti-Semites with *Pesah*, and he is arrested, imprisoned, and tortured for being a Jew, he gradually *becomes* a Jew. He hasn't known about *tefillin* but at a climactic point in the attempts of the police, the chief prosecutor, and the religious inquisitors to break him and to convert him to their "true" faith, he dons *tefillin* proudly, arrogantly, defiantly. He will now become committed; he will now become political; he will now become "religious"!

Yakov Bok will represent the Jew who stands in the twilight between light and darkness. He is the Jew who against his will is thrust into a situation where dark, irrational forces are pitted against him forcing him to dig deeply into himself in order to rediscover the tiniest ember of Jewish self-awareness. And in the darkest darkness before the dawn he joins himself to Israel in Egypt at *ke-hatzi ha-layla* (at about midnight), getting himself ready to exit from bondage. He has begun to hear a Voice, the Voice that will speak to all of Israel at Sinai. It is an overwhelmingly powerful Voice which every individual at Sinai will be graced to hear according to his own individual capacity — the old, the young, the strong, the weak, the wise, the ignorant. But it is a Voice which will dwarf the imprisoning reality of Egypt — and Czarist and Soviet Russia — as it opens up vistas of possibility for the slave who is to be freed and for the nation which is to be born.

Children's Questions

God has announced earlier that Israel is His son — *"beni bekhori"* ("My first-born son"). The theology of anti-pagan ethical monotheism won't allow for this phrase to be interpreted literally. It can only reflect an attitude towards the primacy of the covenant which doesn't preclude God considering all the nations His children and as His children to be brought into the covenant eventually. But as God's firstborn who has been treated by Pharaoh as dispensable refuse, to be worked to death and then incinerated, Israel must be raised to its proper station as "princely child" of the true Sovereign of the world. And Israel will be raised as God's firstborn even as Pharaoh will learn directly through the bitterest irony what it means to lose a firstborn son and to be the hard-hearted instrument for the demise of all of Egypt's firstborn. The tenth plague will indeed be the severest — and most painfully appropriate — short of the final "plague," i.e., utter extinction at the Sea of Reeds.

Moses has made clear to Pharaoh how important children are to Israel. To Pharaoh's desperate petition that Moses take his adult population off for the three-day holy day in the desert which Moses had originally requested, the Israelite leader now replies: *"Bi-ne'areinu u-vi-zkeneinu nelekh"* ("We will go with our adults *and* our children"). Once Moses admits that the adults are intending to take their children with them, Pharaoh knows that the Israelites have no plans to return to Egypt. For the Israelites as well as for the descendants of these Israelites, their children represent their prayer, their hope, their future.

The Rabbis will not be naïve about the loyalty to the covenant of these and future Children of Israel. They will extrapolate from various questions put forward in this portion a number of archetypes. It will be a heretical son who will ask: "What is this worship to you, my elders?" implying that for him it is meaningless. There will be a son who will be so utterly uninvolved that he will be mute in his somnolent spectatorship. And there will be a son whose simplicity will be summarized in the unsophisticated question: "What is all this?" These modes of questioning will characterize the attitudes of the entire generation of Israelites being taken out of Egypt whose views of redemption are mixed. It will remain for the fourth son, whose question is recorded in Deuteronomy forty years after struggling through the Wilderness experience, who will reflect a more mature understanding and appreciation of what the covenant entails: "What do the decrees, the laws and rules which the Lord God has enjoined upon us mean?"

Only after enduring the Wilderness with its disappointments, frustrations, and rebellions, will the people be ready to hear the terms of the covenant renewed and understood — truly understood in detail for the first time. But now, at the threshold of the Exodus, the Children of Israel are collectively bewildered. They seem not quite ready; they are as yet spiritually, morally, socially, and politically "unleavened." Leaving Egypt in haste they not only eat *lehem oni* (bread of affliction). For too long they themselves have been afflicted with an unleavened flatness-of-being.

Be-Shalah   בשלח

Throughout the story of the enslavement the most common form of vocal expression used by the Israelites is *za'akah* (or variations like *tz'akah* and *na'akah*). The word means "crying out, weeping, begging, imploring." When Egyptian overlords whip the Israelites, club them into beaten hulks, these Israelites cry out and their crying out is *za'akah*.

But now the situation has been changed radically. The enemy of Israel is drowning at the Sea of Reeds, destroyed by God who has demanded and achieved freedom for His people. Now the Israelites cry out; but their crying out is *shirah* (song). Up to now Moses has been described as a stammerer. Now he is a poet, a singer!

When does the human being wail, whine, scream? When he's in servitude! When does the human being sing? When he is emancipated from his servitude, knows it, appreciates it, and celebrates it! Thus *za'akah* is the expression of one who is bent, broken, incapable of comprehending on any kind of conceptual level what is happening to him. His cries are instinctual, formless, uncontrollable. On the other hand, what is the expression of one who is emotionally erect, sound, fully cognizant of his ability to prevail, to triumph as a free personality — *shirah*, the structured rapturous invocation of poetry, music, song!

The Song and the Shabbat

Moses is credited with the Song but he is not alone. All of Israel celebrates with him. Moses is the *sheli'ah tzibbur* (representative of the community) of Israel leading them in their song, this Song of the Sea of Reeds, this chorus of victory. The Song captures in a rare moment of unified covenantal dedication and appreciation the joy of survival, triumph, vividly played-out redemption.

It is a collective celebration; but each Israelite among the men, women, and children of all ages is able to experience a sense of personal reward. For the attachment to the larger Israel bestows upon the individual Israelite an independent value even as each individual Israelite's spiritual, moral, and national worth is being validated by the group. In a later generation, Rabbi Nahman of Bratzlav will sing of each blade of grass having a unique song of its own. But out of the chorus of melodies of all the individual blades of grass carpeted together emerges a melody which soars above. It is the melody of the Shepherd. Who is this Shepherd? Is he the human redeemer Moses charged with the divine mission of shepherding God's covenanted Israel from slavery to freedom? Or is the shepherd God Himself fulfilling His oath to Abraham that some day He would rescue his descendants and the descendants of Isaac who have been bound on the altar of covenantal expectation while caught in the thicket of worldly strife?

The integration of individual melodies, the harmonization of individual melodies in a chorus which invokes a transcendent ode to emancipation orchestrated by God Himself blankets the Children of Israel as they emerge from slavery. This chorus wraps the Children of Israel in an aesthetic and ethical aura that will lead them shortly to Sinai and the experience of direct revelation. From within the Song the call of adoration *"zeh Eli ve-anvehu"* ("this is my God, and I will adore Him") will manifest itself throughout the development of the religion of Israel called Judaism as a purposeful goal for humane living. It will inspire the value-concept of *hidur mitzvah*, i.e., beautifying whatever deed or commandment one is performing. At the same time, it will underscore aspects of humane behavior which are to be guided by what the Torah will perceive as imitatio Dei, e.g., just as God is merciful, so are we to be merciful.

The Song does not blot out the unrelieved tensions of maneuvering in the real world with its shadowy contentiousness any more than religion in general and Judaism in particular will pretend to deny the vexing reality of human problems, dilemmas, failures, and tragedies. Shelley's poem "To a Skylark" will evoke in simple yet paradoxical terms the mixture of joy and sadness which characterizes human life — all human life: "We look before and after, And pine for what is not; Our sincerest laughter with some pain is fraught; Our sweetest songs are those that tell of saddest thought." Rephrasing Dickens' line, it is *always* the best of times and the worst of times.

Nevertheless, the Song of the Sea of Reeds, placed as it is between unbroken complaints on the part of Israel, suppresses even for a short while the fears and anxieties of this slave population. This is a slave population which will have to be nurtured with endless patience in order to have them be ready not only for the overwhelming impact of Revelation but for the detailed regimen prescribed by Revelation, i.e., the Torah, so as to enable them to build a covenanted community.

The Song will give Israel the opportunity for a collective burst of uninhibited joy — short-lived perhaps — but authentic joy expressed as a result of total victory over their enemies, their erstwhile oppressors. The Song is an expression of unbridled exaltation of the life-giving power of the incomparable Lord of the Universe: "Who is like You among the gods..." There is no room within the Song itself for brooding, for lamenting over the past or for anxiety-filled anticipation of the future. And if the celebration includes mention of the annihilation or subjugation or general defeat of enemy peoples present and future, it is without moral inhibition. For the victory is perceived as God's victory over those who have in the past or will in the future shed the blood of His covenanted people.

The poetry and poetic moment lauding the victory serve as a prelude to the beginning of serious collective instruction in "mitzvah." The institution of the Shabbat, in contrast to the poetic Song, is introduced to the people by means of prose instructions. The heavenly food — the manna — that will sustain them in the Wilderness will arrive mysteriously enough. But the gathering of the food is to be a daily activity without poetic fanfare — except that the instructions include a special stipulation *not* to go out to collect food on Shabbat. This institution of the Shabbat will grow into a majestic redemptive public monument to human freedom and creativity. But the struggle to build such an institution will be fraught with formidable psychological, sociological, and economic obstacles. The people will be tested as to whether they have enough focused faith to be able to control their acquisitive appetites. Moreover, will they have enough focused faith to be able to recognize day-to-day Godly grace? Will they have the spiritual strength to resist wanting to insure that they will have enough, i.e., not hoarding for a "rainy day"? Even if they will be given double the manna on Friday, can they restrain themselves from going out again on Shabbat?

The Shabbat will become for the Jew the weekly institutionalization of the Song. It will encapsulate in its weekly service the celebration of creation out of chaos and emancipation from humanly imposed bondage. It will offer Israel the weekly light which will pierce the darkness of the work-week, the arena of relentless struggle, whether the darkness is personal or social. The darkness will not always be that imposed by adversaries. There will be times when personal concerns or Israel's national concerns will be so suffused with a self-imposed gloom that the verse already quoted from Job 10:22: "a land whose light is darkness, all gloom and disarray," will not be restricted in its applicability to Egypt.

The individual Israelite's personal view of light may become so lurid, the national mood and situation of Israel may be so full of apprehension, that only through the committed observance of the Shabbat will one be able to draw comfort and assurance as promised in Psalms 139:12: "Darkness is not dark for you; night is as light as day; darkness and light are the same." The Midrash will speak of a king and his disciple whom he wishes to visit. The disciple prepares modestly for the king's arrival with a simple welcoming lamp. The king brings his enormous train of attendants bearing huge golden candelabra. The disciple is totally intimidated and hides everything. When the king realizes what has happened, he assures the disciple that the modest lamp which the disciple has prepared will outshine all that the king has brought. Similarly the light of each individual Jew's modest Shabbat candles will dispel the gloom and doom which will sooner or later afflict in some fashion his personal and collective world.

But alas, the very first observance of Shabbat on the part of Israel is marred by its desecration on the part of those Israelites who simply lack the faith, that is, who lack confidence that the "manna" will return. At this early stage in its newly discovered situation of "freedom," Israel cannot but show its collective immaturity. Even arriving at the threshold of Song has not been easy for this slave population. They will discover, however, that singing a song of triumph *once* is much easier than keeping the Shabbat over and over again, regularly, systematically, meticulously.

Faith at the Sea

The Song — and the capacity to sing the song of emancipation in tribute to the God who has made the emancipation possible — is a collective proclamation of faith. For until this moment the Israelites, notwithstanding the proof of the plagues, have not been genuinely convinced that there is merit to Moses' message of "redemption." Granted, they appear to have been freed of their "shackles"; but having been brought out of Egypt, they reach the Sea of Reeds and discover to their woe that they are to be tested again. From their encampment they see the Egyptians thundering down upon them. As it says in Exodus (14:10): "And *Egypt* was marching after them."

Rashi makes two comments regarding the personification of "Egypt" in the verse by the use of the singular form: (1) the use of the phrase "Egypt marching" in the singular indicates that they marched with "one heart, as one man"; (2) the Israelites imagine that they see the guardian angel of Egypt in the singular descending from the heavens in order to aid the Egyptians. Whichever explanation is noted, the Israelites are clearly suffering and will continue to suffer from a psycho-physical fear born out of a lack of faith in their God and in the destiny which He has promised them. Such fear will paralyze them. And so God must bring His own transcendent power into play. And at this early juncture at the Sea of Reeds He will — emphatically and decisively!

Ibn Ezra adds another note regarding the Israelite paralysis. He is also relating to the question why it is that six hundred thousand heads of Israelite families were still terrified of what must have been at this stage following the plagues a severely decimated Egypt: "The Egyptians had been lords and masters over this generation of Israelites which had only known servitude under the yoke of Egypt. This generation had only known humiliation under these Egyptians. How could they now rise against them in combat?"

Whichever emphasis one prefers as an explanation for the paralysis — Rashi's political-theological emphasis or Ibn Ezra's psycho-sociological one — the slaves' reaction at this stage can only continue to be *za'akah*, certainly not song. To feel that they are our lords, that they represent a world-renowned dominant culture, so that their very "angel" or "god" is leading them over us, what else can we do but cry out for an act of God — assuming Moses is telling the truth, that there is such a God. True, we have seen the terrible afflictions dealt out by such a God on the Egyptians yesterday and in recent weeks and months. But what of today as we stand before this impassable barrier, this *"Yam-Sof"* (Sea of Extinction)? Will it be the end of us?

But more! Israel feels that all its adversaries are with "one heart, as one man." This general mood of the Israelites will be labeled in later generations as the classic ghetto mentality. Moses will bear the burden, therefore, of having to help them develop their own sense of *"be-lev ehad ke-ish ehad"* ("with one heart, as one man"), so that they can meet the threat, any threat, prevail against it, and go on to fulfill their destiny. Moses had been cast forth into the water of fate and had been saved for higher purpose by no less than Pharaoh's daughter, called significantly *Batya* (Daughter of God) by the later rabbis. Now Moses will have to shepherd this people safely through this perilous water-of-fate which will sweep away the vestiges of the Egyptian empire and give this newly born people Israel a chance to develop its "one heart, as one man" in its chosen Land.

Rabbinic tradition will debate whether or not the Jewish people can ever be of "one heart, as one man." The historic reality will always confront the given generation of Israelites, of Jews, with the challenge of faith. Do they as a people have adequate faith in God, in themselves, to challenge the waters of fate, to stand up to the thundering horde of enemies which may attack them in any generation?

There are two competing *midrashim* regarding the Israelites' readiness to challenge the Sea. Rabbi Meir's laudatory *midrash* says: "As Israel stood on the shores of the Sea, the tribes competed with one another as to which of them should go down to the Sea first. For they all wished to show others the way. During the ensuing contentiousness *le-shem Shamayim* (for the sake of Heaven), as it were, the tribe of Benjamin jumped in first. It was thus worthy to become host eventually to the Holy One Blessed be He, i.e., the Holy of Holies in the Temple would be located in Benjamin's territory." Rabbi Yehudah disagrees with Rabbi Meir and presents his own disparaging *midrash*: "None of the tribes nor any individual Israelite was ready to jump in first. Instead they all conferred with each other. And during the interminable procrastination, Nahshon ben Aminadav of the tribe of Judah hurled himself in and led his tribe after him into the fateful waters. Thus, the tribe of Judah would merit the rulership over all Israel."

It is an endless debate throughout Jewish history. The fact that the better-known *midrash* is Rabbi Yehudah's lends support to the ongoing collective guilt feelings prevalent in the House of Israel over periodic lack of faith and lack of individual initiative. God Himself is described as having led the Israelites by way of a circuitous route around the territory of the Philistines at the very beginning of the Exodus. It was clearly more logical to take the shortest route and to go directly from Egypt along the Mediterranean coast to the Promised Land. Yet God chooses differently "lest the newly freed slaves lose heart when experiencing war or the threat of war…" The Philistines were a most formidable adversary who would undoubtedly not give rights of free passage to the Israelites. The Israelites would have to fight. And God has little confidence in the resolve of the slave generation. It isn't that the slaves don't want relief from their bondage. But will they fight for it? Forty years later their children will be prepared for mobilization and under Joshua will fight and conquer as need be. But now, the morale of this generation and their commitment to the ideal which Moses has been preaching to them is too fragile.

The fragility is qualitatively different from what will eventually turn into stiff-neckedness. The Israelites before the splitting of the Sea and the revelation at Sinai are "innocent" in their spiritual weakness. After all, in Egypt they have received an audacious message from Moses who claims he is a messenger of God. It is true that in Egypt they have been witness to a series of disasters which have brought Egypt to ruin. But they have not as yet experienced *directly themselves* God's saving power. At this stage they are in particular need of God's pillars of support and motivation. These pillars turn out to be the pillar of cloud by day and the pillar of fire by night. Rashi sees the pillars supplementing each other so that Israel is never without one or the other. The *Ba'al ha-Turim* sees the pillars as working together, interlocked, as it were, to help Israel forge for itself a capacity for dealing with life under all circumstances — whether needed to guide them through undifferentiated "brightness" or impenetrable "darkness."

The maturation of Israel's faith will be a long, even endless process. It will require a moderation of God's expectations as well which will not be fully achievable considering the ambitious terms of the covenant. God will get angry with them and then will forgive them; He will lose patience and yet will allow Himself to be reminded that He is long-suffering, full of mercy.

How will God manifest this mercy while never relaxing the demand that the covenant must impose upon the human partner? As an illustration, after God's saving power is vividly experienced at the Sea, and after the Song is sung with robust energy and confidence, Israel regresses in its faith and loyalty as soon as it comes upon the bitter waters of Marah. How can they continue without life-sustaining water? God in His mercy shows Moses a tree which will sweeten the water as soon as it is thrown into its depths. But God's accompanying charge will be in the form of an exhortation to keep a regimen of fixed rules, thereby meeting the covenantal test: "If you will heed the Lord your God diligently, doing what is upright in His sight, giving ear to His commandments and keeping all His laws, then I will not bring upon you any of the disease that I brought upon the Egyptians, for I the Lord am your healer." The faith to be cultivated by Israel will have to be strong and stubborn enough to bridge the gap between life's waters of healing and the demands of God's commandments.

Miracles

The above verses anticipate what the entire Torah will mean once Israel arrives at Sinai. The Torah is intended to be a tree of life — life to be lived within the world using this-worldly means. The Torah is intended to offer a spiritual, moral, and cultural discipline to individuals, to communities of individuals, and to the nation as a whole. And the Torah will offer and demand at the same time a faith that this discipline offers the preventive cure for the illness which has plagued empires from Nimrod's Babel to Pharaoh's Egypt. It is a faith that only a God-inspired legislation can hope to be the ultimate healer of any society!

Thus the splitting of the Sea and the Song of the Sea do not celebrate the concept and reality of "miracle" as much as they have set the foundation for establishing in the minds and hearts of Israel a mode of building a society legislatively in appreciation for that "miracle." There are, indeed, constant miracles such as the "manna" and the quail and the tree that sweetens bitter waters. But what is to be the ongoing response of Israel to these daily signs of God's largesse, His goodness, and blessings?

Martin Buber will define "miracle" as not something "supernatural" or "superhistorical." "It is rather an incident or an event which can be fully included in the objective, scientific nexus of nature and history; the vital meaning of which, however, for the person to whom it occurs, destroys the security of the whole nexus of knowledge for him, and explodes the fixity of the fields of experience named 'nature' and 'history.'" But the "miraculousness" of the incident or the event is contingent upon people who are capable of interpreting it as such, i.e., if it "destroys the *security* of the whole nexus of knowledge" for *them*; if it "explodes the *fixity* of the fields of experience for *them*." The two words "security" and "fixity" — if thought of as absolutely attainable by human means — are illusive, dangerous, and at times lethal. What Buber sees as the biblical aspiration for Man's mode of relating to nature and history is an ongoing "abiding astonishment." There is no absolute and final "security" in Man's ability to control and manipulate nature. There can be no absolute and final "fixity" as to the movement of history in Man's understanding and strategic planning. Human assumptions of absolute and final "security" and "fixity" turn inevitably into hard-heartedness and stiff-neckedness.

There is only one ultimate security or sense of security achievable by Man. It is the "security" born out of the intuitive ground of abiding astonishment, the faith that there is a "ground" of purposeful creation. And if there is any "fixity" associated with human history, it only comes out of a commitment to some sense of covenant, i.e., an ordered scheme of coping humanely with the dynamics that have begun to make themselves plain to Israel as exhibiting a higher security as they try to cope with nature. There are "hints," increasingly manifest as Israel begins its journey through history as a new nation, which will enable them to maneuver despite the absence of fixity in life. These "hints," these "signals," have been there in the plagues, in the apocalyptic scene at the Sea, in the manna, in the sweetening tree, and in the victorious battle with Amalek.

But the fullness of the promise — beyond the "hints" and the "signals" — will come at Sinai. It will be there that God's revelation will overwhelm them in its immediacy. The people Israel will experience together what Abraham, Isaac, Jacob, and Moses have each experienced individually: God's Presence promising a future filled with blessings! These blessings will not be achieved without struggle, without the painful, unrelieved attention to daily living and survival in a human "wilderness" of desire and frustration, aspiration and failure. But the promise of blessings is certified by the sense which Israel will have that God is truly with them.

That God will present Israel with a Torah full of commands — positive and negative — will only confirm the seriousness of the promise. A covenant worth its name must be spelled out in detail. For only concern with specific detail testifies to the sincerity of the partners. The climax of the Song of the Sea has been the triumphant call *"Adonai Yimlokh le-Olam va-Ed"* ("The Lord will reign forever and ever"). How is that to happen except through the living day-to-day witnessing of this sovereignty by His chosen witness-nation Israel. And Israel can only be an honest witness through its day-by-day, moment-by-moment fulfillment of the legislated details of the covenant.

The Contemporary Song

The ability of Israel to fulfill what it will be mandated to do at Sinai is dependent upon its ability to settle the Promised Land, to cultivate it legislatively or halakhically as a society which will in exemplary fashion turn back the "wilderness." They will not recreate Eden; the Torah is to be a tree of life not for the lost Eden but for the discovered potentially humane civilization of the post-Eden situation. The Rashbam will see the settlement in Eretz Yisrael as the clear unequivocal confirmation of the triumphant call in the Song that God is to "reign on earth forever and ever!" *"Adonai yimlokh le-olam va-ed!"*

The covenant sealed at Sinai following the experiential certainty of having been saved as a nation at the Sea of Extinction (*Yam Sof*) will become so permanently etched in the collective sensibility of the children of Israel that even after they will have failed twice to establish in Israel a society hospitable to God's sovereignty, they will never forget the promise quoted in the Song. And on the threshold of the modern era, after the lengthy seemingly endless exile, the yearning to return to the Land will be rearticulated by new voices in Israel — voices who may even disavow traditional covenantal frames of reference but will nevertheless claim proprietorship over the Land.

Tchernichowsky will seek to awaken the contemporary House of Israel which has been falling more and more deeply into despair while continuing to sing in daily prayer the ancient Song of national liberation. He will call out to his contemporary Children of Israel ensnared in *galut*: "They say there is a land bathed in radiant sunshine, where is that land, where is that sunshine? They say there is a land held by seven pillars, seven stars shine from every hill, a land where every hope can be fulfilled. Anyone may enter, anyone can meet Akiva! Greetings Akiva, Greetings my master, where are the Holy Ones, where is the Maccabee? Akiva answers, my master responds, all of Israel is holy, you are the Maccabee!"

The call to each and every Israelite to step forward and to re-enter the Promised Land will be a call to each and every modern Jew to sing the song again, the Song of Rebirth. It will be a song which will herald the coming of a new time and perhaps a new collective national revelation, even though there has long before already been a collective national revelation at Sinai. But whether it is at ancient Sinai or thirty-five hundred years after Sinai, the settlement in the Land will become evidence — prima facie evidence — that Israel cares to hear God's word. And Israel will care, for in the profound difficulties of settling Israel, surrounded by enemies with goals similar to Amalek, they will be renewing the ancient covenant. However these new Israelis will be explaining their determination to revive their people's national life in its Land, they will, like Akiva, like the Maccabees, like Moses, be inviting God to reign again, perhaps this time forever!

Yitro

יתרו

Ivan Karamazov's conclusion that "if God is dead, then everything is permitted" is the motivational source for the Serpent's rebellion in the Garden. The Serpent does not wish to acknowledge God; nor does he care to love and respect God's human creatures. The Torah, on the other hand, understands from its very beginning — from "in the beginning" — that there must be a God, that human beings in order to have a meager chance of surviving together, must have a God. Therefore the human creature owes it to his humanity to acknowledge the God who is God.

At the immediate pristine level of *ayeka* the human being is focusing on his own existential self. If this human being hides from the true God, he will deify another creature, be it animal, be it an inanimate force in nature, be it another human being. Adam may hide from God; but he knows that he cannot sequester himself within nature indefinitely without losing his discrete human identity as separate and distinguished from the other non-human creatures in the universe. Whether he will develop a sense of reverie, *yirat shamayim*, or will carry on a constant rebellion against the Deity, or will fluctuate between the two postures before God, there will be God! And God is that God! *"Adonai hu Ha-Elohim!"* ("God is the One Unique God!")

Beyond the response or lack of response to *ayeka*, there are implications, correlatively speaking, for inter-human relationships, summarized in the question *"Ey Hevel ahikha"* ("Where is your human Other")? The Torah presents itself as a program for living out a covenantally grounded inter-human destiny on earth. Human beings — all human beings — are destined to be taken out of bondage in order to build a free society dedicated to human ennoblement. The experimental model of the Garden has failed in projecting the optimally desirable goal for humanity.

And so God has redrawn His covenantal plans in order to reach out in a post-Eden "wilderness" to one family which will grow into a tribe and then into a nation. He has brought this nation out of its condition of enslavement to lead it to a moment of revelation. In essence, God will be repeating at Sinai the *ayeka*, augmented by the second fundamental question "where are your brothers," both questions intrinsic to the covenant. And the Children of Israel will have to answer both questions with the only answer possible in signing on to the covenant: *"Na'aseh ve-nishma"* to be translated "we are here *ready to behave* and *to learn how to behave* in conjunction with our positive answers to the two fundamental questions."

A Chosen People

In order to sign on to the covenant, Israel has not had to have an especially endowed intelligence. Yitro who is not a member of the House of Israel is sufficiently intelligent to recommend to an already harassed and overworked Moses a preferred plan for setting up a judiciary. The *Or Hahayyim* argues that Israel is not superior in any way to the nations; that it has been chosen out of a transcendent grace that has recognized the special spiritual attributes of Israel's *Avot* (the Patriarchs). In other words, one of the mysteries hovering over the question of Jewish identity will be that the Jews — the descendants of early Israel — will perceive and understand that their destiny is not to be based on pride of intelligence per se. At work has been a transcendent grace which has galvanized and mobilized Abraham, Isaac, Jacob, and now Moses, to the task of bringing the descendants of the Patriarchs and Matriarchs into the covenant.

The expectation is that following the exultation of the Song, the nation of Israel will be so fully alive and alert that its spiritual, moral, social, and political antennae will be maximally attuned to transcendent illumination. If not now, when? If not at this moment of feverish thanksgiving at having been saved from extinction, reinforced by the discovery of water and sustaining food for the Wilderness, when? Thus they have arrived at the mountain and have been sufficiently prepared for high purpose by their leader and by the colossal events which have transpired and transported them. Now, here — a supremely immediate "now" and "here" — they are to be given a gift of the Torah!

Regarding "gifts" of such magnitude, there may be a Nietzschean-like reaction: "You take, you do not ask who it is that gives." The presumption is that the gift, if it has worth, must have intrinsic worth; speculation about the source of the gift is superfluous. Buber will protest: "I think that as we take, it is of the utmost importance to know that someone is giving. He who takes what is given him, and does not experience it as a gift, is not really receiving; and so the gift turns into theft. But when we do experience the giving, we find out that revelation exists." The presumption here is that in addition to the gift's intrinsic worth, its source as legitimizing agent is indispensable for underscoring its covenantal purpose.

Is Israel sufficiently primed to move from Nietzsche to Buber? Or will the Serpent be given an opportunity to sabotage this "now-here" moment at Sinai? No, for God will not permit the revelatory moment to be compromised by doubt, let alone sinful cynicism. Doubt, fear, idolatrous fornication may and will come soon enough. But at Sinai in the third month after the Exodus, following the triumph at the sea and its celebration through the Song, there is a window of revelatory opportunity for Moses and his flock. The initial complaints about lack of food and water have been stilled — at least for now — and the antennae are fully "alive" and "attuned." The Children of Israel are alert to receive. And the moment will forever be encapsulated in collective Jewish memory as *zeman mattan Toratenu* (the time of the giving of our Torah).

This moment at Sinai of God's revelation to the entire people has been made possible pedagogically by the cushioning triple definition of the House of Israel as God's treasured people, a kingdom of priests, and a holy nation. The triple defining of Israel as "chosen" will mark the Jew and Jews forever as individuals and groups of individuals who will be seen by other peoples as somehow separate, somehow different. Because of this marking, Jews will be respected but at the same time suspected. They will be accepted, but often rejected. What will obscure the full dimensions of the meaning of the term "chosen people" will be ignorance, prejudice, confused understanding of terms like moral universalism and ethno-centrism. But at the very heart of the world's misunderstanding and often Jewish misunderstanding of the term "chosen people" will be self-idolatry — self-idolatry of hard-hearted Gentiles and stiff-necked Jews.

The world will be stubborn in its reluctance to understand that the very idea of covenant means reciprocity — reciprocity of responsibility. As much as God chooses Israel — and why to a great extent may be a mystery — *Israel chooses to feel chosen* and to accept the responsibility of being chosen by God. Furthermore, Israel is meant to know what Amos will badger them to know: "You alone have I singled out of all the families of the earth; that is why I will call you to account for all your iniquities." It is an article of faith then that God considers Israel a treasured people; and the treasured *People* of Israel will be given the treasured *Land* of Israel which God can do arbitrarily since *"Li kol ha-aretz"* ("the whole earth is Mine"). But should Israel contaminate the Land it will suffer for its iniquities in greater measure than if it had not agreed to be chosen.

Israel will accept that it has been chosen to model God's vision of harmony-on-earth. In its own success in applying the teachings of the Torah — if it succeeds — it will truly become a "kingdom of priests" in that it will serve humanity as the laboratory model. Thus if there is an ethnocentric focus to the very idea of covenant with God, it is part of a universalistic vision which has the very separateness, the very distinctiveness of Israel, its self-understanding as a "holy nation," serving to pull other nations up the ladder of humane living. Moreover, Israel's choice to be "chosen" should not preclude any other nation's similar choice, provided the other nation is willing to subscribe to the spiritual and ethical terms of the covenant.

In Deuteronomy Moses will stress the absurdity in the thought that Israel's having been chosen bespeaks some kind of racial or intellectual or moral superiority inherent in the choice. "It is not because you are the most numerous of peoples that the Lord set His heart on you and chose you — indeed, you are the smallest of peoples." Or, "Know, then, that it is not for any virtue of yours that the Lord your God is giving you this good land to possess; for you are a stiff-necked people."

Israel — despite its distinguished patrimony — is to be considered quantitatively and qualitatively normal. If it is to be a "light unto the nations" it will have all it can do to cultivate its own inner spiritual, moral, social, and cultural radiance without worrying about impacting on other nations. Whatever impact Israel will make on other nations will emerge out of conditions of natural cultural interchange. Therefore, Israel can in no way and will in no way consider itself paternalistic, let alone innately superior to other nations, e.g., genetically or racially. On the other hand, by virtue of Israel's struggle to live out God's Torah-covenant, it will assume in other eyes and thereby in its own eyes a "chosenness" which will become more and more overt through the progress of human history.

Two Views of Chosenness

Generations of anti-Semitic descendants of Pharaoh will brand Israel's "chosen people" concept as the model for various racial, ideological, or national theories of superiority. But such accusations will reflect not only hatred of Jews and Judaism but ignorance of the authentic biblical framework defining the terms for chosenness. The persistent historic ignorance in all its manifestations will pervert any possible understanding and appreciation of the redemptive purpose of "chosenness."

The Book of Isaiah is a clear illustration of the mainstream purpose of the covenant and the universal good projected by the idea of Israel's chosenness. Isaiah dreams of a day when "The Mount of the Lord's House shall stand firm above the mountains and tower above the hills. And all the nations shall gaze on it with joy, and the many peoples shall go and say: Come, let us go up to the Mount of the Lord, to the House of the God of Jacob, that He may instruct us in His ways, and that we may walk in His paths. For instruction shall come forth from Zion, the word of the Lord from Jerusalem." Following this projected hope, Isaiah summarizes the instruction that "nation shall not take up sword against nation; that they shall never again know war." A similar dream is expressed in chapter 11 — the famous "wolf lying down with the lamb" chapter. In short, Isaiah's and Moses' understanding of chosenness is one of dedication to the sociomoral redemption of all humanity.

It is true that in reaction to the historic anti-Jewish animus of major parts of the civilized world, there will emerge among Jewish thinkers such as Yehudah Halevi and the Maharal of Prague and Shneur Zalman of Liady certain theories which will seek to mark the Jew and the Jewish people as different from Gentiles not only in degree but in kind. But these theories will need to be studied, understood, and accepted as part of a larger much more tolerant corpus of Jewish thought.

Unlike Moses who is preparing his people for the task of building a covenanted but otherwise normal society in a sovereign national situation, Yehudah Halevi may serve as a representative *galut* thinker faced with the stark reality of *galut* vulnerability, subjugation, and empirically proven impotency. His *Kuzari* will be written in the eleventh century at a time when in the eyes of Spanish Jewry an apocalyptic confrontation between two powerful forces representing religion puts into bold relief the utter helplessness of that Jewish "exile" community. One cannot deny what one sees, and Yehudah Halevi's Spanish Jewry is witness to the struggle for supremacy of imperial powers on earth, the Christian and Moslem empires. And Yehudah Halevi's Jewish community is an utterly intimidated Jewish community sandwiched between these empires. In such a predicament, Yehudah Halevi's Jews are asking ultimate questions about the worthwhileness of the entire enterprise of being Jewish.

Yehudah Halevi's troubled Jew may conclude that the fact that two great religions fight each other for dominance implies that their claims of superiority cancel each other out. But this will not lead him necessarily to a conclusion that Judaism is to be preferred. Why not reject religion entirely since it appears to be no more than a charade with which to promote imperialism of territory and thought? Why not opt for a total philosophic rejection of faith in a transcendent God when His alleged worshipers-on-earth — in His name — oppress, plunder, and kill? Why not abandon the belief in a particularistic revelation? Must one bow down before the will of some unseen spiritual power who determines and prescribes duties, obligations, and destinies of men? Why not surrender to the clean, hard standards of human reason and human self-reliance?

Halevi's challenge is existentially different from the one facing Moses. Halevi's view of chosenness will express a desperate need to lift the short-term and long-term morale of a deeply despondent people-in-exile. Granted, Moses' Children of Israel have been more than intimidated by their oppressors, the Egyptians. They have been in actual bondage, physically and spiritually. But they have now emerged from this bondage as free men having witnessed God's victory, *their* God's victory over *their* enemies. Halevi's contrary situation requires an attempt to reach a people suffering from defeat and what seems to them endless exile. His message of chosenness, therefore, must be more radical than that of Moses.

There is only one credible response which Yehudah Halevi can give to the overriding question of why one should continue to be Jewish. And the response must do three things at the same time: (1) It must provide the Jewish self-image with a sense of uniqueness; (2) the uniqueness must have moved the question of Jewish "power" outside the arena of empirical measurement; and (3) the special "wisdom" associated with that uniqueness must be beyond the normal achievements of the human intellect. The response for Yehudah Halevi is the *inyan ha-elohi* (the Godly or prophetic apprehension of reality) which Halevi argues has been bestowed uniquely upon the Jew — even in a situation of worldly powerlessness.

Yehudah Halevi will divide the created universe into mineral, vegetable, animal, human — and prophetically Jewish. The fifth category is not to be considered *quantitatively* different from the fourth. The prophet according to Halevi doesn't necessarily have — nor does the Jewish people have — greater wisdom *quantitatively* than humankind. But its prophetic apprehension is something *qualitatively* different. It is to be perceived as somehow standing outside the "mechanical" universe. This prophetic mode is to be a critical mode; but the critique is focused more on the Jew's image of himself in relation to God than it is on the fate of the nations of the world. In this sense, Halevi's *galut* situation has taken him in a different direction than has been intended originally at Sinai. The covenant accepted by the Children of Israel at Sinai will have them confront the world of nations as a free sovereign people with a particular agenda that should not separate them from the rest of the world. They must be a visible interacting force in the world in order to set an example for other people to emulate — assuming Israel is worthy of emulation.

In Halevi's case the qualitative uniqueness of his prophetic mode must be spiritual; and this spiritual dimension must be powerful enough to be impregnable. It will therefore have to have an esoteric quality comprehensible only to the Jewish faithful. But even with Halevi, if there is an elitist exclusivist dimension to this esoteric quality of chosenness (as any faith community will claim for its faithful), it in no way sanctions oppression of other human beings in the name of God. Any attempt, therefore, to cite the Jewish understanding of its chosenness — even according to Halevi's definition — as a model for racial, ideological, or national superiority with imperialistic aggrandizement as reward is plainly pernicious.

But now returning to the situation of Moses and his generation of liberated Jews who are moving out into the world of nations: If there is any reward for chosenness, it is felt by these Children of Israel to be intrinsic to the covenantal faith itself. God's promise in the covenant is to *be* with Israel in the world as He insists He has been throughout the enslavement in Egypt. But the imagery will now soar from being with Israel in its "burning bush" of suffering to seeing to it that it can be protected in the world by "eagle's wings." Rashi's traditional interpretation sees the eagle bearing its young on its wings as opposed to other lesser birds which carry their young below, between their talons. The lesser birds fear the stronger birds who can and will sweep down on them from above. But the eagle has no bird that can soar higher than he. All he has to fear are the arrows from Man below. The eagle would prefer the arrows piercing him rather than his young resting safely above.

Thus God will protect Israel from all dangers — especially the weapons of Man. For Israel in moving towards its Promised Land will learn to utilize power in many different ways. Israel will have to fight for the Land, settle it, build it, and defend it. And it will have to cultivate that Land in order that it not become an esoterically inspired cloister — but that it become a healthy earthly society struggling for international legitimacy and well-being. History will compromise the perfection of the metaphoric protection as seen by Rashi. It will inspire Buber to see in the eagle and its young a pedagogically oriented metaphor. The eagle carries its young, which may be tired or fearful, until it learns to maneuver in flight in imitation of its parent. It can then fly off autonomously, independently, and fight for its life on its own. Will then Israel be guaranteed a permanent avoidance of the "slings and arrows of outrageous fortune?" Hardly! But Israel will learn to cherish its chosenness as it maneuvers its way through human history — diplomatically, militarily, socially, culturally, morally, and religiously. It will remind itself regularly of Joshua's reminder: "You are witnesses yourselves that you have chosen God to worship...."

As noted earlier, it has been Israel's choice as much as it has been God's. The covenant to qualify as a covenant must be fulfilled in this doubly independent manner. God in His utter freedom has chosen to bind Himself to Israel; and Israel in its freedom — and its creation in the image of God requires it to have its own measure of freedom — has committed itself to God's long-term purposes for humankind on earth as it perceives those purposes.

The Commandments

Israel is aware — certainly as it stands at Sinai — of the awesomeness of the covenant. The tradition has Rabbi Yehoshua ben Levi offering a terrifying image in which, as soon as the Lord utters the first of the Ten Commandments, the collective soul of Israel "expires." If such an event has indeed occurred, how is Israel able to hear the next commandment? Heavenly dew comes down with which the "deceased" nation is brought back to life. Another rabbinic tradition holds that all of Israel hears collectively only the first two commandments. The remainder Moses hears and transmits to them. In any case it is the first two which are the most critical for each and every Israelite to hear and to absorb.

What are these two statements that are the charge for the newly born nation of Israel? The first is God's announcement that "I am your God who has taken you out of the Land of Egypt, out of the house of bondage." Every child within the House of Israel will be reminded how in every generation there have been forces mobilized to annihilate it. *Galut* itself will constitute a predicament placing Israel in permanent peril for its very survival. As such, *galut* will always be considered servitude, occasionally benevolent, often malevolent — but in essence servitude! And the nadir of the *galut* predicament will come in the incomparable horrors of the Shoah (the Holocaust). Once the magnitude of the evils perpetrated in the Shoah will have been fully revealed, then there will never again be an interpretation of God's first "commandment" that will fail to include as starkest example of "servitude" the utter helplessness of the Jewish people in the Shoah.

The Midrash which imagines Israel "expiring" or "fainting" at the sound of the first commandment has Israel experiencing immediately the restoration of the spirit of life by means of transcendent dew, a gift of restored opportunity. But once resurrected there can be no return to naïve normalcy. There must be a new national agenda. And the agenda is proclaimed through the second commandment which is concerned with idolatry.

Why idolatry specifically? Because idolatry is the source of all other sins. It is the source of all human pretense. The idolatry being referred to cannot be limited to fetishism. Fetishism would be too trivial an issue. On the purely theological level idolatry refers to the false belief that somehow Man can manipulate the "gods" by discovering the key to the supernal realm which houses these "gods." But infinitely more threatening on the sociomoral and political plane is the non-trivial, non-fetishistic idolatry which proposes that a human being can become a "god," can become a force which has the power — and who will exploit that power — to demand obedience to the point of blind worship from his subjects. And the scope of the might of this god-man is to reach and subjugate all human beings on earth.

It will be this idolatry that will persist in resisting the triumph of ethical monotheism in the world from the moment in which the Serpent challenges God in the Garden until a latter-day Satan incarnate builds gas chambers and ovens in which to exterminate human beings. If then the second commandment calls out to Israel: "You shall have no other gods besides Me," it is against the background of the first commandment with all its resonances of the hopelessness of *galut* and Shoah. The remainder of the commandments then follow. They follow in their attempt to set a legislative foundation for building a treasured human society under a sovereign Israel dedicated to ethical monotheism.

God has His prophet Moses who is charged with the comprehensive task of supervising and administering the building of such a society while continuing to be its political, spiritual, and moral teacher. It is a task which is radically complicated by the fact that he and the Israelites are in transition socially, culturally, and politically. In every conceivable way they are being challenged to create a society alternative to what they have experienced in Egypt. And the alternative to Egypt must be one envisaged not just through the eyes of Israel as erstwhile slaves, but through the eyes of Moses who understands the world through the aristocratic eyes and sensibility of one who has been educated in the palace of the Pharaohs. The question being put to Israel and to Moses their teacher is "How can we truly build a society of human dignity, worthy of being called a society of treasured people?"

When a group of people, any group, finds itself in such a transition, being swept along by a revolutionary process, it cannot effect — except with great turmoil and agitation — the required conversion from being slaves within a totalitarian empire to sovereign caretakers of a Godly inspired, humanely oriented society. Israel is being asked to reject Egypt as a sociopolitical model. This does not entail, however, entirely new legislation in every sphere of human endeavor. Even totalitarian societies have laws of prudential importance, even ethical laws to enable some sense of equity to regulate human interaction for at least certain segments of society. But Israel will be asked, will be commanded to establish overall new standards, a firmer sense of security for all members of society, a spiritual, social, and moral consensus for all, including the underprivileged. As Herman Hesse will someday coin the felicitous phrase — "a simple acquiescence"!

The Torah is given to Israel so that they may have a spiritual and ethical standard, a sense of security, and at the pristine level of social commonality — a simple basic acquiescence among its people. The commandments are intended to be simple, clear, and unambiguous. The more complex legislation will come later. Life is indeed much more complex than the literal reading of the Ten Commandments suggests. Torah will have to be much more than the Ten Commandments pretend to be.

The Ten Commandments are the summarized spiritual and ethical agenda intended for a group of tribes, a new nation that seeks to peel itself down to the spiritual and ethical core of what it is, what it thinks, and what it is prepared to commit itself to without compromise. In these ten statements the nation will be dedicating itself (1) to remembering its servile origins, (2) to its opposition to all humanly conceived idolatries, (3) to its caution against ever exploiting religion for vanities. It will (4) revere the Shabbat and (5) the institution of the family as the centerpieces for its vision of sanctity and domestic stability. It will proclaim apodictically as indispensable sociomoral standards prohibitions (6) against murder, (7) against adultery, (8) against kidnapping, (9) against swearing false oaths, and (10) against coveting that which belongs to others.

Israel has suffered through the long-term trauma of enslavement. They have then experienced a short but highly charged trauma of seeing a unified Egypt thundering down upon them as they stood on the shore of the Sea of Reeds. Rashi, as indicated earlier, describes the moment in terms of Egypt appearing to Israel as with "one heart, as one man." (A simple but nefarious acquiescence!) But at the foot of Mount Sinai, Rashi describes Israel encamped there as *"ke-ish ehad be-lev ehad"* ("as one man with one heart"). Indeed, Rashi continues, all the other encampments will have been fraught with strife and quarrels. But here, at the foot of Sinai, the Children of Israel will be sufficiently of one heart to be ready to receive a standard, a solemn declaration containing a series of planks upon which to build a simple but demanding acquiescence.

This national unity — brief as it may be here at Mount Sinai — will serve as the pristine incomparably unifying moment for the Jewish people throughout the generations. It has been made possible by four elements coming together in the collective mind-set of the Children of Israel: (1) they know that henceforth they are to represent the antithesis to Egypt and all that Egypt represents; (2) they feel blessed by their belief that they truly have signed on to a covenant with God; (3) they are motivated by the dream that they can succeed in becoming a holy nation; and (4) they do not have any hesitation — at this moment at least — in promising to themselves that they will act as a unified people in the future.

Autonomous Choice

For generations afterwards, Jews will debate whether or not the covenant at Sinai was agreed to by Israel under compulsion. Was Israel held by God as a hostage, the situation at the foot of Sinai described as one in which God threatens to destroy them (and the universe) if they don't accept the yoke of the Torah? The Talmud will argue that perhaps there was a measure of coercion at Sinai. The midrashic imagination will not only feature God holding Sinai threateningly over the head of a terrified Israel; commentators will note that God's very Presence is itself a coercive force. But the same talmudic passage will point to a time in Jewish history when Israel will agree to fulfill the covenant autonomously. It will be in the period of the first *galut* in Babylonia — soon to be conquered by Persia — when God will be in eclipse, when prophecy will have been decreed to be officially dead.

The Children of Israel with God in eclipse and with no prophets to represent Him — certainly no Moses — will nevertheless reaffirm at that time during the first *galut* their faith in a unique Jewish destiny. And this reaffirmation will be considered as daring and as courageous an act as their standing-in-awe and committing themselves to *na'aseh ve-nishma* at Sinai. Some will argue that it may be an even greater testimony to Jewish faith precisely because of God's "absence." Perhaps an Ezra of that later time will deserve to stand together with Moses as a prophetic leader sent to re-establish the covenant autonomously with a stubborn people. But it will be a determined people wedded to a Jewish future in Israel despite its memory of failure in sustaining the first Jewish Commonwealth.

It will always be understood, however, that the *naʾaseh ve-nishma* given autonomously by Ezra and his generation will not have been possible without the earlier *naʾaseh ve-nishma* at Sinai, however it was secured. And if the *naʾaseh ve-nishma* at Sinai has been proclaimed by Israel under heteronomous pressure, it is nevertheless a sublime reaffirmation following the failure of Eden. Following that failure of Eden, if Israel's affirmation or reaffirmation at Sinai is not entirely autonomous, God's reaffirmation of His faith in the future of humankind certainly is. And God's choice of Israel as model covenanted partner for a post-Eden "wilderness" for humankind certainly is!

Mishpatim   משפטים

The revelation at Sinai is perceived to be the source and absolute authority of Jewish law throughout the ages. It is correct to assert that however Jewish law has evolved since Sinai, the *authority* to which the Jew submits as he lives out his commitment to the covenant in his daily life comes from Sinai. It is not correct, however, to insist that the *source* for all the laws legislated for Israel in the Wilderness is the revelation at Sinai. There is ample evidence in the Torah itself to confirm the axiom *"derekh eretz kadmah la-Torah"* ("appropriate socioethical behavior preceded the Torah"). When Jethro urges Moses to reorganize his judiciary so that he — Moses — will be able to share the burden of adjudication with others, there must be a corpus of laws and customs that is already known to Moses and the Elders and is being applied. But even before Jethro appears, the episode of the bitter waters at Marah being sweetened miraculously has Moses described as giving *hok u-mishpat* (fixed law, or statute and ordinance) to Israel.

The *Mishpatim*

The phrase *hok u-mishpat* may be interpreted in various ways. The Ramban has chosen to see Moses facing the problem of social and organizational chaos at the very outset of the Exodus. The Children of Israel are faced with a situation totally antithetical to what they have been accustomed to in Egypt, albeit as slaves. Even as slaves — especially as slaves within the Egyptian reality — their day-to-day situation was predictable. But here in the Wilderness, freed from Egypt, they will have to adjust immediately to the *hukei ha-midbar* (laws of the wilderness), as the Ramban puts it. This means that there will be food and water problems, and answers will have to be found. Then there are the *mishpatim* that Moses gives them along with the *hukim* in order to regulate their social interaction. These *mishpatim*, even before Sinai, are to direct them "to love each other, to behave in accordance with the advice of their elders, to conduct themselves modestly within the family, and to welcome strangers who will come to do business with them."

What then are these *mishpatim* — these pre-Sinai laws, if not basic sociomoral norms necessary for building a society of interacting human beings at their most immediate survival level. And these *mishpatim* — as well as others to be added — are given revelatory approval and absolute authority of concern at Sinai. "Authority of Concern" put in simpler terms means "God cares!" The triteness of the expression "God cares" should not dull the sharpness of the spiritual thrust being asserted here at the Sinaitic moment in the Israelite socio-religio-political revolution. The covenant as originally postulated with Abraham is summarized in God's injunction *"hithalekh le-fanai ve-heyei tamim"* ("walk before me in wholeheartedness"). There is a double emphasis here. Whatever Abraham does, he must be *tamim*, that is, he must behave with wholehearted sincerity and uncompromised commitment. But the "walking before God" is an equally vital part of the injunction. Living is "walking." One "walks" through life in tiny, incremental steps as he tries to concretize his dedication to the covenant. For God "cares" about the fulfillment of the covenant — every detail of its fulfillment.

The term *halakhah*, which will come to mean Jewish law, will continue to mean "walking before God wholeheartedly." Those who will label Judaism as a faith dominated by legalism will overlook the word "wholeheartedly"; but worse, they will show an embarrassing ignorance of human nature and human behavior. Judaism at its outset will argue that either the Creator, the Revealer, and the Redeemer of the universe cares about human nature and human behavior in its tiniest detail or utter chaos will doom the universe to self-nullification. So the *mishpatim* which even a godless society needs for sheer existential survival are the tools which are to be considered as sanctified injunctions from God covering every facet of human endeavor.

Halakhah — as any serious legal system — will become heavily weighted with technicalities and procedures along with seemingly infinite analyses of fine detail concerning given issues. As such, it will appear to the uninitiated as "unspiritual." But a spiritually lofty injunction like "you shall love your fellow as yourself" cannot be implemented, acted out, "walked through," so to speak, in day-to-day life, without considering the finest details of the given source of conflict that has inspired the spiritually lofty injunction to begin

with. The commentator Sforno will categorize the ten words or commandments proclaimed at Sinai as general warnings. For example, the tenth commandment warns against "coveting anything that is your neighbor's." The
question to be asked, however, is "How do I know that which is my neighbor's?" In most cases the answer is clear. But there may be situations in which
ownership is in dispute and will involve, therefore, detailed legal discussion.
If and when it does, it is thereby no less spiritual a concern than that manifested in the tenth injunction itself. It is these detailed legal discussions which
are dependent on the *mishpatim*.

When the Torah says *"Ve-eileh ha-mishpatim asher tasim lifnehem"*
("these are the laws which you shall set before them"), it is in effect getting
serious about implementing lofty ethical precepts such as "loving your fellow...." Even with the prescribed *mishpatim* it is not saying that every conceivable human situation can now be imagined and predicted in advance and
have a preordained command or direction towards correct behavior. But with
the Ten Commandments as bed rock principles, elaborated upon by the
mishpatim, a new society will have the legislative tools with which to secure
its existence and social stability, no matter what new problems may arise.

As crucial as it will be for the future judges and legislators to be upstand-
ing figures of impeccable honesty and integrity, the *mishpatim* are placed as
norms to be known by everyone. The Torah is not meant to be the esoteric or
otherwise secret teaching of a given class of spiritual or judicial leaders, be
they priests, judges, rabbis, or other "professionals." Just as the entire people
is meant to be a "kingdom of priests, a holy nation," so is the entire people
meant to be learned in the *hukim u-mishpatim*. This principle is not to be
restricted to Torah interpreted narrowly. It is meant, ideally speaking, to
cover all areas of human endeavor. Of course, no one person can know
enough in all given areas of expertise. He will lean on "judges" or other
experts as he may need them. He will be subject to the decisions of judges
when he comes in conflict with other "learned" members of the community.
But the instruction to Moses to set before *all* of Israel the *mishpatim* means
that every individual Israelite is intended to be both initially in awe of them
and ultimately responsible for keeping them.

The Covenant and the Law

As seen by the Bible, responsibility has been the required attribute of Man from Adam's predicament to contemporary definitions of existential authenticity. A.J. Heschel has spoken of the basic difference between the Greek and the biblical conception of Man: "To the Greek mind, Man is above all a rational being; rationality makes him compatible with the cosmos. To the biblical mind, Man is above all a commanded being, a being of whom demands can be made. The central problem is not: What is being? but rather: What is required of me?"

Heschel has presented a correct but highly preliminary distinction between the two cultural definitions of Man. As a platform for launching Man into the universe as a specially endowed moral creature the distinction is useful; but from the Jewish point of view, Man as a commanded being is not expected to be an automaton. He must respond rationally to the commandments. He must be rational in his struggle to apply the *mitzvot* to his society and to his relationship with that society.

The overriding principle which guides the Torah legislation is that it considers Man in his totality — a creature with spiritual, moral, social, sexual, economic, and political dimensions. The listing of the *mishpatim* here in the Book of Exodus — like other listings in Leviticus and Deuteronomy — is lacking a systematic order. There does not seem to be a sense of prioritization. The topics move from the laws of slavery to those concerned with bodily injury; from the laws concerned with damage-to-property to sexual offenses; from prohibitions against idolatry to warnings against oppressing the disadvantaged; from ritual questions to fundamental ethical obligations such as truth-telling. What is unquestioned is the Torah's attempt to aim at comprehensiveness while apparently neglecting order.

But the key to understanding why there is a lack of order may be found in its acceptance of the world and humanity within the world as part of an organic whole ordered fully and rationally by its Creator, although not fully grasped by any segment within that creation. The Torah plainly refuses to consider any given set of subjects concerning Man, God, and society as less important than other sets of subjects. Every particular is considered essential to the whole. In other words, the detailed projection of *mishpatim* becomes the full embodiment of Torah. The covenant to be implemented requires such a full embodiment.

It can be argued that the program of detailed *mishpatim* is already inherent in the preliminary basic outline of the covenant. In this light a question will be raised by Rashi and the Ramban as to why the *brit* (covenant) was "signed and sealed," as it were, *after* the portion dealing with all the *mishpatim* and not after the giving of the Ten Commandments or even during or before the spectacularly dramatic events at Sinai. It is after the textual review of the *mishpatim* that the solemn ceremony officially accepting the terms of the covenant takes place. Rashi gives an explanation often suggested by commentators who are faced with what may be a chronological anomaly in the Torah: *"En mukdam u-me'uhar ba-Torah"* ("there is no chronological order in the Torah"). According to Rashi, the portion concerning the *mishpatim* was given somehow *before* the Ten Commandments.

The Ramban disagrees: "After the giving of the Ten Commandments, on that same day, God said to Moses, 'thus shall you say to the Children of Israel,' and God began to dictate and command '*ve-elei ha-mishpatim* that you shall place before them' and all the commandments which followed...." At first, Ramban's answer seems more reasonable. Before signing a contract, the parties demand to know all its details. In this case, before signing the covenant the Children of Israel need to be informed that this *brit* touches all aspects of human existence and interaction. At second look, however, Rashi's answer is equally reasonable. Does Israel really need to hear all the details before agreeing to the covenant? After all, they know that they have been rescued from catastrophe at the Sea of Reeds. Why won't they now be ready to commit?

Whichever of the explanations as to when the *brit* was "signed" is preferable, there are two general propositions held to by both Rashi and the Ramban. The first is that the *brit*, the covenant, is indispensable for fulfilling the purpose of human destiny in general and Jewish destiny in particular. And the second — the burden and thrust of the chapter — is that building a covenanted society requires concern for comprehensive detail in every area of human endeavor.

The necessary ongoing dialectic between the solemn resoluteness of the *brit* as a general faith-commitment *not yet relating to specific details* and the meticulous concern for detailed application as a *condition for commitment to the covenant* will be recalled directly and indirectly throughout prophetic history. On the one hand, it will be necessary from time to time to recall the faith-commitment of the *brit*. At the same time, the detailed *halakhah* will need to be vividly realized by a community concerned with the particular. Underscoring the dialectic, there will be times when the *halakhah* will need to be re-addressed and re-legislated to avoid what Ernst Akiva Simon will refer to as an "evolutionary deficit" in halakhic development, i.e., the *halakhah* will have remained frozen in the face of necessary social change. At such times, the *brit* in all its spiritual breadth and depth will be called upon to reinvest the community-of-concern with high general purpose.

The Children of Israel will never again experience the specific set of circumstances that has brought them to Sinai and to the Grand Revelation at Sinai. But they will re-enact the signing of a covenant with an adjoining commitment to keeping the legislated mandates of the covenant when they return to the Land of Israel after the First Exile. In Nehemiah 10:1 the verse says: *"U-be-khol zot anahnu kortim amanah!"* ("In spite of everything we hereby sign an agreement!") Here it will be a people who will differ from those Children of Israel who had come out of Egypt never having experienced sovereignty in implementing the covenant. Here, under Ezra and Nehemiah, it will be a people who will carry the burden of knowing that previous generations have failed in embodying Torah in their sovereign Israelite society. They will face a grim task of resettlement. Most of their brethren will prefer remaining in the Babylonian exile. And God will be in eclipse. There will be no prophets to bring them the word of God directly. There will only be Ezra who will re-teach them the word of God which was given at Sinai. But they will all be ready to sign on again despite the failure. *"U-be-khol zot anahnu kortim amanah!"*

Why the previous failure? Is a sovereign nation in its own land dedicated to a Godly humane covenant pre-destined to fail? Is it not humanly possible to implement the terms of the Torah in the crucible of conflict that is human civilization? The answer will plague Israel, its children the Jewish people, and any nation sufficiently enlightened to the dilemmas associated with living and building communities-on-earth. The Torah itself is sensitive to the dilemmas and is therefore far from utopian in its outlook as a legislative tool for building the hoped-for covenanted community in Eretz Yisrael.

The Problem of Slavery

Illustrative of the non-utopian outlook of the Torah is its recognition of slavery as an undeniable institution. In its day it cannot be otherwise. A translation of the axiom *"derekh eretz kadmah la-Torah"* with an ironic twist might be "the contemporary way of the world is a reality which the Torah must confront and live with." A dramatic climax has now been reached in the collective faith-experience of Israel: the revelation at Mount Sinai and the giving of the Ten Commandments. We have argued before that the chief focus within the Ten Commandments is on the first statement: "I am the Lord who has taken you out of Egypt from the house of slavery." God has emphasized that the very birth of national Jewish being has been rooted in its emergence from slavery to freedom, from slavery to redemption. Isn't it strange, then, perhaps even shocking, that among all the possible topics with which the following *mishpatim* could begin, it chooses the institution of *slavery* — and accepts it! The Torah sees it as an institution which will continue to exist in the Promised Land!

The question must be sharpened: The cardinal importance of the redemption from Egypt has been to free Israel from slavery, an institution — described in the first chapter of Exodus — as degrading, as utterly abusive of the idea that every human being is created in the image of God. How is it then that with all the sociomoral expectations underscored by the giving of the Torah, these first of the listed *mishpatim* assume that the institution of slavery will continue? The Torah, it is claimed, is the product of the revealed will of the Lord of the universe who is a righteous judge. How is it that the sociomoral expectations of this Torah should already be so limited that the Wilderness generation has to be oriented to the continuation of this barbarous institution?

The only serious response to the question argues that the economic structure of that era can in no way strike down the entire institution of slavery. All that the Torah can do is to lighten the moral burden of the institution, relatively speaking. It does so in these *mishpatim*. How much more so will the ongoing halakhic development in the Talmud alleviate the plight of Israelite slaves — more appropriately called "indentured servants." Furthermore, considering the era and the social, political, and economic realities of the era, there will be a certain amelioration of conditions regarding the non-Israelite slave as well.

The Talmud based on the written Torah has the *eved ivri* (the Hebrew slave) arrive at his state from one of two causes. He has stolen and has no way of returning or repaying what he has stolen. He is thereby "sold into slavery" in order to pay off his debt. It can be argued that such purposeful employment is much more preferable than uncreative incarceration. In fact, talmudic legislation will so protect the rights of the *eved* that a descriptive axiom will be coined: "He who acquires a Hebrew slave has acquired a master for himself."

The second cause for the Israelite's descent into slavery is personal debt. A man has failed economically and needs to support himself and family for a limited amount of time, the time it takes him to pay back his debt. This case is legislated clearly in Leviticus 25 where the injunction resonates with the echoes of Egypt: "He shall be as a hired resident within you; do not oppress him *be-farekh* (ruthlessly)"! In other words, the terms for such a debtor are evolving towards an enlightened employer-employee relationship. And it will be the twelfth-century codifier Rambam who will in effect sound the death-knell for Hebrew enslavement with his halakhic association of the institution of slavery with the institution of the Jubilee, i.e., since the Jubilee no longer exists, neither does slavery.

The question still stands! Why couldn't the *mishpatim* legislation begin with one of the more uncompromising moral injunctions such as "He who slays another shall be put to death," or with a treatment of perennially relevant subjects even for enlightened societies such as damages to person and property, borrowing and lending, etc? It is all there in the legislation. Why begin precisely with a topic concerning an institution shameful in its moral assumptions to the extent that the Rabbis — clearly sensitive to its moral complexities — will seek to liberalize the institution as best as they can in their Oral Torah? Why can't the Rabbis uproot the whole institution?

There is a deeper message to be derived from this preoccupation with slavery — right at the outset of the legislation. The Ramban says simply: "The subject of the Hebrew slave is discussed in order to stress that he is emancipated in the seventh year as a reminder of the Exodus from Egypt." But Abrabanel expands the discussion: "The subject of slavery emerges from the first commandment heard at Sinai which is the foundation of all the other commandments. And because the Holy One Blessed Be He took Israel out of Egypt he granted them the privilege to be *His* servants and therefore it was not right for them to be servants or slaves to each other — as it is written *'avadai hem'* ('they are My servants')." Certainly Abrabanel is direct in his condemnation of the institution — at least regarding Hebrew slaves.

Still, neither he nor the Ramban state unequivocally that slavery from a spiritual and moral point of view is intrinsically flawed and must lead to the degradation of the individual who is before all and after all a human being created in the image of God. They desist from such an emphatic statement even though they know it is true; it has to be true, or the whole Torah is a spiritual-moral travesty. They realize, however, that the "way of the world" is not yet ready for a socioeconomic classless society. It may never be ready. In their minds there may be positive movement towards that goal as is indicated by the Rambam's conclusion that just as the institution of Jubilee is not practical, so has the institution of slavery become obsolete. They also know that in the age in which they live, even if according to the *halakhah* Hebrew slavery is forbidden, the institution of "Canaanite" slavery, i.e., the involuntary servitude of "aliens," is still permitted — at least theoretically. Furthermore, they must be aware of the moral weakness in the Rambam's legalistic stratagem that because there is no longer a Jubilee, the institution of slavery can no longer exist.

One could argue against the Rambam's reasoning: If the Children of Israel would ever again achieve sovereignty over the Land of Israel and could even conceive theoretically of instituting the principles of the Jubilee, would Hebrew slavery again be allowed? What would Ramban the Zionist be hoping for as he would concretize his dream to go up to the Land, that ultimately full Jewish sovereignty would be achieved accompanied by the reinstitution of Jubilee *and slavery*? Hardly!

Abrabanel's moderate response to the question of why shouldn't slavery or any variation of the institution of slavery be outlawed unequivocally by the Torah begs further discussion, because he is not just an interpreter of Bible and a moral philosopher. He is a politician who finds himself in a fifteenth-sixteenth-century Machiavellian world that is falling apart around and on top of the Jewish people. The way of the medieval world has been similar for the Ramban who in the thirteenth century has had to escape from "no-win" theological debates with his oppressive Christian "hosts."

Abrabanel in his day is occupied in feverish political negotiations regarding the very existence of his Jewish community in a world of anti-Semites. He struggles philosophically and practically with questions that trouble any nation trying to survive in a "wilderness" or, more to the point, a jungle. He knows that in a jungle, the Torah cannot speak in a terminology of detached moral abstraction, in a language which is politely naïve but totally irrelevant to questions of political life or death. In such a jungle, in which there exist not only institutions like slavery, but war, wholesale expulsions, and annihilations, he is not about to state that slavery is a morally enlightened institution. But he understands that in such a world, slavery or indentured servitude may be a particularly appropriate example with which to underscore the human predicament conditioned by a world of power, exploitation, and ruthless competition for national and communal survival. The particular predicament has to do with the makeup of states and with the relationships of majority and minority populations within those states.

When Abrabanel sees the placement of the subject of slavery in a direct line with the first of the Ten Commandments, he is arguing that in the consciousness of Israel there must be juxtaposed as an eternal model the opposing social strata of slavery and lordship, servitude and freedom, against the background of the reality of majority populations and their sovereign power vis-à-vis the minority populations who live among them with their lack of power. This unnervingly paradoxical combination of opposing images has already been presented to Abraham by God in the ceremony of the "Covenant of the Pieces." Israel will live through a period in which they will be shackled in servitude. But at the appointed time they will be taken out of servitude in order to be prepared for freedom, for lordship, for sovereignty, for responsibility. Facing this kind of political reality, there are two possible options regarding the question of how to survive with moral self-respect.

One either prefers political "servitude" or political "lordship." Political "servitude" entails minority status in an exile situation without serious political responsibility, immune to the moral dilemmas associated with lordship and sovereignty but vulnerable to the power-driven decisions of the majority. In such a situation of political servitude, the "slaves," i.e., the minority — if they are able to — will have to cultivate what Isaiah Berlin will call an "inner citadel" of spiritual pride which will fortify them at least in their own minds and souls against the dominance of the majority.

The "Covenant of the Pieces" recommends, however, another option, the one announced in the Revelation of Torah for this new nation: lordship, sovereignty, independence, and responsibility. And that in the reality of the world as it exists there is no shame in lordship, sovereignty, and independence provided the independent sovereign lord is morally responsible — as morally responsible as he can be under the circumstances. And so there is a critical reminder recorded in the First Commandment that Israel is never to forget that it has emerged from servitude. Any temptation which the children of Israel will have to pervert the responsibility of independence, sovereignty, and lordship — being the majority — will be neutralized, it is hoped, by empathy with those who are now in the minority, i.e., in relative "servitude" to them.

Thus Abrabanel, in his quoting God's allusion to emancipated Israel as *avadai hem* (my servants), suggests more subtly, if indirectly, the strategy for surviving with moral self-respect in a world that oscillates between a "wilderness" and a jungle. The proclamation *avadai hem* means that ultimately no Jew may serve another Jew as a slave. *Avadai hem* then is the emancipation proclamation of every Jew. Is it meant to apply to the non-Jew as well? The first of the Ten Commandments has already proclaimed an end to Jewish serfdom at the hands of non-Jews. The *avadai hem* must be seen to imply as well that in the long run no human being shall be subservient, dependent, enslaved by another; for all human beings are *avadai hem* (God's servants).

In the short-term, however, political realities being what they are, there will be groups who by virtue of less than utopian political, social, and economic conditions will find themselves dominated by others. This means that an Israelite-Jewish sovereignty like all nations will be facing the problem of minority populations, aliens, "servants," who will challenge by their very presence in society the sociomoral norms of the Israelite-Jewish "upper class." This Israelite-Jewish "upper class" — like the upper classes of all nations — will seek and must seek to apply standards of equity and empathy to all people under its sovereignty while retaining its integrity as a sovereign Israelite-Jewish entity. The struggle to find a sociomoral equilibrium within the Israelite-Jewish sovereignty will be relentless. It will have to be if the covenant is understood to be grounded in the great moral absolute of the Torah — that all human beings are created in the image of God. In other words, the first commandment will provide the foundation-stone for constant sociomoral aspiration — particularly in a pre-messianic reality where myriad variations of the relationship between sovereignty and servitude are the "way of the world."

A Medicine for Life

The revelation at Sinai in its awesomeness cannot but be brought down to earth and there be compromised as God knows it will be, having driven Man out of an Eden in which he showed that he couldn't live. But God has not surrendered to despair. His Torah will be described as a *sam hayyim* (medicine for life). It will be bestowed upon Israel through the *hukim u-mishpatim* as a preventive antidote against the moral, social, and spiritual diseases of the "wilderness." Indeed, among the many *mishpatim* and *hukim* appear the two words *"ve-rapo yerapei"* (in healing, he shall be healed). The Hebrew language features such intensive repetitive construction; the two words may therefore be translated "he shall cause him to be *thoroughly* healed."

Nevertheless, the school of Rabbi Yishmael in the tractate *Berakhot* will learn from these words that the Children of Israel are to look both to God and to the human physician to work the cure. The revelation from God and the *mishpatim* in the hands of covenanted human beings will similarly, it is hoped, work the cure for the earthly world. The God of Israel has informed Moses that he is sending a messenger to lead His people to the Land where applying the medicine for life is their mandate. Only the Torah with its prescription for humanizing and sanctifying the *derekh eretz* (way of the world) can secure their confidence in what they are charged to do in order to fulfill their part of the covenant. Only the observance of the Torah's norms can keep Israel itself immune to the sociomoral disease that has destroyed Egypt. The medicine must not only be looked upon as a cure. As human physicians will learn to say: It must be taken as a preventive — a revelatory preventive.

Terumah   תרומה

There is a time for spectacular events which change the destinies of peoples — revolutions, wars, natural cataclysms, transcendent public revelations. And then there is a time for quiet and relative calm; opportunities for reflection and sober-minded self-examination. God Himself wants respite within the journey, some degree of stasis within the dynamic rush of events which are leading Israel — His people — to the Promised Land. The people, weary from having been pulled out of the pit of slavery and saved from near destruction, shaken by the paralyzing awesomeness of Sinai, also yearn for respite, for a period of stability, for a sense of security in predictability. The recommended solution is found in the instruction *"Ve'asu Li mikdash ve-shakhanti be-tokham"* ("May they make Me a sanctuary so that I may dwell among them").

It has been noted by the commentators that the syntax of *"ve-asu Li mikdash ve-shakhanti be-tokham"* requires an extra careful reading. The word *mikdash* (sanctuary) is in the singular; the word *be-tokham* (in them) is in the plural. Cassuto, for example, divides the verse into two separate virtually independent thoughts. The first part, *"ve-asu Li mikdash,"* is saying: "May the *mikdash* be a structure dedicated to Me and sanctified to Me." Cassuto adds that this part of the verse avoids saying *"ve-asu li* mishkan," in which the word *mishkan* would mean "dwelling place." God does not need a dwelling place; only Israel needs a dwelling place for God. When Israel will look upon this *mikdash* set up in their camp they will feel God's indwelling Presence. According to Cassuto, once the representational meaning of the *mikdash* is established, then the second part of the statement will be understood. *"Ve-shakhanti be-tokham"* ("I will dwell amongst them") will mean that just as the Children of Israel have sensed God's glory present on Mount Sinai, so they will sense it among *themselves* on the plane of earthly reality and in the circle of each of their normal everyday lives.

The *Mishkan*

Will Israel have the capacity to appreciate, however, that any attempt to encapsulate God's indwelling Presence in an objectively contained space is fraught with idolatrous potential? Will they avoid such error by recognizing what Isaiah's seraphim will be witness to — "that the whole earth is full of His glory"? They will have to be reminded of it in emphatic terms following the disastrous episode of the "golden calf." Their descendants will be taught it continuously at great cost when they see that both Holy Temples will not be immune to destruction despite their purported "hospitality" to God's indwelling Presence.

In the meantime, here at the commencement of their journey following the Exodus, Israel must have a sense of tangible Presence or, at the very least, a tangible testimony to a Presence. Shmuel David Luzzatto rationalizes the need for the *mikdash* in that having it among them the Children of Israel will be inspired to maintain a solid unity committed to God's covenant of Torah. And so despite the risk of any such tabernacle turning into a house of idolatry, the *"mikdash-mishkan"* is approved.

The risk is recorded well before the Exodus. The persistent concern is that hidden and not so hidden in the consciousness of the people is the temptation to build a *mikdash-mishkan* not in praise of the one true Sovereign but to challenge the one true Sovereign. This people, after all, has come out recently from under a powerful, all-encompassing imperial idolatry. Perhaps they will seek to build another Tower of Babel, a testimony to *Man's* "greatness," not *God's*. Perhaps they will seek to imitate — albeit in a small way — Egyptian temples, pyramids, subtly denying their own covenanted future as a uniquely endowed new people Israel with a new idea, a new spiritual-ethical vision. Perhaps their understanding of the implications of the Torah covenant is at this point in their spiritual-moral development too limited. They may fall into the trap of believing that it will be sufficient to encapsulate God's indwelling Presence in an edifice without allowing for God's Presence or imprint of His Presence in His Torah to impact on their individual and collective lives.

Because of these palpable risks, the instruction *"ve-asu Li mikdash — ve-shakhanti be-tokham"* underscores the latter part of the verse as a pedagogic condition: If God cannot be perceived as dwelling within each and every

Israelite, i.e., being perceived as standing demandingly before each and every Israelite (Psalm 16:8), then the idea of a sanctuary in which God dwells is not only blasphemous — it is perverse. The commentary *Tzeidah la-Derekh* will summarize the idea in his allusion to the later Jeremiah's diatribe at the Temple gates in Jerusalem. Jeremiah will mock the Israelites who fail to execute justice among their citizenry, who oppress the disadvantaged, and indulge in a variety of spiritual and moral debasements and yet persist in coming to "worship" in the Temple. They dare to chant their incantations *"Heikhal Adonai, Heikhal Adonai, Heikhal Adonai* Heimah" ("The Temple of the Lord, the Temple of the Lord, the Temple of the Lord are *these*"). But *these* buildings are fundamentally nothing more than ordinary buildings, if they are allowed to exist alongside social injustice. These latter day *batei-mikdash* cannot possibly be home to God's Presence when His Presence has been shut out of the lives of the people.

As Nahum Sarna has pointed out in further support of the reluctance to "locate" God in a particular abode, the verb *shakhen* (dwell) is not synonymous with the common verb *yashav*. The verb *shakhen* conveys the idea of temporary lodging in a tent and "characterizes the nomadic style of life…the sanctuary is not meant to be understood literally as God's abode…rather it functions to make perceptible and tangible the conception of God's immanence." In other words, God's *Shekhinah* can be present, vividly and providentially present, provided that the Children of Israel are hospitable to such a dynamic Presence.

In essence what is being demanded of Israel as a nation and from each Israelite as a member of the covenanted nation is to let the *mikdash-mishkan* serve as the outer communal concretization of what should be going on in the inner life respectively of the community and individual members of the community. The Malbim will preach: "Each of us must build a sanctuary in the chambers of his heart so that he may prepare himself to be a dwelling place for God's indwelling Presence, an altar, as it were, on which he is prepared to offer up his total being."

Once the Children of Israel have received the respite for which they have been seeking after the excitement of the Exodus and once God Himself has relegated Himself, as it were, to a less active role in the ongoing journey through the Wilderness, then there is an opportunity — in truth a necessity — for focusing more on the individual Israelite and his responsibilities in the covenantal enterprise. It will not just be the individual's lip-service to the commands of his leader Moses. It will be the relentless call to the individual to eschew idolatry and to commit himself comprehensively to the covenant. As it had been with God's questions to Adam and Cain it will be with each later Israelite. As it will be with Joshua's challenge to Israel before his death to decide between the covenant and "other gods"; and as it will be with Elijah's taunting of his generation to choose between God and Baal, so it is with the Israelite in the Wilderness — where is his heart to be?

In a peculiar irony, some of the fabrics to be used in the *mikdash-mishkan* will be a combination of linen and wool otherwise forbidden as *kilayim* or *sha'atnez*. Jewish law will dictate that hybrid mixtures are not to be planted or worn. Yet the tabernacle which is to represent God's indwelling Presence may allow itself the *kilayim*. It is to be a sign to the Israelite that for him the line between what is permitted and what is forbidden is at times very thin, so thin that his committed wholeheartedness will be his only security in ascertaining the path he shall choose.

Making the choices which are acceptable to the covenant will need constant reminders. In later Jewish history, the time of the reading of the Torah portion concerned with instructions for building the *mikdash-mishkan* will coincide with the Hebrew month Adar. And mishnaic law will dictate that on the first of Adar public announcement is to be made reminding Jews of the obligation to donate their half-shekel towards the cost of providing the public offerings for *Pesah*. In addition, Jews are to be instructed to check their fields and gardens for diverse hybrid mixtures. This double instruction reinforces a double message regarding the covenant. On the one hand, each Israelite, each Jew, must consider himself responsible, accountable, as he proudly donates his half-shekel to the public purse. At the same time, the Israelite, this Jew, must beware of the temptations of pluralistic paganism, of the variety of hybrid mixtures seeking to entice him into forgetting covenantal purpose and direction.

The Cherubim

The task of this first generation of free Israelites will be double in its intensity and responsibility. For these free Israelites will have to educate themselves as well as set the pattern for the coming generations to be brought to a full understanding of the covenant. The echo of the response of Moses to Pharaoh, *"bi-ne'areinu u-vi-zkeneinu nelekh"* ("we leave with our young and our old"), will pervade the efforts of this and all future generations of Jews. The central family ritual of *Pesah* has already been instituted with the shared experience of the offering of the paschal lamb. It will prescribe henceforth and through the ages a family *Seder* (Order) with its central focus on the questions of the young. All of Jewish pedagogic history may be summarized as an exercise in the initiation of the young into the covenant.

It is for this reason that the Rabbis see one of the most prominently suggestive images associated with the *mikdash-mishkan* — the cherubim — as representing children. There is no certainty as to what a "cherub" is or what it is to represent. How does it become suggestive of a child? It has been associated with the word *merkavah* (the divine chariot) of Ezekiel. In the talmudic tractate *Hagigah* (13b) there is the following discussion. One verse in Ezekiel (1:10) says: "Each of the four creatures had a human face at the front; each of the four had the face of a lion on the right; each of the four had the face of an ox on the left; and each of the four had the face of an eagle at the back." But juxtaposed to this verse is the report in Ezekiel 10:14: "Each one had four faces: One was a *cherub's* face, the second a human face, the third a lion's face, and the fourth an eagle's face."

In this second version, the Talmud notes, the face of the ox is omitted — or rather exchanged. Resh Lakish explains that Ezekiel was entreating God for mercy on behalf of Israel and exchanged the image of the face of an ox — or of the same family of an ox, a calf — for a cherub. Resh Lakish implores: "Lord of the Universe, *'kategor ye'aseh sanegor'* ('shall a prosecutor become a defender')?" The face of the ox is reminiscent of the golden calf, a prosecutorial image reminding God and Israel of the sinfulness of the people. The *merkavah* represents the *Shekhinah* (God's indwelling Presence) which is leaving Jerusalem, symbolizing the loss of the Temple. The return of the *merkavah* will symbolize the return of the *Shekhinah*, the redemption of Israel, and the rebuilding of the Temple.

The Talmud then continues with its definition of the word "cherub." Rabbi Abbahu sees the word in Aramaic as *ke-ravi'a* (like a child), calling our attention to the Babylonian use of the word *ravi'a* as meaning "child." This "cherub," therefore, this child is purposely associated with the redeeming "chariot" (*merkavah*). For who if not the children will be considered the force within Israel that is to represent future redemption. Isaiah's messianic vision in which the carnivorous animals and herbivorous animals will all lie down together "and a little child shall lead them" will serve to implant in Israel an optimistic eternal light for the future. The child is that future!

The education of the child for living according to the "way of the world" will not be seen by the adult generation as automatic initiation into the covenant. Such initiation will require a particular kind of education aimed at inspiring commitment. Nevertheless, what will become a genuine attribute of Jewish communities in the future will be the concern for learning and teaching, for acquiring and transmitting the skills for survival on the one hand and the tools for spiritual, moral, and cultural enlightenment on the other. That every child is to be taught from the earliest age — at least the male children — will become a self-evident truth in every Jewish community. Ultimately the female segment of society will be included as part of a universal application of the theory. But such dedication to education as such will not necessarily mean initiation into the covenant. Education for purposes of living according to the "way of the world" will not by itself serve the purposes of the covenant. "Derekh eretz kadmah la-Torah" is to mean that the way of the world is the necessary grounding for Torah. But only the value-laden influence of Torah can validate "derekh eretz," i.e., human life-on-earth.

The Rabbis of the talmudic era will sense the urgency of Moses' labor in bringing the Torah to Israel and sharing the details of the Torah with an Israel not fully aware of the pain and suffering which will have to accompany the application of such details to the enterprise of covenantal living. The Midrash *Sifre* will have Moses say to Israel: "You don't know how much I suffered, how much I labored, how I wearied myself during those forty days and nights with God. I came among the angels, among the living beings, among the fiery creatures, any one of whom could have burned up the world and all its inhabitants. I gave my flesh and blood to the effort. Just as I learned it in suffering so shall you; or, just as you will learn it in suffering so shall you teach it in suffering."

The rabbinic authors of *midrashim* such as these will be looking to a particular kind of education, one which will have the power to reconstruct for their exile situation a new world of spiritual and moral values which will have the power to inspire Jews to want to keep living as a covenanted entity — even in exile. Moses' existential challenge of bringing his people from exile into a pre-sovereignty opportunity may appear to be different than the challenge that the later Rabbis will face. It is not! He has brought a distraught, decimated horde of slaves out of their known situation promising them a new world. By new world he means a society in which their every effort will be measured by covenantal standards set by the Creator-Revealer-Redeemer of the Universe. This new world will need generations of Israelites prepared to build a covenanted society. The "child who will lead them" will need to have come through a crucible of struggle that will reflect Moses' sojourn on the Mountain together with the "fiery creatures, any one of whom could have burned up the world and all its inhabitants."

The cherub is seen as guarding — or at least as hovering over — God's revealed word as concretized literally and figuratively in the tablets. It will again be the talmudic Rabbis who will understand the full implications of the Torah and who will elaborate on what is at stake in the Children of Israel's acceptance of the Torah: "What is meant by, 'Thou didst cause sentence to be heard from Heaven; the earth feared, and was tranquil' (Psalms 76:9): if it feared, why was it tranquil, and if it was tranquil, why did it fear? But at first it feared, yet subsequently it was tranquil. It feared lest Israel would reject the Torah, and became tranquil when Israel accepted it.

"And why did it fear? In accordance with Resh Lakish — for Resh Lakish said (with regard to the six days of Creation): 'Why is it written and there was evening and there was morning, *the* sixth day' (Gen. 1:31); What is the purpose of the additional 'the'?" In the case of the other days it is simply stated, a second day, a third day, etc. 'a' being unexpressed in Hebrew. "This teaches that the Holy One, blessed be He, stipulated with the works of creation and said thereto, 'If Israel accepts the Torah, ye shall exist; but if not, I will turn you back into emptiness and formlessness.'"

Resh Lakish thus translates homiletically: "and the continuance of morning and evening depend on *the sixth* day of Sivan, when Israel was offered the Torah." Without the Torah the world must inevitably lapse into chaos and anarchy. In other words, the precondition for the world existing at all is that it be defined by Torah. But this definition also includes the creature called the child of Israel. Man has been the pinnacle of creation, created also on the portentous sixth day, placed in a perfect harmony-filled Garden to work it and to guard it. But Man has failed in his task and has forced God to re-plan His creation towards a more detailed, infinitely more complex civilization in partnership with the descendants of undifferentiated Man. And the spearhead in implementing this plan is now to be one covenanted people led by generations of new Israelites wedded to the covenanted partnership.

Will these Children of Israel reject the Torah and turn thereby into prosecutors of the world thrusting forth the face of Ezekiel's ox-calf of golden vanity? Or will they defend the world by giving it spiritual-moral hope as represented by the face of the child? The answer Israel will give, of course, will be the cherub. Israel will have accepted the Torah, but their "acceptance" assures them of nothing complete. On the contrary, Moses knows how difficult it will be from his recollection of the fiery creatures surrounding him on Mount Sinai, darting in and out at him as he "prepares" the Torah. Israel's acceptance will guarantee them a life of struggle, a life of suffering. Moses will recall for them the original Israel who was Jacob, limping, with his ladder reaching heavenward but with its feet chained to the earth. Each child — each cherub — will be struggling to realize on earth the redemptive promises of the *merkavah* — that redeeming divine chariot looking always to return to Jerusalem in order to grant Israel a renewed opportunity at covenantal sovereignty.

The Synagogue

All of Jacob's children, the Children of Israel, in their struggle to implement the covenant on earth will be tempted to dream of therapeutic apocalypses, prematurely messianic promises that will degenerate into messianic pretense — with frustration and failure inevitable. They will yearn from time to time to return to a pristine never-never land called Eden, to discover there a garden of ideal spiritual and moral values. But as a descendant of Jacob, Moses — at least Moses, if not yet his people — knows that one cannot go back, certainly not to a never-never land. The Torah, the living Torah, is meant to be a program for the future, for the cherubim of the future. And this future must be relevant to living on earth — no matter how corrupt, no matter how initially or perennially inhospitable the world may be and will be to Torah and the covenant. The Children of Israel will have to initiate ways of living in the world, of weaving into its way of life answers to political, economic, familial, and personal identity questions without losing a sense of transcendent purpose.

Moses understands as no one before him and perhaps no one after him how difficult the task will be to transmit the Torah to his own generation of Israelites, let alone to future generations who will not have experienced directly God's revelation. He anticipates the machinations of the Serpent who will plant the doubts and confusions within all Israelites, the learned and the unlearned. He knows that there will be divisions among the people. He knows that there will be divided personalities — those who will be certain that they believe in God exclusively; yet, in reality do not. The interchange between the face of the idolatrous ox-calf and the face of the child will plague all of Jewish history. Throughout Moses' career as leader of this people he is driven and will continue to be driven by his prophetic foreknowledge of what that history will be — a history of sublime achievement neutralized by idolatrous backsliding.

The *mikdash-mishkan* will thus be forced into becoming a vehicle for continuous contact between the source of revelation and the needy recipient — the House of Israel. It will be expected that God's indwelling Presence will be there to recall for the House of Israel or for any individual member of the House of Israel the terms of the covenant — provided that it will be *et ratzon* (the appropriate time) in God's merciful judgment. The particular *mikdash-mishkan* of the Wilderness experience will give way to various tabernacles within the Land of Israel after the conquest. The great *mikdash-mishkan* will eventually be built and will become for the Jewish people *the Bet ha-Mikdash* the permanent House of God. Its central place in collective historic consciousness will outlive its destruction — twice. It will be dreamt of and yearned for in prayer, studied about and prepared for reconstruction when the messianic time will come. But until such time, a vital substitute will be introduced into the national covenantal life of the Jewish people — the Synagogue.

If the original Wilderness tabernacle will have been intended to be the place of meeting where God is ever in readiness to reveal Himself to Israel and to "speak" with them, the Synagogue will become known as the *mikdash me'at* (the miniature tabernacle). There will be a change, however, in the operational activity of the Synagogue as tabernacle. The Rabbis will claim that prophetic revelation will have ceased with the return from the first exile of Ezra's generation. In its place three specific functions will be served by the Synagogue as an integrated surrogate for God's ongoing revelation in the

Wilderness tabernacle or in later sanctuaries like the *Bet ha-Mikdash* itself in the Land of Israel.

The Synagogue will be intended to be a *Bet Midrash* — a House of Study. The aggadic Midrash will state: "If you wish to know Him at whose word the world came into being, then learn the *Aggadah*, for through it you shall know the Holy One, praised be He, and follow His ways." The halakhic Midrash will ask: "What is the meaning of 'And God spoke to Moses saying...'? Moses said before God: Sovereign of the Universe! Cause me to know what the final decision is on each matter of the Law.' God replied: The majority must be followed...." In short, both midrashic traditions, the aggadic and halakhic, will operate on the theological premise that study of the tradition — aggadic and halakhic — bring revelatory insight, Torah insight into the way of the world.

The Synagogue will be intended to be a *Bet Tefillah* — a House of Prayer. For notwithstanding the indispensability of study in the search to ascertain God's will, there are instrumental, utilitarian aspects and purposes to study — legitimate as concern for the "way of the world" is legitimate. Prayer, on the other hand, is an act which in its ideal form is non-utilitarian — even that prayer which is petitionary. Abraham Joshua Heschel will attempt to describe the pristine moment of prayer: "We pray. We are carried forward to Him who is coming close to us. We endeavor to divine His will, not merely His command. Prayer is an answer to God: 'Here am I. And this is the record of my days. Look into my heart, into my hopes and my regrets.'" The assumption will be, in other words, that an authentic opening of one's heart, a focused attention upon the "burning bush" in one's soul will be the regular order of the day for the covenanted member of the House of Israel. With every prayer of praise, petition, and thanksgiving the worshiper will be acknowledging God as sovereign ruler of all. And in his prayer he will be hoping to elicit God's appropriate attention and instruction.

But even prayer along with study will not have exhausted the purpose and function of the Synagogue. For the Synagogue will also be intended to be a *Bet Knesset* — a House of Assembly. Simon Greenberg will speak of the Synagogue as "the institution whose function it is to concretize here and now the concept of *Knesset Yisrael*. And what is *Knesset Yisrael*? It is the Jewish people at their conceivable best." The Talmud will recall Rabbi Yishmael ben Elazar's rebuke of those who will prefer calling the *Bet Knesset* a "*Bet Am*" — a place of ordinary gathering of people — or a place which aims for ordinariness. But the Children of Israel will need to be taught and reminded regularly that revelation or hints of revelation can only come if a people is extraordinarily ready for it. In terms of the covenant, the House of Israel will need to aspire to become its *conceivable best*.

It cannot be otherwise if God is expected to dwell among them in their covenanted Land. It cannot be otherwise if Israel is aspiring to walk in the footsteps of Abraham who signed the first draft of the covenant as he walked the Land which was being promised to his descendants. But at the time, Abraham was "alone-in-faith"; and Abraham had already reached a point of being at his conceivable best. It would now remain for the Children of Israel to aspire to "walk that Land before God with a whole heart" — *"be-lev ehad ke-ish ehad"* ("as a unified people with one heart"). This would be excruciatingly difficult; but it would be a precondition for Israel striving to imitate their father Abraham: aiming as a complex polyglot people to becoming its conceivable best.

Institutionalizing Memory

If the Synagogue is truly to serve as a *mikdash me'at*, as the critical reminder of the original Wilderness *mikdash-mishkan*, it will need to be that place dedicated to intellectual, spiritual, and sociomoral rejuvenation within the larger agenda of settling and building a covenanted society. At lengthy periods in Jewish history, however, in which the settling and building of a covenanted society will be put on hold because of exile, the Synagogue and its support will in effect serve as the most vital institutionalization-of-memory of the covenant and the Land.

The exile community living in close identification with the Synagogue will fulfill those *mitzvot* commanded by the covenant which will maintain them as a corporate entity. The indwelling Presence of the God of Israel within that movable *mishkan* will keep the wandering people alive and alert — even in the "wilderness" — to their long-term Zionist destiny of settling and building again a covenanted society in the Land of Israel.

Tetzaveh

תצוה

God creates the universe with the words *"yehi or"* ("let there be light"). The light is to serve as the redemptive force which dispels the darkness. At the same time it is to illuminate the glories of God's creation. The human being has been made to see but he will not be able to see without light. And the darkness which the human being will experience if he cannot see is not just a physical darkness. It can be a spiritual, moral, cultural eclipse which — even if he can see physiologically — blots out for him all hopeful possibilities in life. Israel has just emerged from the black pit of ancient totalitarian Egypt. It has received the Torah of Light and Life. If to house the Ark of the Covenant which will contain the Torah, Israel has been commanded to build a tabernacle, what better symbol of God's creative renewal than the raising of an Eternal Light in that tabernacle. A Light for Eternal Life!

Along with His creation God has committed Himself to a covenant. He has announced long before the Exodus of Israel from its entombment in the bondage of Egypt that He will never again destroy the world as He did in Noah's generation. This is a covenantal promise which God has made to all of humankind. The agent for carrying out the terms of the covenant on behalf of humankind is to be Israel — at least preliminarily. Israel is to be an embodiment on a collective socio-national scale of the proverb: *"Ner ha-Shem Nishmat ha-Adam"* ("The Candle of God is the Soul of Man"). In other words, the covenant which God has originated with Abram-Abraham is a positive extension of God's "rainbow" sign to Noah's descendants that the world and its human inhabitants are being given another chance. Israel's destiny is to represent a national human effort to avail itself of that chance to bring spiritual, moral, and cultural light into the world for its own as well as for humankind's benefit.

In the future, Isaiah the prophet will enjoin Israel to "arise and shine, for our light has come…for whereas darkness shall cover the earth, and thick clouds the peoples, upon you — Israel — the Lord will shine…*ve-halkhu goyyim le-orekh* (and the nations shall walk in your light)." Isaiah will be articulating that which will be summarized in the "light unto the nations" concept — an idea which will give an additional illumination and responsibility to Jews to fulfill the covenant. All of creation relies upon such fulfillment.

God has "breathed" from His spirit into Man that which is intended to represent as the soul-of-man a transcendent dimension to his existence. Without this additional "breath" Man is a lowly creature, no different from the dumb animals in God's creation. God's "breath" can be bestowed upon a creature as dumb as Balaam's ass and the latter will talk and say poignant things. But God has chosen Man to have the particular kind of *neshamah* that will have the capacity through his potentially autonomous nature to truly carry on with God the necessary reciprocal relationship demanded by the covenant. God has chosen Israel to be fully and actively conscious of His gift of the *neshamah* to human beings. God will seek from Israel, therefore, the kind of spiritual and moral postures which will light God's "candle," as it were, in the world for other human beings to experience. In short, the *Ner Tamid* (Eternal Light) will serve in the Wilderness tabernacle — as in every future tabernacle — to remind Israel of its responsibility to this covenantal reciprocity.

Two Grounds for the Covenant

There is an opening command given to Israel regarding the Eternal Light. They are to "bring clear oil of beaten olives for lighting in order to raise up an Eternal Light." Inherent in the very command are two contrasting images which will be conjured up throughout Jewish history reflecting two contrasting attitudes towards the possibility of covenantal continuity throughout that history. Rabbi Yohanan, on the one hand, will be struck by the image of *katit la-ma'or* (beaten olives). Why, he asks, is Israel to be compared to an olive? To inform us that just as an olive will not give forth its oil except through *katit* (pounding), Israel will not be able to be brought back to the good path from perdition except through suffering. Rami bar Hama, on the other hand, will focus on the image of *le-ha'alot Ner Tamid* (raising up an Eternal Light). *Le-ha'alot* (to raise it up) is meant to cause a flame to be stirred up so that it can burn independently and not because of outside stimuli.

Rabbi Yohanan's preoccupation with the *katit la-ma'or* image of olives or Israel being pounded in order to bring out the best in them is distressing but prescient. For Israel has already experienced in the Egyptian servitude a foretaste of what it will undergo in its later national agony — that anti-Semitism will often be the insidious but potent force which brings Israel to renewed commitment. There will be a school of thought that will insist that Jewish covenantal survival — nay, even Jewish creaturely survival — will be traceable solely and exclusively to anti-Semitism.

The pedagogic scenario will have begun with the understanding of Abram as *ivri*, a nomenclature derived from the Hebrew word *eber* (side). The whole world is on one "side," while Abram is on the other "side." The hyperbolic notion that Abram has to confront, combat, and emerge victorious against legions of idolaters, a whole world of idolaters, has its seed in the *peshat* (the simple meaning) of God's charge to him in Nimrod's Mesopotamia. *"Lekh lekha"* in this context is a rebellion against all that is wrong in Nimrod's civilization, a civilization, which according to the midrashic imagination, has already tried to impose its will upon Abram and failed.

What has been the *shi'bud Mitzrayim* (the enslavement in Egypt) but the attempt to entomb the covenantal idea with Jacob's and Joseph's bones before the idea will have had the opportunity to flesh out its spiritual and social possibilities. But Israel — bludgeoned into a comatose social state — has cried out finally and effectively enough to attract God's attention. And God's attention has initiated the events which will not lead to Jewish creativity in Egypt but which will decisively destroy Egypt and enable Israel to be reborn for creativity elsewhere.

The major post-Exodus pre-Emancipation example of anti-Semitism serving as the catalyst for an awakening of Jewish consciousness and resistance will be the report of the events associated with Purim. The talmudic association of the autonomous acceptance of the terms of the covenant with the period in Persian exile where God is presumably in eclipse underscores the words in the Scroll of Esther *"kiyemu ve-kibelu"* ("they fulfilled as they accepted"). Even without God's awesome immediate Presence hovering over them, Israel emphatically "signs on" again to the covenant. But if it is not God who "pounds" them into an awakening, who or what is it if not the blatant machinations of murderous fools and buffoons — Ahasueres and Haman — who have limitless power at their command. It is their anti-Semitism which fortuitously for the Jews of Persia lacks the serpentine cleverness of Pharaoh's *"hava nithakma"* ("let us deal wisely with them"). Thereupon Mordecai and Esther are able to anticipate the catastrophe in time. Through their resourcefulness at court and through the Jews' readiness to confront and defeat their enemies militarily, they succeed in preventing a proto-Shoah.

Finally it will be the Shoah itself that will be the quintessential spur to revolution in Jewish thinking, confirming what the modern Zionist theorists will have been arguing all along — that anti-Semitism is a virulent germ which requires a revolutionary antibiotic. The post-Emancipation early Zionists will know that the fires of extermination are not just smoldering from the various pogroms and expulsions of medieval Europe. There is a new apocalypse of hatred being stoked into readiness for ignition. And the messianic prophet of the new political awakening will be a Herzl whose inspiration at least at the beginning will be exclusively "negative." Herzl will argue that the Jews need a place of their own, so that the sickness of anti-Semitism can be eliminated. The *katit la-ma'or* (the pounding in order to send forth the pure oil) is unfortunately the necessary catalyst.

Is there nothing intrinsically constructive to be derived from the Jewish spirit itself? Rabbi Yohanan's theory that only a negative phenomenon such as anti-Semitism can bring out the Jewish determination to survive and revive the will-to-live will have strong historic confirmation. But if that is so, the theory is based on a pathological state which, at least in the opinion of those like Rami bar Hama, has to be by definition unhealthy. It is one thing for a person or a people to be prepared for hostility; it's quite another for a person or a people to build a strategy for creative survival based exclusively on external hostility. The reason is twofold: first, Israel is depending upon outside forces to determine its destiny, a position intrinsically weak and tenuous; but secondly, when the outside forces are pathological, then Israel, by waiting, as it were, for the noxious plots of the anti-Semites to impact upon its agenda is tantamount to collaborating with the wicked.

Rami bar Hama's approach — based as it is on his interpretation that "the flame of the Eternal Light must ascend of itself, and not through something else" — will argue for a positive grounding for a Jewish will-to-live. One should sustain the positive in a tradition by emphasizing the intrinsic strength within *us* rather than looking outside for negative spurs to inspire and to motivate. The question being asked throughout the generations will be: Is there nothing intrinsically valuable in the covenant, in Judaism, in being Jewish? Is there no pure olive oil to be lit and to be self-sustaining, reinforcing? No internal light?

The same four examples used to illustrate the negative stimuli to Jewish survival throughout its history may be turned right-side-up to strengthen the Rami bar Hama position. Abram's appearance on the ancient scene may be considered, it is true, a revolt against the pagan status quo of Nimrod's empire. At the same time, however, it may be seen as an independent, intrinsically valid lightning bolt into human history that has forever altered the way human beings have looked at their destiny and purpose on earth. Abram's idea of the ultimate Oneness which unifies all creation and posits the human being, every human being, as worthy to be treated as God's special creature, is an idea which lifts human aspiration well beyond the mere ugly reality of human hostility and conflict.

Similarly the Exodus from Egypt may be seen as the embodiment of the positive idea of national freedom and self-determination. The "Covenant of the Pieces" consummated between God and Abram long before the servitude in Egypt may predict a future negative phenomenon. The promise of redemption, however, comes out of God's positive goal of freeing Abraham and his descendants, the Children of Israel, in order for them to go on their national journey of "*lekh lekha.*" And while the events recorded in *Megillat Esther* describe anti-Semitism at its pre-Shoah starkest, that same period in Jewish history is also marked by the first *Shivat Tziyon* (the return of the first exile from Babylonia to Eretz Yisrael). Ezra and Nehemiah will shepherd a people back to the Land and in the course of building the Second Jewish Commonwealth will expand and deepen the parameters of Torah for their new contemporary situation.

Finally, Zionism may be perceived as chiefly Herzlian-Pinskerian in its antibiotic function of counteracting the disease of anti-Semitism. But others will argue for a positive dimension to Zionism — its reawakening of the Jewish creative spirit, e.g., the resuscitation of the Hebrew language and its literature, the flowering of Israeli agricultural and technological ingenuity and invention, the Gordonian emphasis on human renewal, the sundry examples of social reconstruction and cultural readaptation.

Confronting the Serpentine Darkness

Rami bar Hama's focus on the Eternal Flame renewing itself cannot be seen as rejecting entirely, however, Rabbi Yohanan's preference for the *katit la-ma'or* image. The light that dispels the darkness may be supernal, a direct gift from God to Man who is God's agent on earth. But the darkness doesn't surrender easily. It seeks to envelop as much of life as it can to the constant misgivings of Man. And while God has created the light for Man, who in essence is intended to serve as God's "Eternal Light" on earth, it will be part of Man's covenantal responsibility to assure that the supernal light keeps descending so that Man's light can keep ascending.

Adam has been fortunate to have had the blessing of God's supernal light. The blessing has not guaranteed him, however, an existence free of anxiety. The Midrash says: "The light shone for him thirty-six hours from the time he was created on the sixth day. There were twelve hours during which it shone on Shabbat Eve, then twelve hours over the night of Shabbat, and then twelve hours of Shabbat Day. Once the sun went down on *motza'ei Shabbat* ('the outgoing of the Shabbat'), darkness began to envelop Adam and he was afraid, as it is written in Psalms 139:11 'Should I say that darkness shall strike me (*yeshufeni*), the night shall become light for me (*ba'adeni*)!'

"The word *yeshufeni* conjures up God's condemnation and decree upon the Serpent of the Garden of Eden regarding the enmity which will persist between him and Man: 'Man shall strike (*yeshufkha*) at your head, and you shall strike (*teshufenu*) at his heel!' As the darkness is about to enshroud Man completely, God orders for Adam two flints which the latter then rubs together in order to produce for his immediate use the light which in the future will serve Adam's descendants — on earth." Thus, unlike Prometheus who will have had to steal fire from Heaven in order to teach Man its uses, Adam will have been taught by God to create his own sources of light with which to separate the "darkness" from his life and from his destiny.

But the issue is more complex for Adam's descendants than it will have been for Adam. The play on the word in Psalms 139:11 "*ba'adeni*" — the night shall become light for me in my "*Eden*" situation — cannot mean the same thing for later Israel. Adam loses Eden. Israel will never have an Eden. Israel will plod through the forty-year Wilderness in order to arrive at another spiritual, moral, cultural, political "wilderness" which it will be charged to cultivate into a covenanted garden. But it will still not be an Eden! Adam has had to learn to create his own sources of light for the darkness which he himself has brought on following his surrender to the machinations of the Serpent. And now, granted, Israel has been taken out of darkness by God's supernal light. But because of Israel's vacillations which will become more and more pronounced during the course of its wanderings, the supernal light will not suffice to dispel the darkness unless Israel provides additional light of its own.

The lights of *motza'ei Shabbat* will serve to inspire later generations of Jews to recite the *Havdalah* blessings separating the holy from the profane, the light from the darkness, Israel from the nations, and the seventh day from the other six days of labor. But the clarity of the various separations will often elude Israel. Israel will seek out the holy and the light and the sanctity of the Shabbat. But Israel will lamentably often lose its way as it will try to understand the constructive purpose in distinguishing itself from the "nations." It will often seek to mask its own covenantal identity before the challenge of the Eternal Light. In seeking to hide this true covenantal identity from itself, Israel will often behave like a masked reveler at a Purim masquerade ball. Lawrence Durrell's description of such self-effacement will be acutely applicable to those Jews seeking to escape their identity: "They suddenly found themselves turned to ciphers, expelled into a formless world of adventitious meetings, mask to dark mask, like a new form of insect life…the spirits of the darkness had taken over, disinheriting the daylight hearts and minds of the maskers, plunging them ever deeper into the loneliness of their own irrecoverable identities…"

Israel will yearn for the light and yet will often cower in the darkness of its own uncertainties and insecurities. It will covet the distinction from the other nations as a badge of honor with concomitant rewards. Yet, it will so often lust after cipherhood, longing to be lost in the profane and undifferentiated. It will appear to be seeking to return to primitive creaturehood, preferring the sovereignty of the Serpent to that of God.

The Priesthood

Sensitive to the difficulties which these early Israelites will experience in learning to distinguish between that which will be considered holy and that which will be considered profane, God separates a class of individuals within the House of Israel who will be considered "holy." True, the entire people is to be considered a "kingdom of priests, a holy nation." But it is felt that there will need to be special "caretakers of the holy" — at least until the people have learned to adapt to its requirements. The High Priest is not — nor can he be — the prophet-leader.

Yehezkel Kaufmann shows that whereas there may be some hints at ruler-ship among the accoutrements associated with the High Priest — the crown and his anointment with oil — these are not signs of sovereignty. They are meant to be reminders of sanctity and only as such do they call for particular respect. Kaufmann argues: "Whereas in biblical religion, kingly rule is trans-mitted by inheritance, the High Priest's role is not. The High Priest is not even permitted to appoint a successor which here and there is the right of a king." The point of Kaufmann's argument is that the High Priest's representation of holiness is his sole justification for being in office. Should he ever disgrace his role, it would truly be the nadir of religious perversion.

But what does "representing holiness" entail? First, it entails meticulous attention to the details of ritual. The assumption is — daring as it may be — that God Himself is attending to the order of worship. After all, the worship is intended to be conducted in God's "Presence," appealing to His "Presence," lauding His "Presence." For He is perceived as dwelling among the worship-ers. Every gesture, therefore, every motion, every nod, every piece of costume worn by the priest, every aspect of the sacrificial ceremony, must be as ordered as specified, as commanded.

The initial command to Moses to appoint Aaron and his sons to the priesthood is meant to represent a purposeful arbitrariness by God. Abrabanel will argue that the choice of Aaron and his sons is to inform the people that all is from God. For if anyone should entertain the notion that the choice was Moses', wouldn't he have indulged his paternal instincts and appointed his own sons Gershom and Eliezer as his fellow priests? But just as Moses will obey the transcendent command to appoint Aaron to the priest-hood and Joshua his disciple to ultimate prophetic and executive leadership, the people are to learn obedience to the numinous dimensions of their new status as a holy people.

This view of holiness — and its institutionalization — will not be easy to sustain. Notwithstanding the glorious imagery of the priest's dress and the pageantry which will accompany the ritual ceremonies, the priests can only be the human beings they are. And from time to time there will be a falling short of their concern for correctness. There will be "marring" of the purity of the spirit associated with the sacrificial worship. Aaron himself will lead — under compulsion, it is true — the "golden calf" apostasy. Later on in Jewish biblical history, there will be a range of priestly exploitations of the role for gross spiritual and moral perversities, e.g., the sins of Eli's sons, the degeneracy of the priesthood in Second Temple days. And there will be the gross national misconception — excoriated by the prophets — that sacrificial worship without concomitant moral repentance is religiously efficacious. Nevertheless the original intention is to have the priest represent God's mysterious yet indwelling Presence — the awesomeness of the Presence which will elicit authentic reverence.

There is an additional significance to the role of the priest, in this case the high priest. The priest is to be taken *mitokh benei Yisrael* (from the midst of Israel). There may seem to be a latent paradox here in that the priesthood will become a class. But the real lesson is that whatever validity any select group within Israel may have as a group with a particular function and accompanying apparent privilege, it is dependent upon their serving the people out of which they have emerged. When they are perceived to serve themselves, it is the death knell of their class.

With the copious detail concerned with the glorification of the priesthood, there are the vestments and in particular the ephod with its two shoulder-pieces attached. On these shoulder pieces are to be put the *avnei shoham* (lazuli stones) on which are to be engraved the names of the tribes of the House of Israel. The instruction is for Aaron to bear the names *le-zikaron* (as a memorial) — stones of memorial for the Children of Israel. In this manner the high priest represents all of Israel before God. He is not a prophetic *sheli'ah tzibbur* in the mold of Moses who will be prepared to stand in the breach pleading for his people, arguing on their behalf. The priest is Israel personified in reverential communication with the awesome mystery — confessing, lauding, transmitting back to Israel God's blessings.

The high priest is charged to "remember" Israel. What is remembering? Various commentaries will illuminate the components of remembering. The Ralbag will explain the stones as the simple virtually mechanical reminder that the priest's thought should always be circulating around the Children of

Israel. Thus at the very pristine level of *thinking*, it cannot merely be creaturely ruminating, permitting one's thoughts to wander aimlessly. The High Priest is to concentrate his thoughts, direct his thoughts to the current condition of his charges, the Children of Israel.

But "remembering" the Children of Israel is not just "thinking" about the Children of Israel. Benno Jacob will emphasize the symbolic representation of the stones as the paternal concern or worry of the priest for his people. Thus *zikaron* (memorial) will be a prayer of blessing, a mute prayer of the priest on behalf of his people Israel. The thought then is not just directed to Israel's concern in a cool emotionally detached manner. The priest is to *worry* about their condition, to see himself as totally identified with their concerns, anxieties, hesitancies, doubts, guilts — in short, to feel Israel's collective identity in himself.

But then remembering is not just *thinking* and *worrying* about the Children of Israel. Cassuto's brief comment will underscore the service dimension: *"Zekher ve-semel le-khakh she-ha-kohen mesharet be-shem kol shivtei Yisrael"* ("the stones are a memorial symbol that the priest *serves* in the name of all the tribes of Israel"). The cognitive and empathetic dimensions of "remembering" must be actualized in willful *service* on behalf of the Children of Israel, on behalf of all the Children of Israel. The volitional dimension is the key concretive agent that brings otherwise ungrounded cognitive and empathetic reflections — well-intentioned though they may be — to actualized behavior.

Light for a People and the World

The high priest is dressed opulently as an enraptured people looks to its newly planned tabernacle to bring them as close to God as possible as often as possible. Their delight is a multi-colored illumination before the fact of their recent emancipation from darkness and before the promise of a brightly burnished future.

The *Midrash Tanhuma* will promise the light of the Holy Temple in Jerusalem as the spiritually energizing force for Israel in this world. But the Psalmist will have promised even more with the coming of a Messianic time when there will be an especially lustrous candle to welcome the redeemed future. That candle on earth will be Israel itself — a people sanctified in its own Land — in whose light all the nations shall walk.

Ki Tissa כי תשא

The events surrounding the sin of the "golden calf" — God's reaction to the wholesale apostasy, Moses' behavior towards God on the one hand and towards his people on the other — may be summarized in the tribute paid to Moses in Psalm 106:23: "God would have destroyed them had not Moses His chosen stood before Him in the breach, turning back His wrath lest He should indeed destroy them."

Among the prophets in the Israelite pantheon of prophets Moses is considered unique. There are obvious reasons for his distinctiveness, the principal one being that it is he who receives the Torah and is known henceforth throughout Jewish history as *Moshe Rabbenu* (Moses our teacher). Within his lifetime he is clearly the central indispensable personality orchestrating everything that happens to the Children of Israel from the time he first goes out to them in Egypt until he leads them through the Wilderness to the borders of the Promised Land. He has served as God's agent in bringing Israel out of Egypt. It is he who has shepherded Israel to Sinai in order to have this people experience an unparalleled collective revelation. He has been and will continue to be throughout the forty years in the Wilderness Israel's spiritual leader, administrator, executive, legislator, and judge as well as sociomoral critic.

His supreme role, however, may be seen as the perennially tortured intermediary — he who stands in the breach representing in all situations at all costs the permanent unbreakable covenantal bond between God and Israel. No matter how severe the Israelite "breach," Moses will stand in the "breach" as Israel's *meilitz yosher* (righteous advocate). He is their pre-eminent *sheli'ah tzibbur* (representative of the community) refusing to permit God to repudiate the covenant by rejecting the people.

At the same time, Moses is the great admonisher. True, he will not allow God to abandon *Am Yisrael* (the People of Israel). But once he comes down the mountain and witnesses the idolatrous revelry, he smashes the tablets, grinds the "golden calf" to powder, and forces Israel to drink the bitter waters of faithlessness. He initiates a civil war which will see three thousand of his people slain but which he has deemed necessary in order to unify a stubborn, dangerously immature rabble. His fighting slogan *"mi Ladonai elai!"* ("whoever is for God follow me!") is to shock the rabble into renewed attention to the covenantal task and obligation.

The Golden Calf and the Sin

What is wrong with the building of a golden calf to represent God? As long as it is intended to represent God, what is the sin? The Israelites are quoted in the text as proclaiming upon seeing the idol: *"Eleh Elohekha Yisrael"* ("this is your god, O Israel")! Such a proclamation is not necessarily a repudiation of God. Moses has been delayed in coming down to them. It may be argued on their behalf that they need the security of something substantial to represent this new God whom they cannot see. Nevertheless, the sin is serious enough to arouse God's anger to the extreme. Why is God's invisibility so crucial to the new religious message that Moses is trying to bring to the people? Briefly put, God will be accentuating the logical impossibility of manufacturing a likeness of Him with His later words to Moses: "No human can see Me and live!" The impossibility underscores the heresy. For any attempt to picture what is impossible for human beings to picture is an act of human vanity — as all idolatry has already proven to be. And idolatry is *the heresy!*

What is it then that impels the Israelites to commit this act of idolatry — *the heresy* — when they've already had evidence that this God insists with all His omnipotence and all His omniscience on being invisible? The Children of Israel are manifesting a need to rebel against *maturity*. They are described as *"va-yakumu le-tzahek"* ("they rose to make merry"). They rose to play! What is maturity? At the most basic level as established in Eden it is being able to conduct one's life with rational understanding and according to a set of established standards of self-control. It means being able to master one's impulses. Unlike animals, who never attain "maturity," human beings have been expected — according to norms as pristine as Eden — to set controls over themselves, to assume responsibility for their actions. Maturity entails making demands on oneself and fulfilling them.

On a more subtle level, maturity is recognizing the complex fluidity of a new situation and a readiness to assume responsibility for dealing with the new situation. Here is a people — the Children of Israel — living through a turbulent time, suddenly being asked to be mature, to be mature despite having been imprisoned among the pagan "children" of Egypt. What is required of the Children of Israel now that they have been liberated from their pagan prison? They are expected to rise to a level of higher, more demanding, socioreligious standards and values than they have experienced in Egypt. Instead of facing up to this required elevation in spirit, intelligence, and vision, they prefer a regression in order to "play" with a god fashioned after their own infantile desires and previous socioreligious patterns. The building of the "golden calf" is blasphemous — it is literally a backsliding — because it manifests a refusal to see that a new idea of God is emerging. This is a God who creates, reveals His moral will, and is a redeemer of the enslaved and downtrodden. His will is all-determinative. He does not need to be seen — nor touched! Conforming to His will is sufficient to feel redeemed.

The tragic frustration which Moses experiences is a consequence of an intersecting of two moods summarized in two biblical statements: On Mount Sinai Moses is inspired to fashion a Torah which is to be a "Torah of the Lord which is perfect in its renewing of life" (Psalms 19:8); but in the face of this opportunity Israel's behavior is base, as it is said in Daniel 9:7, "with You O Lord is the right; whereas with us is the shame."

This tragic juxtaposition between *Torat Yisrael* at its best and *Am Yisrael* at its worst is represented in the following *midrash* from *Tanhuma*: "On the day that Israel made the 'calf,' on that day the 'manna' came down from Heaven. Israel took from the 'manna' and offered it up before the 'calf.' Despite Israel's behavior the 'manna' continued to come down...." What does the "manna" represent if not God's gift to Israel! It is meant not only to sustain them physically; but it is to teach them the lesson of newness, novel expectation, challenge, demand, the constant surprise of life! And in "appreciation" for this gift of life — this *Torat Hayyim* — the Children of Israel offer thanksgiving to an inert, unchanging, frozen idol! All this while God's gift — the "manna" — is never withheld!

Moses at the *sneh* (the burning bush) had tried himself to concretize the idea of God by asking God for His name or essence. The answer *"Ehyeh asher Ehyeh"* would inspire in Moses and eventually, it was to be hoped, in Israel a sense not of Ultimate Being but of Ultimate Becoming. Israel would have to learn a mature lesson: that all things are in a state of evolution — especially human relations. Slavery and hedonism can be made extinct if people learn to realize that change for human betterment is not only possible — it is inevitable! They must be made to see that they are never to be satisfied with the status quo. For there is always something left undone for human betterment. The idea of change, therefore, cannot and must not be concretized in an image of an icon, of a statue, of a golden calf. An icon or a statue like the "golden calf" represents the antithesis of change because a concrete image of any kind represents completion, petrifaction, death.

Moses' Tactical Arguments

And so Moses stands in the breach which has been caused by Israel's refusal to apply with sufficient seriousness its commitment to a new set of terms for human relationships — relationships with God and with Man. Nevertheless, Moses is his people's unconditional advocate. He presents a defense on behalf of his people which will employ debating tactics based upon an underlying value-concept which generates these tactics. The Midrash says in the name of Rabbi Nehemiah: "At the time Israel was indulging itself in the 'deed,' Moses was appeasing God by pleading: 'Lord of the Universe, they've provided you with assistance and You are angry with them! This calf which they have made will assist you. You'll give light to the sun, the calf will give light to the moon; You'll provide the dew, the calf will provide the winds; You'll bring rain, the calf will make vegetation grow.' The Holy One Blessed be He retorted: 'Moses, you are as misguided as Israel, the calf is as nothing, i.e., it has no substance or power!' Moses then said: 'If such is the case, they why are You so angry with Your people?'"

Moses has employed as his first debating tactic the trivialization of Israel's sin, considering their idolatrous background. Moses is saying to God, as it were: "You're too big to be so small! If the calf or any other humanly manufactured icon or statue has no power, is merely dust, then what are You afraid of, O Lord!"

But what if the sin, despite Moses' relegation of the calf to insignificance, is considered great because of the fact of Israel's disobedience per se, Israel's stiff-necked lack of appreciation of God's largesse in having freed them from bondage? After all, Adam's sin in the Garden per se was also "trivial"; yet the consequence was catastrophic. Moses thereby reminds God of His oath to Abraham, Isaac, and Jacob-Israel: *"asher nishbata lahem Bakh"* ("to whom You swore *by Your Self*"). Rabbi Elazar asks for the meaning of *Bakh* (by Your Self). And he has Moses argue: "Lord of the Universe, if You had sworn to our ancestors by heaven and earth I could say that such an oath is limited, because even the heaven and earth are not eternal. But now that You have sworn by Your own great name — Your very essence — which lives and endures forever, so does Your oath live and endure forever." In other words, let the sin not be considered trivial; but nevertheless the commitment to Israel, Moses reminds God, is *unconditional*. It is as eternally binding as God's very Being.

But what if despite Moses' second argument — unassailable as it seems to be — God nevertheless as *kol yakhol* (all-Powerful) decides to reject and abandon this people Israel? Moreover, what if God is prepared to continue the covenant with a new core-people which He will choose through the discipleship of Moses: "I will destroy them and make of you a great nation."

Yohanan Muffs in his "Prayer of the Prophets" has Moses reacting to such a proposition by "embarrassing" God with an imputation that He is being faithless: "O Lord, You say that You are going to abandon Israel and make of me a great nation. How will You be able to face the Patriarchs after You will have destroyed their seed and will have broken the covenant by making of me and my seed a new Israel! This is impossible, impossible!" Thus Moses' final tactic is a double prosecutorial attack: (1) he accuses God of contemplating a violation of His own promise to Abraham, Isaac, and Jacob; and (2) in an expression of total self-effacement he rejects God's offer to begin a new covenantal arrangement with himself — Moses — as "patriarch" of a new nation. In the midst of Israel's heresy, Moses insists on his people's survival as permanent partner with God in His original covenant.

"Ahavat Yisrael — The Love for Israel"

In the light of the three debating tactics used by Moses — the trivialization of the sin, the reminder that God's commitment to Israel is unconditional, and the self-effacement of Moses in the tempting moment of self-aggrandizement if it involves abandoning Israel — what then is the underlying value-concept generating these debating tactics? *Ahavat Yisrael* (the Love for Israel).

Moses' love for this people has been an acquired love. He has come to them from the "outside" — from "outside" their plight, their servitude. He has grown up inside Pharaoh's palace — no less — and then gone out to this people, to these afflicted Israelites and become one of them. True, he has had to run away from them when their quarrelsome temperaments balked at his attempt to make peace among them. But after a period of quiet regeneration in Midian, he has been charged by God to love this people — to love them enough to face down an emperor and the full power of his empire without fear and without hesitation.

Like Abraham at the *akeidah*, Moses rises above God's expectation of a human being. Once Abraham shows that he is ready for the most supreme personal sacrifice, God realizes that He has found someone who is truly reverent, determined, unswervingly faithful. Similarly, once Moses rejects the special fame offered by God of fathering a new people, a new faith, a new religion in favor of remaining with his brethren the Children of Israel, this rabble of a newly emancipated confederation of tribes, then he too — like Abraham — will have proven himself an authentic spiritual and moral teacher of humankind.

Moses has already learned that it is not easy to love Israel. Before he descends from Mount Sinai, he knows only too well how seriously they have sinned and that they will continue to sin. Even with his tactical defense before God he is still basically begging for mercy. At the same time he is courageous enough to argue his several points in favor of justice being weighed as well by the Supreme Judge of all the earth: "Lord of the Universe, whence have you taken them, if not from Egypt where the worship of the lamb is endemic to the population?" Moses is arguing in essence that it was too much for God to expect — that Israel could have become sufficiently mature overnight to reject idolatry entirely.

Moses contends that even under ordinary circumstances it may have been too much to expect. But the circumstances have hardly been ordinary. Emancipation and revelation are hardly ordinary events. Under these circumstances, Israel may have erred. It may have even sinned egregiously! But, in truth, Egypt as the dominant culture could not but have conditioned Israel towards a belief in idolatry. And if Egypt has represented human arrogance, hubris, a great civilization built upon human misery and exploitation, how can one expect that Israel would not be infected at least somewhat with the "way of life" and the "way of belief" of Egypt?

Yet, no! Moses has to give credence to God's position as well. After all, God in His grace has appeared as a Redeemer, has destroyed this empire built on human arrogance, and has bestowed freedom on this people Israel which has suffered under the evil empire. God has then revealed His will as absolutely against immorality *and idolatry*. Granted, things happen quickly and covenanted demands are made upon this people immediately. And, granted, this people will have to look beyond themselves and beyond their idolatrous conditioning. Having had the pain and shame of the enslavement removed and having been privileged to experience the unique epiphany at Sinai, how can they not be prepared to move further on God's chosen path! Instead they have disobeyed — and how could they have chosen this most disgraceful mode of disobedience!

In other words, Moses' love for this people is not based on a blind acceptance of their spiritual and moral weaknesses. He knows that Israel cannot be exonerated for its disgraceful reaction to the supreme blessedness of God's act of redemption. In his advocacy of Israel's case before God, Moses may be trying to "blame" God for being too harsh. Instead he blames Egypt for their overwhelming influence upon these erstwhile hapless slaves. But Moses knows that the sin of the "golden calf" is still Israelite responsibility.

The degree of their responsibility is illustrated by the talmudic discussion (Babylonian Talmud, *Megillah* 25b) of the compounded sin associated with the "golden calf." According to this passage, Moses has come down the mountain and confronts his brother Aaron. Aaron's explanation is at best weak and at worst an outright falsehood. The Talmud legislates that the particular passage be read publicly in the future but not translated. For in the passage Aaron states: "Let not my lord be enraged. You know that this people is bent on evil…so I said to them, whoever has gold take it off. They gave it to me and I hurled it into the fire and out came this calf." On this passage Rabbi Shimon ben Elazar says, "A person should always be careful in his responses; for on the basis of Aaron's response to Moses heretics deny God." For to suggest that "out came this calf" is to suggest that the calf had independently divine powers.

In other words, why shouldn't this passage be translated? For two reasons!

The first is that it underscores Aaron's complicity with the people in a total overthrowing of God's rule. Aaron's use of the word *hitparaku* (take off) in connection with the gold is taken to mean the general abandonment of the yoke of God's rule. *Hitparaku* is suggestive of an instruction to "become *hefker*" (to become free of the yoke, free of ownership). God is not sovereign! Secondly, the passage describes the people Israel as *paru'a* (out of control). It cannot be a mere accident of language that *paru'a* and Pharaoh are of the same root. But Israel "out of control" means that the people will be a menace to any who may oppose them. In other words there is a double sin: throwing off the yoke of transcendent sovereignty and standards; and the madcap deterioration of Israelite society into moral and social chaos. Such a passage, the Talmud decides, is too embarrassing to translate in public.

But the embarrassment of the talmudic Rabbis has itself a double — almost paradoxical — fallout. First, the Rabbis are asserting that it is an embarrassment to show the degraded state of Israel which has been so blessed and yet becomes quickly blind to their good fortune. Second, what is the feared embarrassment of the Rabbis if not a reflection of what they have learned through the centuries from their teacher Moshe Rabbenu — *ahavat Yisrael* (love for Israel)! For these Rabbis the most severe spiritual and moral blemishes of Israel should never be publicized; they dare not be read publicly, let alone as part of a permanent public ritual!

It is that same love for Israel which will motivate Yehudah Halevi in his *Kuzari* to underplay the less than ultimate sinfulness of the worship of the "golden calf" by the Children of Israel in the Wilderness. He stresses that the sin was not a total abandonment of the worship of the Lord who had taken them out of Egypt. True, it was an act of rebelliousness against a few of the commandments that the Lord had warned them about, e.g., making an artifice to represent God, etc. But Israel was in a psychological-spiritual-aesthetic predicament. They had experienced a series of unparalleled redemptive events and they wished to express their feelings about these events. That they decided on a mode of worship which was unacceptable was unfortunate. Could they be entirely blamed? Again, it can be argued, it was all they knew from their experience in pagan Egypt.

It is that same love for Israel which will fertilize the sympathetic imaginations of other commentators who seek a *zekhut* (a merit) for the people of Israel. The *Ha'amek Davar* asks the question: "How is it possible for Moses to have gotten away with seizing the "golden calf" in the presence of all the revelers, burning it and grinding it into dust without opposition when it was this same group of uncontrollable revelers who had forced Aaron to manufacture the "calf" in the first place? The answer is that Moses was wise enough and clever enough not to smash the tablets while he was out of sight on the mountain even though his emotional impulse might have been to do so. Instead, he decided on the mountain to wait until he would come down in order to smash them in the sight of Israel. He would do this *"li-shbor et lev ha-am"* ("to break the people's heart"). He was confident that they would become emotionally overwrought upon seeing the treasure that was the tablets being crushed before their eyes. Their guilt-ridden embarrassment would neutralize any impulse to protest.

Such a *peirush* (commentary) serves as an example to show that whenever the *peshat* (the simple meaning) of the Torah appears to be harsh regarding the reputation of Israel, the Midrash and the later commentators imitate Moses and, as it were, defend Israel before God. They insist on putting Israel in a better light. Israel has certainly sinned a great sin and the *peirush* itself seems to be intent upon putting Moses in a clever light. Yet the real purpose of the *peirush* is to show that Israel was capable of having a broken heart, of having its emotional — and intellectual — sensibilities overturned by the loss of this wondrous treasure — the Torah — and that God would deem them fit to be given the Torah again.

There is no more supreme example of the love for Israel than the person of Moses himself. And how the commentators throughout the ages have interpreted the *peshat* underscores the *ahavat Yisrael* of Moshe Rabbenu. Enforcing the earlier image of this incomparable *sheli'ah tzibbur*, the classic line within the text — with no further commentary really necessary — representing Moses' literal self-effacement is *"ve-ata im tisa hatatam, ve-im ayin, meheni na mi-sifrekha asher katavta"* ("and now if You are ready to forgive their sin, fine; but if not, then wipe me out of Your book which You have written").

The commentators vie with each other in presenting increasing degrees of empathy for his people on the part of this *meilitz yosher*. Rashi has Moses saying to God: "If You won't forgive them, wipe me out of Your book, that is, out of Your whole Torah, so that it shouldn't be said about me that I wasn't capable of begging and eliciting mercy for them." Moses will have failed, in other words, in what he considers his principle portfolio — serving as a righteous and effective advocate of this people. Moses is echoing one of the complaints of the people as they face various crises during the wandering in the Wilderness, namely, how can God let them perish after having taken them out of their near hopeless situation. Moses' empathy here is sufficiently all-inclusive; for without Israel, his life and mission have no validity.

Sforno has Moses reasoning as follows: "Whether You wish to forgive them or not to forgive them, cancel out my merits from Your records and place these merits on their account so that they may deserve forgiveness." Moses is prepared to extend his empathy sufficiently so that whatever merits he may have earned should be transferred to the benefit of Israel. Moses presents God with an example of compassion which will, it is hoped, "embarrass" God into extending the appropriate forgiveness. This is not a case of Moses exhibiting a lack of ego. On the contrary, Moses is appealing to God on the scale of justice to accept his judgment — Moses' mortal judgment — as to the worthwhileness of continuing to maintain the covenant with this people.

The most extreme of the interpretations is that of the Ramban who has Moses offering himself *instead* of Israel on the altar of atonement for sin: "If you are not ready to forgive them, then erase me from the Book of Life *instead* of them. Let me suffer their punishment as described in the prophetic text (Isaiah 53), 'He was wounded because of our transgressions, crushed because of our iniquities; he bore the chastisement that made us whole and by his bruises we were healed.'" The Ramban then has God rejecting Moses' offer with the judgment that there is to be no vicarious atonement. The sinners are to be punished, not Moses who is innocent! Ramban attributes to Moses a hyperempathy which is rejected by God because it undercuts any concept of moral fairness. Nevertheless the commentator has succeeded in underscoring Moses' boundless love for his people.

In short, summarizing these commentaries, Moses feels increasingly like the parent whose children have erred, have sinned, have failed. As a loving parent, he is prepared either to take the blame, or to claim that whatever merit he the parent may have, it should be accounted instead to the children, or — as a last resort — to offer himself for punishment instead of them. Rightly or wrongly from the point of view of strict justice, Moses refuses to entertain the possibility of living without Israel. In essence Moses has challenged God to modify His teaching regarding the indispensability of Torah for the continued existence of the world. God must now include Israel itself as equally indispensable to the world even if it has sinned against God and the Torah. God allows Himself to be convinced. He thereby reminds Moses and the people that their mission and destiny have not been changed. They are to be brought to the Land of Israel — notwithstanding their rebelliousness, their stubbornness, their heresy.

Teshuvah

Moses proves to God that his love for Israel doesn't mean that he will accept uncritically their spiritual heresy and moral profligacy. As God's deputy and as the teacher of a stiff-necked Israel he is not prepared to countenance any act of rebellion on the part of Israel against God and the Torah. In the name of God and the Torah he is prepared to plead, to cajole, to admonish, to threaten Israel with the full measure of his and God's authority. But at the same time he is not prepared to reject them, to repudiate them, to abandon them. He will always plead on their behalf for another chance. For already in his crisis-filled ministry on behalf of both God and Israel, Moses will have recognized the necessity for the concept and healing process of *teshuvah* (repentance).

Teshuvah is the necessary opportunity which God must allow a sinful Israel — and by extension a sinful humankind. Without *teshuvah* for human beings, there can be no hope for God's creation. God Himself has known this ever since He vowed never again to bring on a deluge to destroy humankind. Yet *teshuvah* — for whatever reason known only to God — was unavailable to the people of Sodom by the time God had brought Abraham into the picture. Perhaps the evil within Sodom had become so great that its fate anticipated the hard-heartedness of Pharaoh. They had by the time of God's final decree of destruction forfeited the *opportunity* to do *teshuvah*. With Israel — and Moses insists upon it — it is different. Israel as human, notwithstanding its covenantal obligation to be holy, will err, will disappoint, will frustrate, will rebel. But it will always be given the chance to continue covenantal realization. Moses will never permit Israel to forget the various signs in the *mitzvot* which stamp the people as chosen for partnership in mending God's creation. He will similarly never permit God to forget His attribute of mercy which will make *teshuvah* for this people possible.

The tradition teaches that the Torah was given in forty days and the human soul was formed in forty days. Whoever keeps the Torah, his soul is kept, and whoever does not keep the Torah, his soul is not kept. What has happened at Sinai is that Israel has discovered its collective soul but then has lost it with the "golden calf" heresy. Israel knows that it has lost it; but with Moses standing in the breach, Israel through *teshuvah* will have its soul restored. And its soul will continue to be restored throughout Israel's later history, again and again and again.

Va-Yakhel   ויקהל

Who built the tabernacle in the Wilderness? In verse 36:8 of the Book of Exodus it says: "And every wise-hearted individual among them that wrought the work made the tabernacle…" At the same time verse 37:1 informs us that it was Bezalel who "did everything." And then towards the close of the Book of Exodus it is said: "Thus was finished all the work of the tabernacle…and the children of Israel did according to all that the Lord commanded Moses." The *Or Hahayyim* commentary clarifies the possible confusion by saying: "Though it was Bezalel and his fellow craftsmen who actually performed the tasks, *sheluho shel adam kemoto* (a man's agent is as himself). Therefore, the entire effort was attributed to Israel." Although Bezalel only did what God instructed, it was the Children of Israel who delegated him and approved him as their *sheli'ah li-dvar mitzvah* (their agent to perform God's command).

In other words, even though Bezalel and his expert artisans have planned and in effect built the sanctuary in the Wilderness, all of Israel is credited with the achievement. Bezalel and his team are the *shelihei tzibbur* (the delegates of the people), which means that they — like Moses who is the supreme *sheli'ah tzibbur* — derive their legitimacy only insofar as they truly represent the people. The *Or Hahayyim* adds that in building a society, everyone is expected to "carry his weight," i.e., to perform to the limit of his capacity, and in turn all members of the society will benefit from the full cooperation of all. Thus the injunction "you shall love your fellow as yourself" is given further exemplification. One's fellow citizen is like you in the sense that his welfare affects positively your welfare and vice versa. Each one is thereby part of the other's organic "health" and vice versa.

The Children of Israel settled in Egypt as a group, as a family growing into tribes that became somehow unified and retained their familial and tribal unity even within the grand Egyptian empire. They became a nation even as they were bound into servitude. They have now been taken out of their bondage as a nation; they have celebrated the victory over their enemies at the Sea of Reeds as a nation; they have stood awestruck at the foot of Mount Sinai as a nation. Even when they apostatized around the "golden calf" they have done it as a nation. In summary, they, together with Moses as their *sheli'ah*, represent a particular view-of-redemption which will be a permanent mark of the religion of Israel: there is no personal salvation without the accompanying salvation of the group, of the community of Israel, of the nation of Israel.

The building of the *mishkan* (tabernacle), therefore, must be a national enterprise. Not only has the proclamation by God *"va-asu Li mikdash ve-shahanti betokham"* ("they shall make Me a sanctuary so that I may dwell among them") made the collective emphasis in covenantal purpose very clear, but let us note that the recording in Scripture of the detailed plans of the building project and the carrying out of the project immediately precede the Book of Leviticus with its own detailed agenda for the nation. This third Book of the Torah will in turn detail the ideal spiritual, ritual, ethical, and social norms to be observed as a fleshing out of the injunction *"kedoshim tihyu"* ("be you holy") — an injunction not merely for the individual Israelite but for the nation of Israel as a whole.

The Miracle of the *"Mishkan"*

Just as Bezalel as *sheli'ah tzibbur* represents the nation in building the *mishkan*, his very name is a homily to the nation as a whole and to each separate individual within the whole. Bezalel walks and acts and lives *be-tzel El* (in the shadow of God). The Children of Israel as a *tzibbur* and each child within the *tzibbur* are to see themselves similarly as charged to walk and to act and to live as appropriate to being in the shadow of God.

Walking, acting, and living in the shadow of God as the homiletic application of Bezalel's name answers a number of troubling questions for the Ramban. If the Children of Israel had really been slaves in Egypt, how could they have developed a sufficiently free sensibility to manifest genuine creativity — the kind of creativity that could produce a tabernacle and have a sufficient appreciation of its importance? Where and how would they have been trained to develop the artistic and technological skills required for constructing such a tabernacle with a concomitant understanding of its fine detail?

And in the light of the tabernacle representing no less than an object hospitable to the indwelling Presence of the new invisible God, how would they have gained the spiritual sensitivity to worship this God with the appropriate *yirat shamayim* (centralized reverie)?

The answer to all three questions is given in Bezalel's name. (1) The yearning for freedom, (2) the intuitive feel for aesthetic beauty, and (3) the aspiration to reach spiritual transcendence are gifts from God. They represent God's protecting and animating shadow over humankind which mysteriously endows groups and individuals with capacities to lift themselves beyond their normal creaturely habits. Peter Berger has coined the term "signals of transcendence" to refer to those elevating and illuminating characteristics of ordinary human beings that enable them to hope, to laugh, to create redemptive visions out of the dross of life.

1. Where does the elemental *ze'akah* or "crying out" for relief come from when the slave suffers the beatings of the taskmaster? The answer may be that the slave's cry is no different from the whelp of a dumb animal in pain. But what turns the slave's instinctive cry for relief into an intuitive longing for radical change in his existential situation, beginning with his escape from sociomoral imprisonment? From where does the call for freedom emerge? Joseph Campbell, having studied all the mythologies of humanity in his four-volume study *The Masks of God*, argues: "Among all the beliefs of mankind, the biblical idea of God must be clearly set apart." And the key attribute of the biblical God relevant to the question of Man's search for freedom from the yoke of other men is that God in His utter freedom has bestowed a dimension of that freedom in the heart and soul of every human being.

2. From where does the erstwhile slave bogged down in the bitter mud of an aimless drudgery-filled existence derive an aesthetic sense, an eye and an ear and a feel for order, for form, for beauty? The talmudic tractate *Berakhot* sees Bezalel's talent as "knowing how to combine the letters by which the heaven and the earth were created." The concept and fact of creation already bespeaks order and form. What God sees and judges to be "good" and "very good" in his daily appraisal of His own work of creation is not a moral judgment or social commentary. It is an aesthetic appraisal and judgment. Man and societies of men do

not yet exist. And when they will have been created, their capacity to live and to love and to build with one another in amity will elicit from God an aesthetic appraisal of His total creation. Again, the ordinary human being in his having been created "in the image of God" may not have the formidable artistic and technological gifts of a Bezalel. Yet even as a slave he has witnessed beauty. As a free man, he will seek it, will discover it, will manufacture objects testifying to its existence.

3. The capacity to *experience* the transcendent — in its most pristine form — is immediately available, even to the slave. *Understanding* dimensions of the transcendent may require an extra measure of cognitive sophistication, although God has instilled in Adam the capacity to both *experience and understand* dimensions of the transcendent. When Adam as human being attempts to hide from the transcendent he fails utterly. For he has *experienced* the presence of God and *understands* the significance of that experience. Adam may rebel against God. Like the Serpent he may deny God or His Presence. But he will only succeed in substituting himself or another immanent creature or thing for the true omnipotent, omniscient mysterious Creator of all. In other words, of the three gifts that God has given the human being, the awareness of the transcendent holiness of God is the most pristine, the most all-inclusive in that even babes sense the numinous. And mature human beings like Adam — as long as they are not idolatrous — never lose this sense of the numinous.

The Shabbat as Holy

Freedom, aesthetic beauty, and the sense of the holy must be made palpable in the lives of the Children of Israel. Institutions are necessary to normalize and formalize these values in the hearts and minds of the Children of Israel — especially the sense of the holy. Freedom and aesthetic beauty are properties which pagans can share with ethical monotheists. But the idea and the sense of the holy — at least as it is intended to be understood by Israel — need living testimony beyond feelings and intuitions. The *mishkan* itself is a daring, outrageously daring, projection of Israel's faith that God's indwelling Presence can be contained anywhere, let alone in a relatively small sanctuary. As a constant reminder, therefore, of the fundamental impossibility of such containment, yet at the same time as another non-spatial way of institutionalizing the individual and communal dedication to God as Creator and Emancipator of humanity, God commands the observance of the Shabbat.

On the opening injunction regarding the covenantal indispensability of the Shabbat, Rashi explains that it is precisely as the Israelites are to begin the work of actualizing the plans for the *mishkan* that they need to be instructed regarding the Shabbat. They need to be reminded that even work associated with a tabernacle intended to house God's Presence does not override or preempt the observance of the Shabbat. The *mishkan* may be important in the socio-aesthetic-spiritual scheme for worshiping God. The Shabbat is more important! Building a *mishkan* or other temple dedicated to the worship of God may be a sublime testimony to Man's commitment of creative effort to the Creator. Desisting from all forms of building on the Shabbat is a more eloquent testimony!

The prohibition against lighting a fire on the Shabbat is absolute. The *Sefat Emet* commentary indicates: "There is a light which illuminates and there is a light which burns. The light which burns is the light which works to make things, to manufacture objects for use by human beings." The building of a *mishkan* and its dedication as a tabernacle for use as a sanctuary in which to worship God may have high purpose. Nevertheless it is still a product of human effort in which the light which has burned in order to eliminate refuse from the product brings to fruition that which is the antithesis of transcendence. For it is man-made. Therefore, to light a fire on Shabbat for what is to be man-made must be forbidden.

"The light which illuminates," on the other hand, "can't be seen, is not a manufactured product." The *Sefat Emet* sees such light emanating from the love of God as exemplified in the Shabbat glow or realized in the loving relationship between husband and wife. The two letters *yod* and *he* — God's shortened Name — which inform the two letters *aleph* and *shin* ("esh" — "fire") common to the Hebrew words for husband and wife (man and woman) represent God's lifting of a human loving relationship to the level of holiness. Here Man and Woman "in love" are experiencing something which is not tangible but which for them is a sublime illumination. The light of this love cannot be extinguished. Its "passion is mighty as Sheol; its darts are darts of fire, a blazing flame which cannot be quenched by floods" (Song of Songs

8:6–7). Analogously, the transcendent "reality" of the Shabbat provides an incandescent signal of all-pervading transcendence to human existence precisely through the cessation for one day of all human labor.

The Shabbat institutionalizes for every Israelite, for every Jew, the unquenchable illumination of the "burning bush." Moses' experience of the revelatory message is meant to be transmitted to an Israel and to a humanity that needs to be reminded regularly of two loves — the love for God and love for one's fellow human beings. In its two rationales for keeping the Shabbat rest, the Ten Commandments will spell out respectively: (1) Shabbat rest is imitatio Dei. Just as God rested from His labor of creation on the seventh day, He has blessed the Shabbat day and set it aside for human rest; and (2) Shabbat is to represent the erasure of all human status distinctions. Ultimately, there are to be no subjugations, no servitudes; for God has taken Israel out of the land of "straits" with a strong outstretched arm in order to dispense freedom, beauty, and transcendent possibility for all human beings regardless of class.

Millenia after the Exodus, when the Children of Israel will establish a third Jewish commonwealth under basically secular auspices, its secular Supreme Court will adjudicate questions related to public observance of Shabbat and the possible violation of one of the state's basic constitutional laws: Freedom of Occupation. The Court will issue the following ruling prohibiting — except under extreme national emergency — the opening of places of employment on Shabbat. Even the secular Court will argue that the prohibition is *constitutional* in that "it is in keeping with the values of Israel as a Jewish and democratic state. It was legislated…for achieving social welfare goals that are realized simultaneously with fulfilling national-religious considerations." The Court will also take cognizance of the danger that if normal business will be allowed to be conducted on Shabbat, Jewish employees will be forced into surrendering their traditional day of rest.

The Shabbat and its own "non-active" method for institutionalizing holiness neutralizes the temptation among the people to turn the *mishkan* into a "golden calf." The twin message of the Shabbat, the double foci of the Shabbat — that God is the Creator and that no human being is to be enslaved to another human being — can be and must be the message and foci of the *mishkan*. But because Israel in the immediate past has shown its vulnerability to idolatrous impulses, an object like a *mishkan* is easier to pervert than the Shabbat. For the Shabbat seeks to transcend space and objects of space.

Does then the Shabbat completely dwarf the *mishkan* in importance? The response of the Torah is that holiness-in-space has its "place." The *mishkan* as sanctuary, later the Temple, and still later the Synagogue, will provide at their best the opportunity for close communion with God's *Shekhinah*. There is a legitimate claim that the Shabbat with the other holy days represent with great eloquence holiness-in-time. And there is an argument well concretized in Torah legislation as to the intention of programming holiness-in-behavior into the pattern of daily life. But there is also a human need for holiness-in-space. Ritual and ceremonial beauty associated with spatial sanctuaries, altars, and service-vessels is a natural expressive desire of human beings. Such beauty cannot be denigrated just because ritual and ceremonial objects can themselves be looked upon as objects for idolatrous worship. The sanctuary and its vessels can enhance the worshiper's experience of holiness, the worshiper's longing to commune beyond the mystery, to be able to find comfort in touching the sublime, in piercing the numinous.

Prayer is possible outside the sanctuary. There has been prayer recited well before the building of the *mishkan*. But that later Jewish law will postulate that praying with the community is a greater *mitzvah* than praying alone underscores the importance of identifying oneself with the collective fate and destiny of the covenanted community. It is of no particular significance to the covenant which has been sealed at Sinai that an individual is privately "holy" or "pious" except insofar as it strengthens the potential-for-holiness of the immediate and extended community and nation. The *mishkan*, therefore, as the later Synagogue, serves as that place signifying communal and national holiness.

The Holy-Secular Paradox

The community will discover that it needs to set aside areas like a *mishkan*, like a synagogue, to be designated as holy for an additional reason: in order to distinguish it from other areas in society which — while not profane in the negative sense — will be considered "profane" in the neutral sense, i.e., "secular." It was explained earlier that the term "secular" in the Judaism which has its birth in the Bible and its classical communal growth and development in the Talmud and Midrash is not meant to have a necessarily negative connotation.

Traditional Judaism sees the whole world as *hol* meaning "secular," meaning "unsanctified," or some might say "profane" in the value-neutral sense of the word. Judaism is then seen as mandated to sanctify the whole "profane" world; for that which is profane has an evaluative connotation that lies somewhere between spiritually neutral and negative. In the *Havdalah* prayer which the Jew will recite at the conclusion of every Shabbat, for example, he will praise God who separates the holy from the "secular." Analogously, God will consider "darkness," the "nations," and the "six days of creation" as polar alternatives to "light," "Israel," and "the Shabbat." But obviously the "six days of creation" cannot and should not be considered "profane" in the negative sense. Neither can nor should the "nations" be placed in an irremedial or irredeemable category. "Secular" then — without the connotation of profaneness in the negative sense — really means *derekh eretz* (the way of the world).

In other words, "secular" should be seen as referring to those areas of human experience that concern day-to-day worldly activity as opposed to "spiritual" aspiration. But these secular areas of human experience, the secular domain as the "way of the world," is never to be considered as other than God's world. And the *mishkan*, the Holy Temple, and the Synagogue are those spatial institutions which are built to embody the dream of ultimate holiness — by definition unachievable — for all of God's creation. As such, they are meant to be, if possible, totally removed from the dangers and temptations of the inevitably profane aspect of the secular "way of the world." This is in order for these spatial holy institutions to represent critical alternatives to the as yet unsanctified areas of the way of that world.

Institutions like the *mishkan*, the Holy Temple, and the Synagogue thus form one side of a permanent dialectic between socio-institutional holiness and secularity. But the dialectic which characterizes the confrontation between holy and secular is paradoxical. Holiness or *kedushah* represents the attempt to sanctify the lives of human beings and the institutions that serve human beings. Israel itself is meant to be a covenanted *goy kadosh* ("holy nation"). But Ernst Akiva Simon will note the paradoxical predicament that religion which aspires to sanctify the entire world will face: "When religion attempts to sanctify all areas of the life of the individual and the collective, e.g., eating, drinking, dress, work, leisure, state and society, love and war, it will provoke inevitably a destructive opposition from within those areas under its jurisdiction which will seek autonomous opportunity for healthy growth." Why?

Certain secular areas of human life insist on asserting their own autonomy in order to better cultivate their own unique ways of looking at the world and living in the world — *for the betterment of that world*. In the long run, the world is perceived as having been made better by the secular "heresy." The areas of science and medicine, art and education, and even statecraft are prime examples of these therapeutic "heresies." For these areas, when controlled by institutional religion, inevitably suffer deleterious inhibition. For the more the religious establishment tries to sanctify the *entire* world, the more it leaves itself open to two self-destructive temptations. First, in feeling that it must control all aspects of the world, it becomes totalitarian and anti-human. Second, in its embrace of the world in its profaneness — "profaneness" used derogatively — it cannot help but become as corrupt, as profane as that world. What is left for it to do is to recede, to retreat, to carve out a place for itself in the spiritual-moral realm in order to keep itself "pure" and hope thereby to influence *certain critical* secular areas not to become impure, immoral, and antisocial.

A paradox is a paradox by virtue of its insolubility. But human beings live with paradoxes, particularly when covenantal dreams are confronted by the stubborn realities of life-on-earth. The *midrash* on Jeremiah 23:24, "Do I not fill the heaven and earth," says Rabbi Yehoshua of Sikhnin in the name of Rabbi Levi. "We may use the analogy of a cave near the seashore. When the sea erupts, the cave is filled with water and yet the sea is not any less. So it is with the Holy One Blessed Be He, even though it is written that the glory of God fills the *mishkan*, even so his splendor still fills the heaven and earth. And don't say that God contracted His indwelling Presence to the dimensions of the *mishkan*; He contracted it even to the dimensions of the Ark of the Covenant."

The image of God suggested by the *midrash* is that He is infinitely expansive and yet able to contract in order to continue His revelatory communications through a dialogue of prophetic insight and communal prayer. Israel building this sanctuary in the Wilderness will be sensing the same up-and-down in-and-out process of covenantal struggle which Jacob had seen in his dream of the ladder. Moses has not as yet shared with his people the full legislation for holiness as recommended by the Torah. Yet they will need to prepare themselves for the struggle — a struggle full of frustrations, spiritual, moral, and social. For they will need to plan on building a society that will not surrender in frustration to the "holy-secular" paradox.

In order to make possible the effort, a very special kind of leadership will be necessary. The successors of Moses will need to be "disciples of Bezalel" in the sense that they will be charged with walking *be-tzel El* ("in the shadow of God"). They will have to be blessed with the *hokhmat-lev* ("the wisdom of the mind-and-heart") that will have been associated with the architect of the *mishkan*. They will have to be aristocrats of the spirit in that they will have to understand the terms in which the covenant is to be fulfilled, the only terms under which the covenant has any possibility of being fulfilled. They must never forget that all they do is done *be-tzel El*. They will thus be dedicated to cultivating among the Children of Israel an appreciation of the responsibility of freedom, the opportunity to create a beautiful civilization, and a humble aspiration for ongoing transcendent insight.

Israel's Torah Intuition

This "spiritually aristocratic" leadership will have an intuitive capacity to measure constantly the temper of the times, the readiness of human beings for spiritual, moral, social, and cultural growth without the necessity for political upheavals. It will seem as though they will have been blessed with a wisdom that has preceded birth. The Talmud will report it as follows: "Rabbi Simlai delivered the following discourse: What does an embryo resemble when it is in the bowels of its mother? ...A light burns above its head and it looks and sees from one end of the world to the other, as it is said, 'When his lamp shined above my head, and by His light I walked through darkness' (Job 29:3). It is also taught all the Torah from beginning to end, for it is said, 'And he taught me, and said unto me: "Let my heart hold fast my words, keep my commandments and live"' (Proverbs 4:4), and it is also said, 'When the converse of God was upon my tent' (Job 29:4). As soon as it sees the light an angel approaches, slaps it on its mouth and causes it to forget all the Torah completely, as it is said, 'Sin croucheth at the door' (Genesis 4:7)."

The *Midrash Tanhuma* teaches the same lesson when it comments on God having filled Bezalel by means of the "spirit of God"; that this kind of *hokhmah* ("wisdom") God only adds "to those who already have it." God will not risk dispensing wisdom to those whose "foolishness" will lead them into misapplying the wisdom. Thus the embryo will have been blessed with the supernal light which blesses its very core-of-being. Rabbi Simlai has the angel "slapping it on its mouth causing it to forget the Torah" so that the devilish Serpent that is the *yeitzer-ra* ("the drive to sin") will not abuse the newly born child as it comes out into the world, not yet strong enough to apply the Torah to this world of temptation. But the child will grow to know the world, the "way of the world." It will become re-educated in Torah with a sense that somehow he had always known from the beginning how to apply the Torah intuitively to the "way of the world" as it is.

The particular blessing bestowed upon an artist like Bezalel is a childish rapture at seeing the world with all his senses, the colors and sounds, the aromas and tastes and feel-of-things. The Rabbis who will see in the cherubim winged children will have a similar sense that the emergence of a people from slavery into a new world of possibility is analogous to a new birth. These Children of Israel have learned the whole Torah before its birth as a free nation. Abraham, Isaac, and Jacob after all were gifted with God's revelation long before Sinai. The newly born Israel may have forgotten everything in the darkness of bondage. And the "golden calf" episode has brought home to them the truth that "sin croucheth at the door." But they will learn anew. Their teacher Moses will see to it as he prepares them for their new life as a free people in their Land. The shadow of God will hover over them as they study their Torah of Life, as they seek to spread their tabernacle of holiness little by little over more and more of life in their Land and beyond — life as it is in the secular "way of the world" that is the world.

Pekudei ‎פקודי

The events which precede the building of the *mishkan* have been apocalyptic. Enslavement, emancipation, revelation, apostasy, collective rebuke, and collective repentance! And then the pause, the cessation of upheaval with the building of the tabernacle and its appurtenances! Israel slows its revolutionary pace. In fact, it brings it to a halt in order to compress within the modest tabernacle its spiritual yearnings and apprehensions which it intuits can be addressed to God in day-to-day communion. There needs to be a time and a place for static contemplation and reflection. The pillar of cloud and the pillar of fire need to rest as the *mishkan* itself represents God "at rest" giving "ear," so to speak, to Israel's yearnings and apprehensions.

As Eldad has pointed out, within the very images of the "pillar of cloud" and the "pillar of fire" is a tension between the static and the dynamic. The word *amud* ("pillar") comes from the root "to stand," representing stasis or equilibrium, predictability, reliability. The images of cloud and fire, on the other hand, represent volatility. They are the antithesis of predictability and reliability. They serve as dynamic signposts, trackers beckoning to the Children of Israel to journey deeper into the Wilderness on their way to the Promised Land. And so the internal tension suggested by the "pillar of cloud" and the "pillar of fire" is each in turn contrasted with the static phenomenon that is the *mishkan*. Not that the *mishkan* doesn't move! It does move; it is transported; it is meant to move or be moved. Furthermore, it is meant to house God's *Shekhinah* ("His indwelling Presence") which is certainly not static. Nevertheless all this movement does not undercut the *mishkan*'s essential function — to be a place for calm and respite, meditation and consultation.

The Role of Art

The experience of Israel as recorded in the Book of Exodus has been dynamic in the extreme. It will resume its dynamic pace in the Wilderness wanderings and certainly once the conquest and settlement of the Promised Land begin. But here, as the *mishkan* is erected and dedicated, there must be a temporary hiatus in order to review and to anticipate. The entire regimen that will be presented to Israel in the Book of Leviticus — that will be *demanded* of Israel — may be seen as bestowed upon a people that has now stopped or at least has slowed down enough to ask itself what are the specific parameters of the covenant.

The hiatus, the pause in the dynamic push to begin to concretize the Ten Commandments and its accompanying "way of the world" norms, has allowed for Bezalel and his fellow artists and craftsmen to exercise their aesthetic gifts. The purpose has been principally to build a house for "God to dwell therein." But an adjoining motivation has been to allow for the arousal among the people of their own pristine spiritual and aesthetic sensitivities. The *mishkan* and all its appurtenances represent the early Israelite realization of beauty-on-earth dedicated to the Creator-Revealer-Redeemer that is God.

Bezalel has been described as having been graced by God with *hokhmat-lev* ("wisdom of the heart"). This wisdom is a special realization of God's love manifested in His dispensation of certain special gifts of artistic creativity. The artist's special vision, the keen sensibility that inspires him to combine the sights and sounds of pristine reality about him, is able to produce objects that enrapture fellow human beings. This gift of vision, shared, as the saying goes, among babes, prophets, and madmen, has a freshness, an immediacy, which cleanses the soul as it stimulates the imagination. Objects produced by this gift of vision have the capacity to bring pleasure while evoking, as in the case of Israel in the Wilderness, transcendent emotions and ruminations.

The intuitive aesthetic sensibility, the potential capacity in all human beings, even slaves, to enjoy beauty, not to mention the refinement of such a sensibility through appropriate aesthetic education, needs to be integrated *approvingly* within the body politic, within the covenanted community. There must never be within the community of Israel a cultivation of the idea that any product of the aesthetic sensibility is perfect enough to be worshiped. Moses, and certainly God, are attuned to the constant possibility that

aesthetic experience can degenerate into idolatry. For this reason Moses plays
the role of patron of Bezalel's efforts. He must in order to bring home to the
people two lessons.

The first is that notwithstanding the freedom that art must be granted in
order to realize its own visions, no matter how unconventional at times those
visions may be, the ultimate goal of the covenant is not to worship the work of
art but to worship God as Creator-Revealer-Redeemer. The second lesson is
that the covenant recognizes the value of aesthetic "education" only insofar as
it contributes to the development of a spiritually sensitive and morally committed person and community. Art for art's sake — even when not worshiped
— is a trivial pursuit. Art for the sake of human enlightenment is the desideratum.

Moses — as cited earlier — is the supreme *sheli'ah tzibbur* of Israel. He is
the central representative of the community as well as its governing leader,
prophetic critic, and supreme teacher. The summary sentence which
describes the desired relationship among God, Moses, and Israel and which
applies to all aspects of the national agenda is: "*Va-ya'asu benei Yisrael ke-khol
asher tziva Adonai et Moshe ken asu*" ("And the Children of Israel did all that
God commanded Moshe that they do"). The assertion here is that there is to
be reciprocal participation in building not only a tabernacle, but the community and the nation as well. But furthermore, there must be a source of human
authority which inspires and regulates human effort and enterprise. God is
the ultimate ruler; but He must be joined by mortal judges and rulers who
will be charged with interpreting and executing, as well as they can, God's
will!

It has been Moses who has had the power, the stature, and the dignity to
keep the mixed multitude of slaves together. It has been Moses — unlike
Aaron — who has been able to enforce the anti-idolatrous norm. He has done
this even at the cost of three thousand slain following the "golden calf" heresy. It may be, as Yehudah Halevi will argue much later, that the sin of the
"golden calf" episode was not substantively catastrophic, i.e., it was not a
rejection of God as such. Nevertheless an anti-idolatrous standard has had to
be established and enforced, and Moses as leader has had to exercise firm and
decisive leadership. And it will be Moses who will oversee the imposition of
many arbitrary rules as to normative procedures in the sanctuary. It will be
Moses who will be the supreme executive, legislator, and judge in spelling out

and actualizing the Torah laws among the people. Indeed, the covenant's durability at this critical early juncture in Israel's history will depend on Moses being able to realize among the people the constantly repeated condition *"ka-asher tziva Adonai et Moshe"* ("as God commanded Moses").

The *Mishkan* and Humility

This condition, this slogan *"ka-asher tziva Adonai et Moshe"* is repeated as a punctuating signature no less than eighteen times in this concluding portion of the Book of Exodus. It is true that the portion emphasizes the meticulous obedience to every tiny detail in the building of the *mishkan*. But this meticulousness is meant to be carried over to the people's attitudes towards the keeping of all the laws of the Torah. The attention to detail is meant to be not only a direct and immediate confirmation of Israel's readiness to obey the terms of the covenant. It is meant to test Israel's emotional sincerity. For sincerity is best measured in any project or enterprise by the obsessive concern for detail.

The connection between the finely detailed construction of the *mishkan* and the carefully programmed halakhic development of the covenanted Israelite and by extension the entire House of Israel is represented in the eyes of the *Ba'al ha-Turim* commentary by this number "eighteen." *"Ka-asher tziva Adonai et Moshe"* ("as God commanded Moses") is written as a qualification for each item in the *mishkan*, eighteen times in total. In compensatory recognition for Moses' willingness to be erased completely from God's book of life during the appeal to save Israel from God's wrathful judgment, Moses' name is now mentioned eighteen times. In parallel fashion to these eighteen citations, the later Sages will legislate for every Jew to recite eighteen blessings in his *Amidah* prayer — *the* prayer — three times daily. And a nineteenth blessing will be added, according to some traditional opinions, to condemn apostates and other enemies of Israel. This will further stress the tightly bound connection between Israel's worship of God, God's tabernacle, and the primary leader and teacher of Israel Moshe Rabbenu.

This *Amidah* prayer will become the individual as well as communal extension of the *mishkan* — to be carried liturgically by the Children of Israel throughout their later history. The post-Eden and post-Deluge covenant which God has established with Abraham to be renewed with his descendants at Sinai has been intended to be more tolerant of the weaknesses of human beings than was God's initial expectations of Adam and the Deluge generation. At the same time, God has not been prepared to surrender His dream, His image of Man's corrigibility, if not perfectibility. God knows that "the devisings of Man's mind are evil from his youth." The Torah is designed, therefore, to program meticulously Man's behavior so as to make of him an aesthetically pleasing creature which for God, as understood by Abraham, Moses, and the prophets, will mean an ethically committed, spiritually enlightened human being.

But such a covenant will call for a commitment on the part of the human being — the Israelite, the Jew — to a special kind of humility. Without the readiness to admit to imperfection, to moral and spiritual weakness, there cannot be any pedagogic threshold. Just as the *mishkan* itself is to represent Israel's humble search for the assurance and comfort of God's indwelling Presence, the individual Israelite's daily prayer of praise and petition similarly must bespeak a posture of humility. The aesthetic link of the number eighteen between the two liturgical-aesthetic phenomena — *mishkan* and daily prayer — has Abraham's humility and Moses' humility as pedagogic pillars.

The Midrash has Abraham saying: "O God, You know that I could have disputed You when You told me to sacrifice Isaac. And if I had disputed You, You would have had no reply — for I would have reminded You that only yesterday You said that in Isaac I would have seed called after me.... But I did not dispute You, but made myself like one who is deaf and dumb." In Abraham's case, his humility is manifested in his self-effacement, i.e., in his acceptance of God's decree to sacrifice his genealogical future. Abraham at that time could not present "his case" before God because he feared that it would not reflect a purely disinterested desire for understanding God's purposes, but rather his own personal "conceit," that is, his love for his son. In his absolute attention to God's command, however — at least at first before attending to his son's neutralizing appeal — Abraham shows that he is truly prepared to suspend, if not erase entirely, his own ego.

As for Moses' humility, summarily stated in Numbers 12:3 as "he was more humble than any other man on earth," there are three climactic crossroads in his lifetime of personal self-effacement: (1) when he steps out of his Egyptian palace and forfeits his imperial office and dignity in order to identify with the Hebrew slaves; (2) when he leaves Midian in order to undertake the self-destructive task of emancipating a stubborn stiff-necked people; and

(3) when he refuses God's offer to become the father of a new nation, preferring utter self-extinction rather than seeing his people Israel rejected and abandoned.

Thus every future Israelite, every future member of the Jewish people, standing in prayer, will begin with the first liturgical blessing of the *Amidah* citing Abraham's merit before God. And then the entire daily *Amidah*, the prayer seeking to prepare the Jew for confronting the "way of the world" with its eighteen/nineteen blessings, will attach this Jew to the merit of his primary teacher and model — Moshe Rabbenu.

The *"Shekhinah"* and *"Mashi'ah"*

Moses has been rewarded in the building of the *mishkan*. He has been the "contractor," appointed by God to direct and ratify whatever Bezalel and the others will have been doing. Moses' achievement with the *mishkan* is analogous to his infinitely more challenging task of teaching and orchestrating the lives of a new community of tribes. And if his "success" with the latter task will be limited, at least the building of the *mishkan* will have brought him uncompromised satisfaction.

The peak of his delight as well as that of the entire people is cited in one of the summary verses: "Thus was completed all the work of the tabernacle of the Tent of Meeting. The Israelites did so; just as the Lord had commanded Moses, so they did." The Alshikh recognizes the kindly exaggeration regarding the Israelites' participation. God always helps those who perform a *mitzvah*; but He is delighted to reward those who do the *mitzvah* even partially as if they have performed it fully. Again to the question as to this erstwhile slave population possessing the necessary mental, psychological, and spiritual capacities to produce a work of the imagination such as the *mishkan*, the only answer can be "Godly inspiration." And just as God has inspired Bezalel and Oholiab and the other more professional workmen, He has inspired Israel as well. They have been under Divine Providence and have thereby been able to build a temporary *Bet El* ("House of God"), just as they had had the God-given poetic imagination to join Moses in composing the Song of the Sea.

God's largesse in letting His creative power rest on Israel sufficiently to stimulate its creative imagination and then crediting it with the reward of the entire labor must be balanced by God's clear enunciation of His indisputable authority and the acceptance by Israel that all is according to God's instructions. The *Ha'amek Davar* says: "Since it is clear that Israel has a passionate desire for God's *Shekhinah* to rest among them, it may occur to them that their *desire* is the causal influence on the *Shekhinah* being there. Therefore it must be repeated again and again that only God's command is to be considered a cause. His grace has made the building of the *mishkan* possible; His grace will permit the *Shekhinah* to dwell among them."

The contribution in tandem of God's *middat ha-rahamim* ("attribute of graciousness") and *middat ha-din* ("attribute of divine correctness") is thus complete as far as Israel and the *mishkan* are concerned. Israel gets credit beyond what it deserves; at the same time the tabernacle is built because God wills it! The entire vision and rationale for building a tabernacle in order to house the *Shekhinah* comes out of these wedded attributes of God.

By now Israel is certainly aware of God's power. Israel has seen it in the destruction of Egypt and the Egyptians. It has experienced its overwhelming immediacy with non-destructive consequences in the revelation at Mount Sinai. Yet it wants to be near to this God, to cleave to Him, if possible, with the requisite *yirat shamayim* ("reverie"). But how can Israel dare to think of being close to God when He exudes so much power? Despite the power inherent in His *middat ha-din*, God has learned through His *middat ha-rahamim* to be sensitive to Israel's propensity to sin, to rebel, to lose heart and faith. For God is Himself ready for intimacy with this people. He has Himself commanded, after all, the building of the tabernacle in the first place. In this He has proclaimed His need for Israel!

God and Israel have both suffered through the "golden calf" debacle. They know what each is capable of doing when "loosely" or "casually" committed to the covenant: God when provoked can destroy! Israel when not disciplined is an idolatrous, salacious mob! And so the idea of building a *mishkan* was not a mistake. Since the "golden calf" apostasy the idea of dedicating a place that would represent the coming together of God and Israel in regular ritual confirmation of the covenant is now felt to be even more necessary. From Israel's point of view, the *mishkan* means that God *is*, that He is *with us*, that he *cares about us*. Moreover, through the vehicle of the *mishkan* Israel asserts that it believes that its words and its acts will count. From God's point of view, Israel is the chosen — arbitrarily chosen, chosen because of the merit of its ancestors — but chosen, and as the chosen, it needs help. God must Himself help their words and acts to rise higher than they could otherwise. God will understand Israel's waywardness and will offer them, therefore, a Torah which will recommend itself to every conceivable area of Israel's life in order to help them keep the covenant maximally!

The *mishkan*, in short, is there as a reinforcement of the covenant, a daily reminder as the synagogue will become a reminder that there is a covenant between God and Israel, that it is firm and immutable. Will there be those within Israel who will nevertheless withdraw themselves from the *Shekhinah*? Will there be crises of faith, losses of "nerve" in the face of catastrophes natural and human? The *rasha* of the *Pesah Seder* will immortalize for Jewish culture the call of the heretic: *"Ma ha-avodah hazot lakhem"* ("What is this worship to you, Israel")? Tauntingly, the wicked one will exclude himself from the Israelite-Jewish collective and deny the *ikar* ("the fundamental principle"), i.e., God and His covenant. The *rasha* will retroactively deny the emancipation of Israel. Had he been there, he would have chosen to remain enslaved — anonymous, undistinguished, a cipher, lost in a primordial chaos of purposelessness.

But as the *mishkan* is built bringing to a close the Book of Exodus, there is no mention of *resha'im* ("wicked backsliders"). All is harmony. The book ends with the description: "For over the tabernacle a cloud of the Lord rested by day, and fire would appear in it by night, in the view of all the house of Israel throughout their journeys."

This summary description of the "state of the nation" as it journeys through history will reflect its collective faith in God's eternal commitment to the covenant. Israel has emerged from slavery to redemption, from darkness to light; it has experienced a messianic deliverance which will henceforth serve as the therapeutic dream of a people when it finds itself again and again in situations of political and spiritual darkness. What will sustain Israel throughout the future exiles will be visions — no matter how faint — of the *"ikveta de-mashiha* ("the footsteps of the Messiah").

Israelite history will echo the traumatic events surrounding its birth: servitude, suffering, struggle. And if and when there appear signals that promise redemption, they will be accompanied by anxiety, apprehension, and most tragically among many Jews — apathy! Jews will ask themselves after the short exile and after the long exile: "Why have we been chosen for the redemption, why our generation in particular?" Such a question, it will be argued, is the question of the spiritually timid, if not faithless. For it will be felt that those who ask "why are we worthy" are themselves delaying the coming deliverance. It is as if they are asking "why are we alive?" One doesn't ask "why" when one is enslaved and sees the "footsteps" leading to freedom. One lives and one fights to march in step with the "footsteps."

Israel will have already learned that emancipation from servitude is not a simple exercise. There will always be forces in the world which will deny God's fundamental teachings. These forces will deny God's ultimate sovereignty. The awareness that these forces exist and undercut the realization of dreams of human betterment is nowhere more poignantly expressed than the passage in Psalms 89:52: "Your enemies have taunted, O Lord; they've taunted the footsteps of Your Messiah. Blessed be the Lord for evermore, Amen and Amen." It is an odd yet provocative thought that in a situation where your enemies are taunting You, O Lord, you are blessed! Rabbi A.I. Kook will suggest an explanation: "The evolutionary process of Messianism contains within itself negative forces, for they too serve towards the divine end. The light reaches downwards, even unto the utmost depths of primal causes motivating the *mohin de-katnut* ('the lowest most vulgar level of awareness'), only so it can prepare the way for the final stages."

The Children of Israel will have already anticipated in their experience in Egypt the *hevlei Mash'iah* ("the pangs and writhings preceding the dawn of the Messianic era"). The servitude, suffering, and struggle to survive under the yoke of bondage will have only been partially neutralized, even with the Exodus. Anxiety regarding future enemies, the future search for economic and political sustenance, and the concern for internal social stability will persist, even and especially after the Revelation.

There will be no less apprehension than there was in enslavement for a people that will know and appreciate the difficulties of surmounting apathy and the day-by-day frustrations entailed in living, not to mention living according to the terms of the covenant. Indeed, the birth pangs of moving into a new and over-all "better" situation will inevitably be accompanied by twinges of uncertainty. And asking questions such as "why are *we* worthy" will indeed be ultimately pointless. In a perverse way it will harbor a conceit; for in truth every generation will be potentially worthy providing it rises to the call for messianic deliverance and tries through struggle to actualize the potential.

The Weight of Covenantal Struggle

The essential question will be whether or not Israel will develop and sustain the kind of spiritual aspiration that will urge it constantly to respond to historic opportunities for independence and growth. A special strength will be required for such constant response; for the response-ability, i.e., the ability to respond, will indeed be a required constant! Rabbi A.I. Kook will claim the potential strength for Israel in the following lament: "Israel in the innermost recesses of her soul seeks to perfect herself, but she is not truly conscious of this tendency in her. She does not know to articulate the Divine Name, nor does she know that the name of the Lord is called upon her, 'for her eyes are towards the earth and she does not yet look heavenwards.' All is the light of the Lord and His glory but neither she nor the world are clearly aware of the fact."

From Rabbi A.I. Kook all the way back to Moses, the task will be and will have been knowing that Israel carries the *mishkan*. It carries that "institution" which houses God's indwelling Presence along with Jewish and human destiny. Such a burden will continue to be heavy, often excruciatingly heavy. Bearing such a burden will be impossible without an accompanying sense of transcendence. God's promise to Himself and to humankind that there can be a Messianic era, i.e., a better time for humankind, is not yet the fulfillment. It is only a promise. But even a promise is a spark of divinity, the spark which can help free the cords of despair which inevitably seek to strangle the Messianic dream.

Israel thus takes up its journey to its Promised Land propelled forward by covenantal purpose accompanied by clouds and fire — pillars of Godly concern and caring. The question for Israel will be "how much it itself feels concern, how much it itself cares."

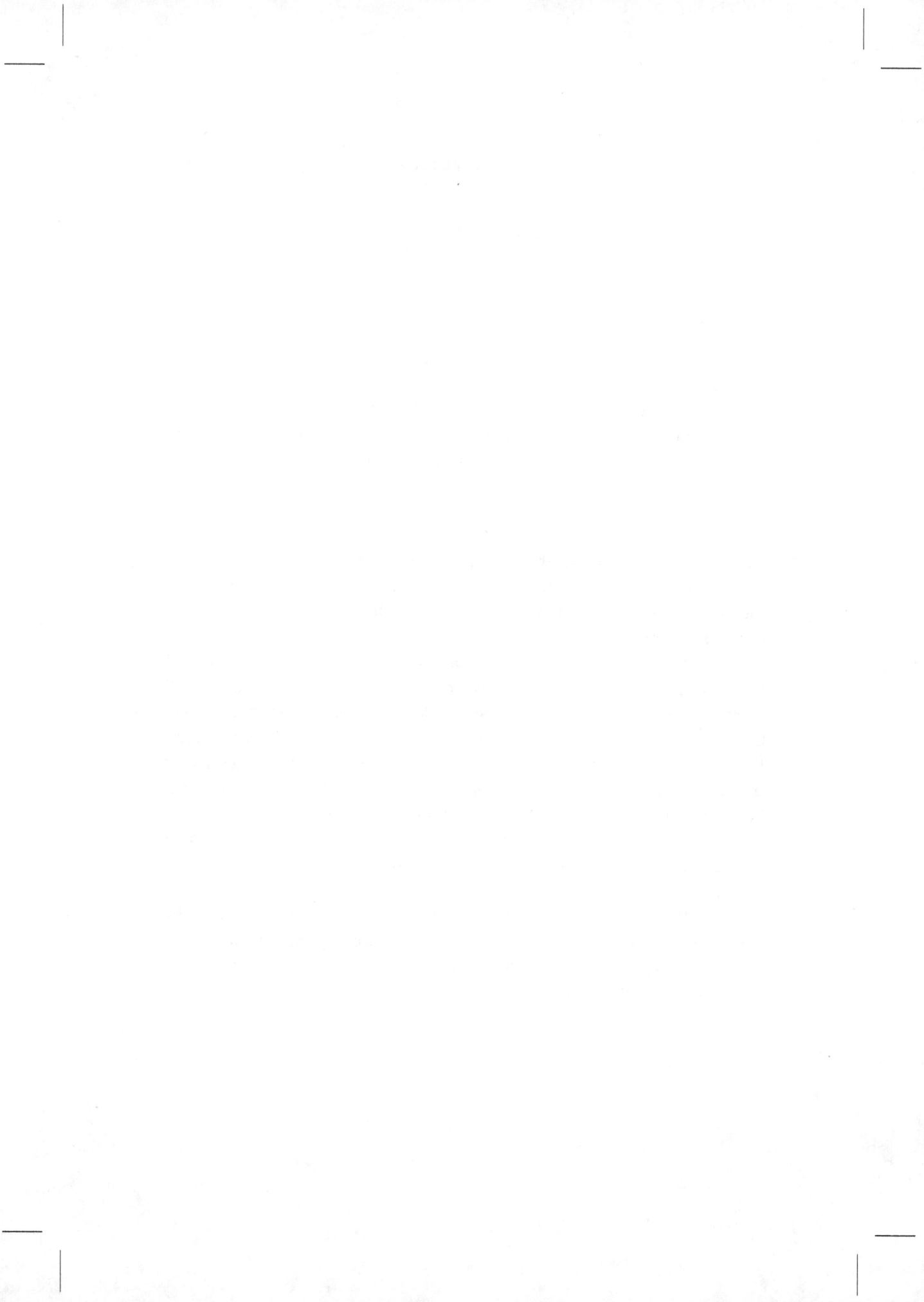

www.ingramcontent.com/pod-product-compliance
Lightning Source LLC
Chambersburg PA
CBHW081423090426
42740CB00017B/3165